JAMES MILL

Political Writings

EDITED BY
TERENCE BALL
Professor of Political Science
University of Minnesota

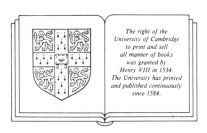

The right of the
University of Cambridge
to print and sell
all manner of books
was granted by
Henry VIII in 1534.
The University has printed
and published continuously
since 1584.

CAMBRIDGE UNIVERSITY PRESS
CAMBRIDGE   NEW YORK   PORT CHESTER
MELBOURNE   SYDNEY

Published by the Press Syndicate of the University of Cambridge
The Pitt Building, Trumpington Street, Cambridge CB2 1RP
40 West 20th Street, New York, NY 10011–4211, USA
10 Stamford Road, Oakleigh, Victoria 3166, Australia

© in the introduction and ancillary editorial matter
Cambridge University Press 1992

First published 1992

Printed in Great Britain by The Bath Press, Avon

A catalogue record for this book is available from the British Library

Library of Congress cataloguing in publication data

Mill, James, 1773–1836.
Political writings / James Mill; edited by Terence Ball.
p.   cm. – (Cambridge texts in the history of political
thought)
Includes bibliographical references.
ISBN 0 521 38323 4 (hardback). – ISBN 0 521 38748 5 (paperback)
1. Political science.   I. Ball, Terence.   II. Title.   III. Series.
JC223.M652   1992
320′.01 – dc20   91–16227   CIP

ISBN 0 521 38323 4 hardback
ISBN 0 521 38748 5 paperback

Contents

Preface

James Mill has had the double misfortune of being overshadowed by two thinkers with whom he was closely associated – his patron and mentor, Jeremy Bentham, and his first-born son, John Stuart Mill. Even the short work for which he is best known, the *Essay on Government*, is remembered mainly for the "famous attack" it called forth from the Whig historian Macaulay. Yet, when all is said and done, Mill was in his own time a formidable figure who earned the respect even of those who disagreed with him (including his nemesis Macaulay). Historian, political philosopher, psychologist, educational theorist, and economist, Mill repeatedly crossed the curricular and disciplinary boundaries that we take for granted today. Like his model Plato, Mill believed that all knowledge was of a piece, and must be grasped by the sort of "theory" that offers a "commanding view" of the whole.

The present volume can scarcely begin to do justice to the sweep and ambition of Mill's thinking. My main purpose in collecting these writings is to give the modern reader a brief but reasonably representative sampling of Mill's political writings, and in a way that shows his strengths and weaknesses as a political theorist and polemicist. In keeping with Mill's own design, this collection begins with the *Essay on Government*, departing, as branches from a trunk, in different directions to treat such allied topics as the protection of rights, a free press as a safeguard of those rights, the importance of education in enlightening the citizenry, and punishment as the primary weapon in the government's arsenal against anyone who violates the rights of fellow citizens. These are followed by a more topical polemic on the secret ballot (1830). This collection concludes with an appendix containing Macaulay's critique of Mill's *Essay on Government* (1829) and Mill's heretofore unnoticed reply in his *Fragment on Mackintosh* (1835). Taken together, these selections will, I hope, enable the readers to form their own estimate of Mill's stature as a political theorist.

For helping me to understand the meaning of Mill's political writings I am much indebted to Isaiah Berlin, the late John Dinwiddy, Knud Haakonsen, Douglas Long, the late John Rees, Alan Ryan, Donald Winch, and William Thomas. I am also grateful to Donald Winch, William Thomas, Quentin Skinner, and Raymond Geuss for their detailed and very helpful comments on the introduction, and to Richard Fisher of the Cambridge University Press for his tact and patience.

Although he is much missed by his friends and admirers, John Rees's example endures. All Mill scholars are in his debt, and I record mine by dedicating this volume to him.

Introduction

James Mill (1773–1836) is arguably among the most underrated and least understood of modern political thinkers. He is pictured today, if he is remembered at all, as Bentham's faithful disciple and mouthpiece, and as the Gradgrind who imposed upon his long-suffering son the extraordinary education described at length in the latter's *Autobiography*. Although this present-day picture does, like any memorable caricature, contain a grain of truth, it obscures much more than it reveals. In particular, it misrepresents the way in which Mill's own contemporaries regarded him, and it underrates his influence and importance as a political thinker.

Mill's interests were by any measure remarkably wide, not to say encyclopedic. They ranged from education and psychology in his two-volume *Analysis of the Phenomena of the Human Mind*, to political economy (he persuaded his friend David Ricardo to write on that subject, as he did in his *Principles of Political Economy*), to penology and prison reform, to the law and history, and, not least, to political theory. On these and other subjects he wrote five books and more than a thousand essays and reviews. Little wonder that his contemporaries, critics and admirers alike, stood in some awe of the elder Mill.

One of James Mill's contemporaries, Harriet Grote (wife of the historian of Greece), thought him "a propagandist of a very high order, equally master of the pen and of speech." (We must, of course, recall that "propagandist" in nineteenth-century parlance meant merely a propagator of ideas, not a special pleader or paid liar.) Others were more critical. Karl Marx criticized Mill the economist for cloaking "bourgeois" biases in "scientific" garb. Others thought Mill dangerous for rather different reasons, including his commitment to democracy and a radical extension of the franchise. In his celebrated attack on Mill's *Essay on Government*, the Whig historian Macaulay singled out Mill as the most dangerous of the philosophic radicals, not only for his extreme political views but also because of his pernicious influence on the young.

Whether friendly or critical, Mill's contemporaries agreed that he was a force to be reckoned with – a fact forgotten or overlooked by succeeding generations of commentators as the elder Mill's reputation was eclipsed by those of Bentham and his son. Historians of political thought have only recently begun to recognize the extent of his influence. The work of William Thomas (1979), John Rees (1985), Robert Fenn (1987), and others has gone some way toward reassessing Mill's stature as a political thinker. These follow Donald Winch's (1966) reassessment of Mill's reputation as an economist and W. H. Burston's (1969, 1973) reappraisal of Mill's educational theories. It is with Mill the political theorist that the present volume is principally concerned.

Life

"When a man has risen to great intellectual or moral eminence," Mill wrote, "the process by which his mind was formed is one of the most instructive circumstances which can be unveiled to mankind." Yet the circumstances under which James Mill's mind was formed remained veiled during his lifetime. Mill, unlike his son, never wrote an autobiography or even a sketch of his early life, the details of which remained undisclosed even to his children. Why this should be so, I cannot say. But we can at least piece together the few scraps that we do possess.

James Mill was born in 1773 in Scotland. His father, also named James, was a shoemaker and smallholder of modest means, and was by all accounts quiet, mild-mannered, and devout. His mother, Isabel, was an altogether more forceful figure. Determined that her first-born son should get ahead in the world, she changed the family name from the Scottish "Milne" to the more English-sounding "Mill," and kept young James away from other children, demanding that he spend most of his waking hours immersed in study. Unlike his younger brother and sister, he was exempted from performing household chores. His "sole occupation," as his biographer Alexander Bain remarks, "was study." (A regimen rather like that imposed by his mother upon her eldest son was later to be imposed upon his firstborn son, John Stuart Mill.) In this occupation young James clearly excelled. Before the age of seven he had shown a talent for elocution, composition, arithmetic, and languages, Latin and Greek in particular. The parish minister saw to it that James received special attention at the parish school. At age ten or eleven, he was sent to Montrose Academy, where his teachers, Bain tells us, "were always overflowing with the praises of Mill's cleverness and perseverence." Sometime before leaving Montrose Academy at the age of seventeen, Mill was persuaded by the parish minister and his mother to study for the ministry.

Word of Mill's decision soon reached Lady Jane Stuart, wife of Sir John Stuart of Fettercairn and patroness of a local charity founded for the purpose of educating poor but promising boys for the Presbyterian ministry. Mill, eminently qualified on both counts, became the recipient of Lady Jane's largesse. As it happened, she and Sir John were just then looking for a tutor for their fourteen-year-old daughter Wilhelmina. They offered the job to James Mill; he accepted; and when the Stuart family moved to Edinburgh, he accompanied them.

Arriving in Edinburgh in 1790, Mill enrolled in the University, where by day he pursued a full course of studies and in the evenings presided over the education of young Wilhelmina. Each experience left its mark. The Scottish universities at Edinburgh and Glasgow (and to a lesser extent Aberdeen and St. Andrews) had earlier been the hub of the Scottish Enlightenment and were still the premier universities in Britain. They had numbered among their faculty such luminaries as Francis Hutcheson, Thomas Reid, John Millar, Adam Ferguson, Adam Smith, and would – if the orthodox town council of Edinburgh had not forbidden his admission – have included David Hume as well. At Edinburgh, Dugald Stewart, under whom Mill studied, carried on the tradition of Scottish moral philosophy. In addition to moral philosophy, Mill's course of studies included history, political economy, and the classics, including Mill's favorite author, Plato. Mill's mind never lost the impress of his Scottish education. As his eldest son was later to remark, James Mill was "the last survivor of this great school."

From 1790 to 1794 Mill served Wilhelmina Stuart not only as a teacher but as a companion and confidant. Her admiration for her tutor quite likely turned to love, and the feeling was apparently reciprocated. But that match was not to be. However promising his prospects, Mill was no aristocrat, a social fact which he was not allowed to forget. In 1797 Wilhelmina married a member of her own class and died shortly thereafter. Mill never forgot her; he spoke of her always with wistful affection and named his first-born daughter after her.

Upon completing his first degree in 1794, Mill began studying for the ministry. For the next four years he supported himself by tutoring the sons and daughters of several noble families. The experience was not a happy one. For repeatedly forgetting his "place" in "polite society" he suffered one insult after another. He harbored ever after an abiding hatred for an hereditary aristocracy.

Licensed to preach in 1798, Mill was unable to secure a position. He was for a time an itinerant preacher, riding on horseback from one parish to another, his saddlebags stuffed with sermons said to be learned but largely incomprehensible to his hapless parishioners. It is possible that Mill had already begun to lose his faith. At any rate, he had by the early 1800s become restless and disillusioned, and in 1802 he left for London and a "career in authorship." When he arrived in London he was twenty-nine and full of schemes for improving his situation. Little came of these, however, and he had to eke out a precarious existence as a journalistic odd-jobber and literary hack.

Mill's pen proved to be a prolific one. From 1802 until his appointment to the East India Company in 1819 Mill's literary labors were by any standard prodigious. Besides some 1,400 editorials, he wrote hundreds of substantial articles and reviews, as well as several books, including his *History of British India* in three large volumes. Some of these were doubtless labors of love; but most were labors of necessity, for Mill had to support himself and his wife Harriet, whom he married in 1805, and a growing brood of "brats." The first of nine, born in 1806, was named John Stuart in honor of his father's Scottish patron.

In 1808 James Mill met Jeremy Bentham, with whom he soon formed a political and literary alliance. The two were in many respects kindred spirits. Both wished and worked for religious toleration and legal reform; both favored freedom of speech and press; both feared that the failure to reform the British political system – by, among other things, extending the franchise – would give rise to reactionary intransigence on the one hand, and revolutionary excess on the other. But the two men were of vastly different temperaments and backgrounds. Bentham, a wealthy bachelor, was an eccentric closet philosopher who fancied himself a modern law-giver and man of the world. Mill, poor, harried, and hard-working, was the more practical and worldly of the two. He was also the better writer and abler propagandist.

A hedonist by temperament and philosophy, Bentham believed that the pursuit of pleasure and the avoidance of pain were the twin aims of all human action. His philosophy, Utilitarianism, held that self-interest – understood as pleasure or happiness – should be "maximized" and pain "minimized" (Bentham, incidentally, coined the terms). And, as with individual self-interest, so too with the public interest. The aim of legislation and public policy was, according to Bentham, to promote "the greatest happiness of the greatest number." Mill agreed, after a fashion. A dour Scots Presbyterian and something of a Platonist, he took a dim view of unalloyed hedonism. Like Plato, he ranked the pleasures in a hierarchy, with the sensual pleasures subordinated to the intellectual ones.

Despite these differences, Mill proved an invaluable ally. He helped to make Bentham's ideas and schemes more palatable and popular than they might otherwise have been. But he also influenced Bentham's ideas in a number of ways. For one, Mill led Bentham to appreciate the importance of economic factors in explaining and changing social life and political institutions; for another, he turned Bentham away from advocating aristocratic "top-down" reform into a more popular or "democratic" direction.

Their partnership was unique and, for a time, fruitful. With Mill's energy and Bentham's financial backing, Utilitarian schemes for legal, political, penal, and educational reform gained an ever wider audience and circle of adherents. This circle included, among others, Francis Place ("the radical tailor of Charing Cross"), the Genevan Etienne Dumont, the historian George Grote, the stockbroker-turned-economist David Ricardo, and – not least – the young John Stuart Mill. Each in his own way enlisted in the Utilitarian cause. The cause was furthered by the founding of the Society for the Diffusion of Useful Knowledge and, later, by the launching of the *Westminster Review* and the founding of University College London (where Bentham's body, stuffed and mounted in a glass case, can still be seen today). This small band of "philosophic radicals" worked tirelessly for political changes, several of which were later incorporated into the Reform Act of 1832. But Bentham and Mill, while maintaining a united front for political purposes, became increasingly estranged. Bentham was irascible and difficult to work with, and Mill on more than one occasion swallowed his pride by accepting financial help and personal rebuke from the old man.

In 1818, after twelve years' work, Mill's massive *History of British India* was published. Early in the following year he was appointed Assistant Examiner at the East India Company. His financial future finally secured, Mill no longer needed Bentham's largesse. The two men saw less and less of each other. Their political alliance continued even as their personal relationship cooled. Their uneasy friendship effectively ended some years before Bentham's death in 1832.

Mill did not exaggerate when he remarked that his "life had been a laborious one." Besides being a tireless reformer and prodigious writer, he supplied his son John with one of the most strenuous educations ever recorded in the annals of pedagogy. The elder Mill gave young John daily lessons in Latin, Greek, French, history, philosophy, and political economy. Literature and poetry were also taught, although with less enthusiasm (James Mill, like Plato, distrusted poets and poetry). John was in turn expected to tutor his younger brothers and sisters in these subjects. Each was examined rigorously and regularly by their stern Scots father, and the nine children, like their mother, lived with an abiding fear of his rebuke. The Mill household was not a happy one. Although the elder Mill mellowed in his later years, largely because his fear of financial ruin abated with his advancement in the East India Company, his children remembered him mainly for his "temper" and his humorless sternness.

Mill's strained relations with his wife and children stand in stark contrast with those he had with others. Young men especially sought him out for the pleasure of his company and the vigor of his conversation. As John Black, the editor of the *Morning Chronicle*, recalled on the occasion of Mill's death in 1836:

Mr. Mill was eloquent and impressive in conversation. He had a great command of language, which bore the stamp of his earnest and energetic character. Young men were particularly fond of his society ... No man could enjoy his society without catching a portion of his elevated enthusiasm ... His conversation was so energetic and complete in thought, so succinct, and exact ... in expression, that, if reported as uttered, his colloquial observations or arguments would have been perfect compositions.

The same cannot, alas, be said of Mill's writings, which tend to be both dry and devoid of decoration.

Mill as writer and theorist

The elder Mill strove to write, he said, with "manly plainness," and in that endeavor he certainly succeeded. The reader is never at a loss to know just where his sympathies lie. Mill's manly plainness is particularly evident in his *History of British India*, which he calls a "critical, or judging history." His judgments on Hindu customs and practices are particularly harsh. He denounces their "rude" and "backward" culture for its cultivation of ignorance and its veneration of superstition, and leaves no doubt that he favors a strong dose of Utilitarian rationalism as an antidote. Although his *History* is in part a Utilitarian treatise and in part a defense of British intervention in Indian affairs, it is more than the sum of those two parts, important though they are. Mill's *History* shows, perhaps more clearly than any of his other works, the continuing impress and importance of his Scottish education. The criteria according to which Mill judges and criticizes Indian practices and customs derive from the view of historical progress that he had learned from Stewart and Millar, amongst others. This view holds that "man is a progressive being" and that education is the chief engine of progress. And this in turn helps to explain not only Mill's harsh judgments on the Hindus but his continuing emphasis on education.

Virtually everything that James Mill ever wrote had a pedagogical purpose. Mill was a relentlessly didactic writer with a schoolmaster's penchant for laying out, summarizing, and repeating his central points, in a manner more likely to be irritating than illuminating to the modern reader. Mill's most important political essays – *Government*, in particular – take the form of clipped, concise, deductive arguments.

It is a style which his contemporaries either admired or detested, as can be seen for instance in F. D. Maurice's novel *Eustace Conway*. When the Benthamite Morton discovers Eustace reading Mill's *Essay on Government*, he asks his opinion of Mill. Eustace replies:

> "I think him nearly the most wonderful prose-writer in our language."
> "That do not I," says Morton. "I approve the matter of his treatises exceedingly, but the style seems to me detestable."
> "Oh!," says Eustace, "I cannot separate matter and style ... My reason for delighting in this book is, that it gives such a fixedness and reality to all that was most vaguely brilliant in my speculations – it converts dreams into demonstrations."

Most of Mill's critics were not so gentle. Macaulay criticized Mill and his fellow Utilitarians for "affect[ing] a quakerly plainness, or rather a cynical negligence and impurity of style." In so doing "they surrender their understandings ... to the meanest and most abject sophisms, provided those sophisms come before them disguised with the externals of demonstration. They do not seem to know that logic has its illusions as well as rhetoric, – that a fallacy may lurk in a syllogism as well as in a metaphor." In Mill's case, the style of reasoning and writing was characteristic of the man and thinker. If it was plain and unadorned, it was at least clear and cogent. And that, surely, is a virtue too often lacking among political theorists.

James Mill made no bones about being a theorist, which was, for him, a title to be worn proudly. Theory, he wrote, gives a "commanding view" of its subject and serves as a guide for improving practice. Theory precedes practice or "experience" and is not simply derived from it (although theory may in some sense be a distillation of experience, rightly understood). Amidst the often-contradictory welter of appearance, theory serves as a reliable weather vane and guide. This view of theory is much in evidence in all his writings, and in his political essays in particular. The most important of these – and the most controversial – is *Government*.

Whether justly or not, Mill's modern reputation as a political theorist rests on a single essay. The *Essay on Government*, Mill later wrote, was meant to serve as a "skeleton map" with whose aid one could find one's way across the vast, varied, and ofttimes dangerous terrain of politics. Government, Mill maintains, is merely a means to an end, viz. the happiness of the whole community and the individuals composing it. We may, he says, simply assume that every human being is motivated by a desire to experience pleasure and to avoid pain. Pleasures and pains come from two sources, our fellow human beings and nature. Government is concerned directly with the first and indirectly with the second: "Its business is to increase to the utmost the pleasures, and diminish to the utmost the pains, which men derive from one another." Yet, "the primary cause of government" is to be found in nature herself, since humans must wrest from her "the scanty materials of happiness." Nature and human nature conspire to make government necessary. It is man's nature not only to desire happiness but to satisfy that desire by investing as little effort as possible in obtaining it. Labor being the means of obtaining happiness, and our own labor being painful to us, we will, if we can, live off the labor of others. To the degree that others enjoy the fruits of my labor, my main incentive for working – namely my own happiness – is diminished.

The primary problem in designing workable political institutions is, accordingly, to maximize the happiness of the community by minimizing the extent to which some of its members may encroach upon, and enjoy, the fruits of other people's labor. This cannot happen, Mill maintains, in a monarchy (wherein a single ruler exploits his subjects) or in an aristocracy (wherein a ruling elite exploits the common people). Nor can communal happiness be maximized in a direct democracy, since the time and effort required for ruling would be subtracted from that available for engaging in productive labor. The only system that serves as a means to the end of individual and communal happiness is representative democracy, wherein citizens elect representatives to deliberate and legislate on their behalf and in their interest. The problem immediately arises, however, as to how representatives can be made to rule on the people's behalf rather than their own. Mill's answer is that frequent elections and short terms in office make it unlikely that elected representatives will legislate only for their own benefit. After all, representatives are drawn from the ranks of the people to which they can, after their time in office, expect to return. Given what we might nowadays call the incentive-structure of representative government, representatives have every reason to promote the people's interests instead of their own. Indeed, in a properly structured system, there will be an "identity of interests" between representatives and the electorate.

Mill's views on representation stand mid-way between two extremes. On the one side are Jean-Jacques Rousseau and other "participatory" theorists who argue that to allow anyone to represent you or your interests is tantamount to forfeiting your liberty. On the other side are assorted Whig defenders of "virtual representation" – Edmund Burke and, later, Sir James Mackintosh and T. B. Macaulay – who hold that representatives elected by the few may best represent the interests of the many. On this view, one need not have a voice – or a vote – to be well represented in Parliament.

Against Rousseau and other opponents of representation *tout court* Mill maintains that representative government is "the grand discovery of modern times," inasmuch as it allows the interests of the many to be represented efficiently and expeditiously by the few – so long, that is, as the many have the vote and can therefore hold the few strictly accountable for their actions while in office. Properly structured, such a system serves to enhance liberty, since it frees most people from the burdensome and time-consuming business of governing, thereby allowing them to get on with their more productive individual pursuits.

But it was against Whigs who defended "virtual representation" and advocated slow and piecemeal reform of the representative system that Mill's main arguments were directed. He holds that the very idea of virtual representation is a recipe for misgovernment, corruption, and the triumph of the aristocratic or "sinister interests" of the few at the expense of the many. The public interest can be represented only in so far as the public, or a considerably enlarged portion thereof, has the vote. Mill is a radical individualist in that he insists that each person is the best, perhaps indeed the only, judge of what his own interests are. And if – as he also insists – the public interest is the sum of all individual non-sinister interests, it follows that the wider the franchise, the more truly representative the government would be. Whig defenses of virtual representation and moderate reform are thus actually arguments against representative government.

Mill's individualism might appear to stand in marked contrast with his paeans to, and apparent privileging of, one particular group – the "middle rank, ... that intelligent, that virtuous rank ... which gives to science, to art, and to legislation itself, their most distinguished orna-ments, and is the chief source of all that has exalted and refined human nature . . ." It is to this middle rank that common laborers look for advice and guidance, especially in matters moral and political. Although such remarks have struck many modern commentators as a militant defense of middle-class power and privilege, it is, in fact, nothing of the sort. Mill rarely uses the phrase "middle class," preferring instead the more archaic "middle rank." And this, once again, underscores the continuing importance of Mill's Scottish education. The notion of "ranks," as analyzed at length in John Millar's *Origin of the Distinction of Ranks* (1806), had left a deep impression. Millar's (and Mill's) "ranks" are not (quite) "classes" in our modern sense – that is, purely descriptive, fairly distinct, and normatively neutral socio-economic entities – but are instead meant to pick out people of particular intellectual merit and to mark gradations of moral and civic influence.

Mill is quite careful to distinguish between a "class" and a "rank." The members of a "class" are united by shared (and usually selfish or "sinister") interests. Members of the "middle rank," by contrast, are marked more by their public-spiritedness than by their wealth or any other social or economic characteristics. They are "universally described as both the most wise and the most virtuous part of the community which" – Mill adds acidulously – "is not the Aristocratical [class]." Members of the middle rank owe their position not to accident of birth but to "the present state of education, and the diffusion of knowledge" among those anxious to acquire it. By these lights the "radical tailor" Francis Place, the stockbroker David Ricardo, the wealthy philanthropist Jeremy Bentham, the Quaker editor William Allen, and even James Mill himself – although not all "middle class" by modern standards – belonged to the esteemed middle rank. Clearly, then, the idea of a middle rank cuts across the kinds of class divisions with which we are familiar today. Hence any attempt to classify Mill as an apologist for "the middle-class" *simpliciter* is anachronistic and rather wide of the mark.

The idea that Mill was an apologist for middle-class interests was, of course, a later development. But what of his contemporaries' views of the *Essay on Government*?

For so short an essay, Mill's *Government* proved to be remarkably controversial in his own day. Tories and Whigs thought its message wildly and even dangerously democratic, while many of Mill's fellow Utilitarians – including Bentham, John Stuart Mill, and William

Thompson – believed that he did not go nearly far enough in advocating an extension of the franchise. Although more "democratic" in private discussion, Mill publicly advocated extending the franchise to include all male heads of household over the age of forty, leaving them to speak for and represent the interests of younger men and all women:

> One thing is pretty clear, that all those individuals whose interests are indisputably included in those of other individuals, may be struck off without inconvenience. In this light may be viewed all children, up to a certain age, whose interests are involved in those of their parents. In this light, also, women may be regarded, the interest of almost all of whom is involved either in that of their fathers or in that of their husbands.

This paragraph, his son later remarked, was "the worst ... he ever wrote." Most of Mill's critics were quick to seize upon it, if only because its conclusion contradicts two of Mill's oft-stated premises – namely that each of us is the best judge of our own interests and that anyone having unchecked power is bound to abuse it. As William Thompson argued in *Appeal of One Half the Human Race* (1825), Mill's premises pointed to the widest possible extension of the franchise, and not to the exclusion of "one half the human race."

Although none of Mill's other essays – save, perhaps, "The Church, and Its Reform" (1835) – proved so controversial, each expands upon points made in passing in the *Essay on Government*. *Jurisprudence* deals extensively with rights – what they are, by whom they are defined, and how they are best protected. In a similar vein – and in a way that anticipates (and arguably influenced) the younger Mill's *On Liberty* (1859) – *Liberty of the Press* defends the right of free speech and discussion against arguments in favor of restriction and censorship. Free government requires the free communication of ideas and opinions, and good government requires an informed and critical citizenry. For both, a free press is an indispensable instrument.

As I noted earlier, it is virtually impossible to separate Mill's political and pedagogical concerns, for, as William Thomas rightly remarks, "Mill's radicalism is at bottom a programme of education." Certainly no other political thinker, save perhaps Plato and Thomas Jefferson, set greater store by education than did James Mill. By "education" Mill meant not only formal schooling, but all the influences that go into forming one's character and outlook. His *Essay on Education* outlines and anticipates the main themes of his *Analysis of the Phenomena of the Human Mind*, Mill's most comprehensive inquiry into what his son would later call "ethology, or the science of character-formation." In *Education* Mill describes the conditions most conducive to creating good men and, more particularly, good citizens. Civic or "political education," he says, is "the key-stone of the arch; the strength of the whole depends upon it."

Just as one's character can be well moulded by a good education, so too may one's character be badly moulded through miseducation. The latter, Mill maintains, is especially evident in the criminal class. Criminals commit crimes and are sent to prison because they have been badly educated. Punishment, properly understood, is a kind of remedial education, and prison, properly structured, presents the opportunity to re-mould inmates' misshapen characters. *Prisons and Prison Discipline* delineates the types of punishments likely to deter offenders or, failing that, to re-mould and re-educate criminals to be productive members of society. One sometimes suspects that Mill might have wished that society furnished all the "educational" opportunities available in a well-ordered prison. Had the late Michel Foucault read James Mill, he might well have singled him out as the theorist of "the carceral society" or "regime of normality" in which human beings are subtly shaped into docile subjects.

And yet this is unfair, for Mill envisaged a society inhabited by active citizens, always on their guard against rulers or representatives who would violate their rights and deprive them of their liberties. This, after all, is the central theme of the *Essay on Government*, and the thrust of the argument of Mill's article "The Ballot," published in 1830 as a contribution to the public debate preceding the passage of the 1832 Reform Act. Mixing logical acuity with withering ridicule, "The Ballot" is, in the main, a masterful demolition job, with Mill knocking down arguments against extending the franchise and introducing the secret ballot.

Always the critic, Mill was himself a frequent target of criticism, much of which came from quarters hostile to the kinds of sweeping reforms favored by Bentham and the philosophic radicals. Mill's *Essay on Government* first appeared in 1820, and was subsequently reprinted in editions of his *Essays* in 1823, 1825, and 1828, which reached an ever wider audience, including (Mill boasted) "the young men of the

Cambridge Union." Fearing that the cause of moderate reform was in danger from Mill and the philosophic radicals, Whig polemicists weighed in against Mill. One of them, Sir James Mackintosh (1765–1832), was an old Whig war-horse with a plodding and ofttimes pompous prose style. The other, T. B. Macaulay (1800–59), was a much younger and altogether more formidable foe.

Mill vs. Macaulay

Macaulay's "Mill on Government," published in the March 1829 issue of *The Edinburgh Review*, is a remarkable mixture of logical criticism, irony, mordant wit, and droll parody. That Mill's *Essay on Government* is remembered today may owe something to Macaulay's memorable critique. Yet, ironically, this celebrated Whig critique owed much of its logical brilliance to arguments apparently borrowed – without acknowledgment, as was then the custom – from one of Mill's most radical Utilitarian and feminist critics, William Thompson, who in his *Appeal of One Half the Human Race* had tellingly turned Mill's own logic against him. In this respect Macaulay merely followed Thompson's lead. To note this is, however, to take nothing away from Macaulay or the brilliance of his broadside against Mill.

The most remarkable feature of Macaulay's critique is that it seems to be largely aloof from particular political issues, focusing instead on what we would nowadays call methodological matters. Against his older adversary the twenty-eight-year-old Macaulay defends the "historical" or "inductive" approach to the study of politics against Mill's abstract, ahistorical, and "deductive" method. We learn more from "experience" than from "theory," Macaulay contends, and had best beware of the simplifications and "sophisms" to be found in Mill's *Essay on Government*. The most pernicious of these is the "law" that men act always on the basis of self-interest. This law, Macaulay counters, is either trivially true (because logically circular) or patently false; in either case it hardly suffices as a foundation upon which to erect an argument for radical reform, much less a comprehensive theory of politics. And if Mill's methodology fails, the entire edifice – including his supposedly "scientific" arguments in favor of radical reform – collapses.

We might expect that James Mill, feisty fighter that he was, would respond quickly and with no holds barred. But he did not. Why?

His eldest son offers one possible explanation. In his *Autobiography* J. S. Mill remarks that

> I was not at all satisfied with the mode in which my father met the criticisms of Macaulay. He did not, as I thought he ought to have done, justify himself by saying, "I was not writing a scientific treatise on politics. I was writing an article for parliamentary reform." He treated Macaulay's argument as simply irrational; an attack upon the reasoning faculty; an example of the saying of Hobbes, that when reason is against a man, a man will be against reason.

Yet, John Stuart Mill's account of his father's reaction to Macaulay's "famous attack" (as the younger Mill termed it) is misleading in at least two respects. In the first place, the elder Mill did not, and given his premises could not, distinguish between a "scientific treatise on politics" and a coherent and compelling argument for "parliamentary reform." For he believed that any reforms that were workable and worth having could be based only on an adequate scientific theory of society. The *Essay on Government* was intended to be both, if only in brief outline. Second, the younger Mill leaves the impression that his father, although angered by the attack, never replied to Macaulay. This is false.

The Westminster Review published several paltry replies to Macaulay's attack, none of them by Mill (who had earlier had a falling out with Bentham and its editor and refused for a time to write for that journal). Thoroughly dissatisfied with *The Westminster Review*'s replies, James Mill tried, without success, to persuade his friend and fellow Benthamite Etienne Dumont to reply to "the curly-headed coxcomb, who only abuses what he does not understand." In the meantime there appeared Sir James Mackintosh's *Dissertation on Ethical Philosophy* (1830) in which Mill's *Essay on Government* was singled out for special censure. There was nothing new in this; but what caught Mill's eye was that Mackintosh's mode and manner of argument was borrowed, as the author acknowledged, from "the writer of a late criticism on Mr. Mill's Essay. – See Edinburgh Review, No. 97, March 1829." "This," says Mill with evident relish, "is convenient; because the answer, which does for Sir James, will answer the same purpose with the Edinburgh Review." Of course, the "writer of a late criticism" to whom Mackintosh refers was none other than Macaulay, whom the elder Mill then proceeds to answer in the guise of replying to Mackintosh (see the final selection in the present volume). Hence – *pace* J. S. Mill's recollection – his father did reply, and at some length, to Macaulay's attack.

In his reply Mill reiterates and defends the arguments advanced in his *Essay on Government*: all men – including rulers and representatives – are moved by considerations of self-interest, and therefore the only security for good government is to be found in making the interests of representatives identical with those of their constituents. But, unlike the cool, detached, and ostensibly deductive *Essay on Government*, Mill's reply contains a good deal of vitriol. He writes like a schoolmaster who, having lost all patience with a slow-witted pupil, is content to ridicule him before his cleverer classmates. The sight is not a pretty one, and all the more so because Sir James was only three years dead when Mill's *Fragment on Mackintosh* appeared. (Originally scheduled for publication in 1832, Mill's *Fragment* was delayed and toned down because of its target's death.) But then, the intended audience – Macaulay and his readers – were still alive and active, and, Mill thought, very much in need of re-education. Whether, or to what extent, such a splenetic rejoinder could accomplish this aim is surely open to doubt.

The particular political context in which Mill and Macaulay quarreled has long since ceased to exist. But to remember that earlier quarrel by recovering the context in which it occurred might be to enlarge upon and add historical depth to the ostensibly non-political and normatively neutral "methodological" disagreements of our own day.

Mill today

Reviewing the quarrel between Mill and Macaulay today, the modern reader may well experience a sense of *déjà vu*, not because the question of parliamentary reform remains relevant and timely, but because the epistemological and methodological questions raised by this debate are with us still. What is the nature of political knowledge, and how is it to be obtained? What sort of "science" can "political science" aspire to be? What is the connection between political theory and the practice of politics? Mill's answers may appear to resemble those of modern "rational choice" theorists, and Macaulay's those of their empirically minded critics. After all, Mill maintains that any scientific theory worthy of the name must proceed from a finite set of assumptions about human nature, with the self-interest axiom at their center. From these one can deduce conclusions about the ways in which rational political actors will (or at any rate ought to) behave. Macaulay, by contrast, claims that people act for all sorts of reasons, including – but by no means limited to – considerations of self-interest.

The *Essay on Government* – and Macaulay's attack – earned for its author an unenviable reputation as an egregious simplifier of complex matters. Yet Mill remained unrepentant since such simplification was, in his view, the very purpose and point of theorizing. To theorize *is* to simplify. But, as his critics were quick to note, it is one thing to simplify and quite another to oversimplify. In a modern echo of Macaulay's estimate, Joseph Schumpeter contrasts Mill's "monumental, and indeed path-breaking, *History of British India*" with the *Essay on Government*, which "can be described only as unrelieved nonsense" because of its simplistic assumptions and its equally simplistic conclusions. A more charitable estimate is provided by Brian Barry. "The results [of Mill's reasoning]," Barry observes, "may appear somewhat crude, and yet it seems to me a serious question whether James Mill's political theory is any more of an oversimplification than, say, Ricardo's economics. The difference is, of course, that Ricardo's ideas were refined by subsequent theorists, whereas James Mill's *Essay on Government* had no successors until the last decade or so." These successors, on Barry's telling, include such "economic" and "rational choice" theorists as Mancur Olson and Anthony Downs, amongst others – a judgment in which Alan Ryan concurs. Although "an eminently dislikable document," Ryan writes, Mill's *Essay* "has virtues that ought not to be neglected." Not the least of these is that it "stands at the head of a line of thought extending down to Joseph Schumpeter and Anthony Downs, a line of thought that provides many of the explicit or implicit assumptions with the aid of which we still practice political science."

Although surely right in one respect, Barry's and Ryan's assessments are anachronistic in another. It is true that there is, methodologically speaking, a family resemblance between Mill's axiomatic-deductive reasoning in *Government* and, say, Downs's *An Economic Theory of Democracy*. But it is important to note that Mill, unlike

Downs and other ostensible successors, was never content to take interests or preferences as simply given or somehow fundamental, full stop. The author of the *History of British India* and the *Analysis of the Phenomena of the Human Mind* was no less concerned with distinguishing between sinister and non-sinister interests, supplying a causal explanation of their origins and development, rendering judgments about them, and attempting to alter the conditions that shape (or more often misshape) men's and women's characters; hence his interest in law, education, punishment, penology, psychology, and other avenues of "character-formation."

All this is, of course, a far cry from the modern disciplines of economics and rational choice theory. Mill's aims were not only explanatory but critical, educative, and, by his lights, emancipatory. The point of almost everything he wrote – from his massive "critical, or judging" *History of British India* to the shortest essay – was, to borrow a phrase from Marx, not merely to understand the world but to change it.

Chronology

1826 John Stuart Mill's "mental crisis" fueled by fear that he was a "manufactured man"

1829 Publication of *Analysis of the Phenomena of the Human Mind*; Macaulay's "famous attack" on Mill's *Government* appears in *Edinburgh Review*

1830 Appointed Head Examiner at India House; death of George IV; William IV becomes king; general election brings Whigs to power

1831 Growing agitation for reform; working-class riots in Derby, Bristol, and elsewhere; Reform Bill introduced

1832 Passage of Reform Act; Bentham dies

1833 Factory Act regulates child labor

1835 Publication of *Fragment on Mackintosh*; founding of *London and Westminster Review* to which Mill contributes controversial article, "The Church, and Its Reform"

1836 Mill dies

Bibliographical note

There is no complete edition of James Mill's voluminous writings. Mill's *Essay on Government* is available in several editions, one edited by Currin V. Shields (Bobbs-Merrill, 1955) and another in *Utilitarian Logic and Politics*, edited by Jack Lively and John Rees (Oxford: Clarendon Press, 1978); the latter also includes Macaulay's "famous attack" and the ensuing debate but not, unfortunately, Mill's own reply in the *Fragment on Mackintosh*. His *History of British India* is still to be found in many libraries, but is most readily accessible in the single-volume abridgement edited and introduced by William Thomas (University of Chicago Press, 1975). Mill's *Analysis of the Phenomena of the Human Mind* (London, 1829; 2nd edn 1869) has been reprinted by Augustus M. Kelly Publishers (1967), as has an abbreviated edition of his *Essays* (1986); the latter unfortunately omits "Education" and "Prisons and Prison Discipline" – two particularly important essays in Mill's oeuvre. Happily, Mill's *Essay on Education* is available, along with his other educational writings, in *James Mill on Education*, edited and introduced by W.H. Burston (Cambridge University Press, 1969). Mill's major economic writings are conveniently collected in *James Mill: Selected Economic Writings*, edited with an introduction by Donald Winch (University of Chicago Press, 1966).

Mill's handwritten *Commonplace Books* in five fat volumes – four in the London Library and a fifth at the London School of Economics – have never been published, although they should be.

There has as yet been no systematic book-length attempt to place Mill in his intellectual and political context. Although dated and not mainly about Mill, Elie Halevy's now-classic *The Growth of Philosophic Radicalism* (London, 1929) is still hard to beat. Halevy, however, overlooks the importance of the Whig thinkers with and against whom Mill and other radicals argued about politics. The second and third chapters of William Thomas's *The Philosophic Radicals* (Clarendon Press, 1979) does a much better job of situating Mill's thought in the political context of his time. The only biography of Mill is by Alexander Bain, *James Mill: A Biography* (London, 1882; reprinted by Augustus M. Kelly Publishers, 1966). A bold if somewhat idiosyncratic attempt to write a "psychobiography" of the Mills *père et fils* is Bruce Mazlish's *James and John Stuart Mill: Father and Son in the Nineteenth Century* (Basic Books, 1975). In a subsequent work, *The Revolutionary Ascetic: Evolution of a Political Type* (Basic Books, 1976), Mazlish views the elder Mill as a prototype for such twentieth-century "revolutionary ascetics" as Lenin and Mao Zedong, with results that are perhaps more suggestive than successful. Altogether different interpretations of Mill's role, reputation, and contribution to political theory and practice are to be found in Joseph Hamburger's *James Mill and the Art of Revolution* (Yale University Press, 1963) and the same author's *Intellectuals in Politics: John Stuart Mill and the Philosophic Radicals* (Yale University Press, 1965), and William Thomas's aforementioned *The Philosophic Radicals*. The most valuable bibliographic guide, Robert A. Fenn's *James Mill's Political Thought* (Garland, 1987), is meticulous in tracking down and identifying Mill's more obscure journalistic writings.

The secondary literature on Mill as a political theorist is sizeable and growing. Knud Haakonsen deftly traces the complicated debt that Mill owed to his Scots predecessors in "James Mill and Scottish Moral Philosophy," *Political Studies*, 33 (1985), pp. 628–36. On Mill's continuing methodological debt to his Scots teachers, see Neil de Marchi, "The Case for James Mill," in A. W. Coats (ed.), *Methodological Controversies in Economics* (JAI Press, 1983), pp. 155–84.

The extent to which Mill was a democrat who favored a wide extension of the franchise is a subject of continuing controversy. In his *Essay on Government* Mill undoubtedly pulled his punches and downplayed arguments in favor of radically extending the franchise. See, *inter alia*, Joseph Hamburger, "James Mill on Universal Suffrage and the Middle Class," *Journal of Politics*, 24 (1962). For a lively and not infrequently intemperate exchange about the intent and meaning of Mill's *Essay on Government*, see William Thomas, "James Mill's Politics: The Essay on Government and the Movement for Reform," *Historical Journal*, 12 (1969), pp. 249–84, followed by Wendell Robert Carr, "James Mill's Politics Reconsidered: Parliamentary Reform and the Triumph of Truth," *Historical Journal* 14 (1971), pp. 553–80, answered by William Thomas, "James Mill's Politics: A Rejoinder," *Historical Journal*, 14 (1971), pp. 735–50, and replied to by Carr, "James Mill's Politics: A Final Word," *Historical Journal*, 15 (1971), pp. 315–20.

The claim that Mill's views, at least as regards punishment, owed as much to Plato as to Bentham, is defended by Terence Ball, "Platonism and Penology: James Mill's Attempted Synthesis," *Journal of the History of the Behavioral Sciences*, 18 (July, 1982), pp. 222–9.

On Mill and India, see Duncan Forbes, "James Mill and India," *Cambridge Journal*, 5 (1951/2), pp. 19–33; Eric Stokes, *The British Utilitarians and India* (Oxford, 1969); and William Thomas's introduction to the aforementioned one-volume abridged edition of Mill's *History of British India*.

James Mill's view of women remains a matter of some dispute, much of which centers on a single controversial paragraph in the *Essay on Government*. The most systematic and sustained critique of this aspect of Mill's thought – William Thompson's *Appeal of One Half the Human Race* (1825) – has recently been reprinted, with an introduction by Richard Pankhurst (Virago, 1983). The conventional view (endorsed by Pankhurst, amongst many others) that the elder Mill was a male chauvinist from whom his "feminist" first son learned nothing of value is disputed by Terence Ball, "Utilitarianism, Feminism, and the Franchise: James Mill and His Critics," *History of Political Thought*, 1 (Spring, 1980), pp. 91–115, and, in a less scholarly and more accessible version, "The Feminist and His Father – A True Detective Story," in W. Phillips Shively (ed.), *The Research Process in Political Science* (Peacock, 1984).

The context and background of the Mill–Macaulay exchange is sketched by Lively and Rees in their introduction to *Utilitarian Logic and Politics* and by Donald Winch in "The Cause of Good Government: Philosophic Whigs versus Philosophic Radicals," in Stefan Collini, Donald Winch, and John Burrow, *That Noble Science of Politics: A Study in Nineteenth-Century Intellectual History* (Cambridge University Press, 1983), chapter 3.

For a critical comparison between James and John Stuart Mill's defenses of democratic rule and representative government, see Alan Ryan, "Two Concepts of Politics and Democracy: James and John Stuart Mill," in Martin Fleisher (ed.), *Machiavelli and the Nature of Political Thought* (Atheneum, 1972), pp. 72–113. Ryan, like Brian Barry in *Sociologists, Economists and Democracy* (Collier-Macmillan, 1970), takes the *Essay on Government* as his sole text and views James Mill as an early advocate of the "economic" approach to the study of politics. For a critique of the use, misuse, and abuse of Mill in this connection, see Terence Ball, *Transforming Political Discourse* (Blackwell, 1988), chapter 6.

The extent of the elder Mill's influence on his son, particularly in *On Liberty* (1859), is discussed sketchily but very suggestively in John C. Rees's posthumous *John Stuart Mill's "On Liberty"* edited by G. L. Williams (Oxford: Clarendon Press, 1985), esp. chapters 1 and 2.

Biographical synopses

Since a number of names mentioned in Mill's essays may not be familiar to some modern readers, the following synopses will, I hope, supply some illumination and a starting point for further inquiry. The interested reader is invited to turn to other, more comprehensive reference works such as *The Blackwell Encyclopedia of Political Thought*, edited by David Miller *et al.* and the original and secondary works cited therein.

BACON, Sir Francis (1561–1626), English statesman and philosopher of science whose *The Advancement of Learning* (1605) attempted to link new advances in the natural sciences to social and political progress.

BENTHAM, Jeremy (1748–1832), English political philosopher and legal reformer whose creed, Utilitarianism, held that "the greatest happiness of the greatest number" was the standard by which all laws, practices, and policies should be judged.

BLACKSTONE, Sir William (1723–80), English jurist whose *Commentaries on the Laws of England* (1769) was criticized by Bentham for its complacent acceptance of the hodgepodge of precedent and tradition from which much of English law was drawn.

CONDILLAC, Etienne de (1750–80), French psychologist and philosopher whose *Traité des Sensations* (1754) purports to trace the origins of ideas and other mental phenomena to sensory experience.

EDGEWORTH, Maria (1767–1849), English educationist and co-author of *Practical Education* (1798).

HARTLEY, David (1705–57), English physician and psychologist whose *Observations on Man* (1749) traced ideas and other mental phenomena to physiological sensations or "vibrations" in the human brain.

HELVETIUS, Claude (1715–71), French educational theorist whose doctrine that *l'éducation peut tout* – "education makes everything possible" – greatly influenced James Mill's views on education and human improvement.

HOBBES (sometimes spelled Hobbs), Thomas (1588–1679), English political philosopher and author of *Leviathan* (1651) which, proceeding from individualist premises, purports to arrive at authoritarian conclusions. Mill, like Hartley, relied heavily upon Hobbes's doctrine of the association of ideas.

HOWARD, John (1726–90), English prison reformer whose *State of the Prisons* (1777) exposed the evils of the English prison system. Cesare Beccaria, Jeremy Bentham, and James Mill, along with various Quaker reformers, were among Howard's most ardent admirers.

HUME, David (1711–76), skeptical Scottish philosopher who held that our most fundamental ideas, e.g. cause and effect, are merely the result of sensory impressions or experiences that, through custom, habit, or "constant conjunction," we eventually come to associate with one another.

KANT, Immanuel (1724–1804), German philosopher and author of the *Critique of Pure Reason* (1781) in which he argued – against Hume and other empiricists – that sensory experience yielded knowledge only because such experience was organized by and mediated through preexisting categories of understanding, such as time, space, and causality.

LOCKE, John (1632–1704), English empiricist philosopher and author of the *Essay Concerning Human Understanding* (1690) in which he traced the origin of ideas to sensory experience.

MACAULAY, Thomas Babington (1800–59), British historian and Whig critic of Bentham, Mill, and philosophic radicalism.

MACKINTOSH, Sir James (1765–1832), Whig polemicist whose *Dissertation on Ethical Philosophy* (1830) was highly critical of Bentham's and James Mill's political aims and philosophical arguments.

MILL, John Stuart (1806–73), eldest son of James Mill and author of *On Liberty* (1859) and many other works in political theory, ethics, economics, and philosophy of science.

REID, Thomas (1710–92), Scottish philosopher and author of *Inquiry Into the Human Mind* (1764), which was highly critical of Locke, Hume, and the British empiricist tradition.

ROUSSEAU, Jean-Jacques (1702–71), French-Swiss political philosopher with whose views on various matters – including representation and education – Mill took strong exception.

SMITH, Adam (1723–90), Scottish philosopher and economist whose *Wealth of Nations* (1776) views rational self-interest as the foundation of human action and association.

THOMPSON, William (1775–1833), Irish radical, socialist, sometime Utilitarian and feminist whose *Appeal of One Half the Human Race* (1825) was highly critical of James Mill's *Essay on Government* for its proposed exclusion of women from the franchise.

A note on sources

The first five essays – *Government, Jurisprudence, Liberty of the Press, Education,* and *Prisons and Prison Discipline* – were published originally in the *Supplement to the Encyclopaedia Britannica* (London, 1819–23), and later reprinted under the title *Essays on Government, Jurisprudence, [Etc.],* by James Mill, Esq., author of the History of British India (first published 1823; corrected and enlarged edition London: J. Innes, 1825; reprinted 1828); the 1828 edition has been used here. [Two essays in that collection – *Colony* and *Law of Nations* – have been omitted.] "The Ballot" was first published in *The Westminster Review,* July 1830, pp. 1–39, and subsequently reprinted as a pamphlet. Macaulay's "Mill on Government" appeared in *The Edinburgh Review* (March, 1829) and is reprinted here from *The Complete Works of Lord Macaulay,* 12 vols. (London: Longmans Green & Co., 1898), vol. 7, pp. 327–71. Mill's heretofore unnoticed reply to Macaulay comes from his *Fragment on Mackintosh* (1835; 2nd edn London: Longmans, Green, Reader, and Dyer, 1870), pp. 275–96.

All Mill's essays in the present volume are reprinted in their entirety, with the exception of several long quotations from other authors which have been omitted. Spelling and punctuation have been modernized only where Mill's original might mislead or confuse the modern reader.

GOVERNMENT.

I.
The End of Government; viz. the Good or Benefit for the Sake of which it exists.

The question with respect to Government is a question about the adaptation of means to an end. Notwithstanding the portion of discourse which has been bestowed upon this subject, it is surprising to find, on a close inspection, how few of its principles are settled. The reason is, that the ends and means have not been analyzed; and it is only a general and undistinguishing conception of them, which is found in the minds of the greatest number of men. Things, in this situation, give rise to interminable disputes; more especially when the deliberation is subject, as here, to the strongest action of personal interest.

In a discourse, limited as the present, it would be obviously vain to attempt the accomplishment of such a task as that of the analysis we have mentioned. The mode, however, in which the operation should be conducted, may perhaps be described, and evidence enough exhibited to shew in what road we must travel, to approach the goal at which so many have vainly endeavoured to arrive.

The end of Government has been described in a great variety of expressions. By Locke it was said to be "the public good;" by others it has been described as being "the greatest happiness of the greatest number." These, and equivalent expressions, are just; but they are defective, inasmuch as the particular ideas which they embrace are indistinctly announced; and different conceptions are by means of them raised in different minds, and even in the same mind on different occasions.

It is immediately obvious, that a wide and difficult field is presented, and that the whole science of human nature must be explored, to lay a foundation for the science of Government.

To understand what is included in the happiness of the greatest number, we must understand what is included in the happiness of the individuals of whom it is composed.

That dissection of human nature which would be necessary for exhibiting, on proper evidence, the primary elements into which human happiness may be resolved, it is not compatible with the present design to undertake. We must content ourselves with assuming certain results.

We may allow, for example, in general terms, that the lot of every human being is determined by his pains and pleasures; and that his happiness corresponds with the degree in which his pleasures are great, and his pains are small.

Human pains and pleasures are derived from two sources: – They are produced, either by our fellow-men, or by causes independent of other men.

We may assume it as another principle, that the concern of Government is with the former of these two sources; that its business is to increase to the utmost the pleasures, and diminish to the utmost the pains, which men derive from one another.

Of the laws of nature, on which the condition of man depends, that which is attended with the greatest number of consequences, is the necessity of labour for obtaining the means of subsistence, as well as the means of the greatest part of our pleasures. This is, no doubt, the primary cause of Government; for, if nature had produced spontaneously all the objects which we desire, and in sufficient abundance for the desires of all, there would have been no source of dispute or of injury among men; nor would any man have possessed the means of ever acquiring authority over another.

The results are exceedingly different, when nature produces the objects of desire not in sufficient abundance for all. The source of dispute is then exhaustless; and every man has the means of acquiring authority over others, in proportion to the quantity of those objects which he is able to possess.

In this case, the end to be obtained, through Government as the means, is, to make that distribution of the scanty materials of happiness, which would insure the greatest sum of it in the members of the community, taken altogether, preventing every individual, or combination of individuals, from interfering with that distribution, or making any man to have less than his share.

When it is considered that most of the objects of desire, and even the means of subsistence, are the product of labour, it is evident that the means of insuring labour must be provided for as the foundation of all.

The means for the insuring of labour are of two sorts; the one made out of the matter of evil, the other made out of the matter of good.

The first sort is commonly denominated force; and, under its application, the labourers are slaves. This mode of procuring labour we need not consider; for, if the end of Government be to produce the greatest happiness of the greatest number, that end cannot be attained by making the greatest number slaves.

The other mode of obtaining labour is by allurement, or the advantage which it brings. To obtain all the objects of desire in the greatest possible quantity, we must obtain labour in the greatest possible quantity; and, to obtain labour in the greatest possible quantity, we must raise to the greatest possible height the advantage attached to labour. It is impossible to attach to labour a greater degree of advantage than the whole of the product of labour. Why so? Because, if you give more to one man than the produce of his labour, you can do so only by taking it away from the produce of some other man's labour. The greatest possible happiness of society is, therefore, attained by insuring to every man the greatest possible quantity of the produce of his labour.

How is this to be accomplished? for it is obvious that every man, who has not all the objects of his desire, has inducement to take them from any other man who is weaker than himself: and how is he to be prevented?

One mode is sufficiently obvious; and it does not appear that there is any other: The union of a certain number of men, to protect one another. The object, it is plain, can best be attained when a great number of men combine, and delegate to a small number the power necessary for protecting them all. This is Government.

With respect to the end of Government, or that for the sake of which it exists, it is not conceived to be necessary, on the present occasion, that the analysis should be carried any further. What follows is an attempt to analyze the means.

II.
The Means of attaining the End of Government; viz. Power, and Securities against the Abuse of that Power.

Two things are here to be considered; the power with which the small number are entrusted; and the use which they are to make of it.

With respect to the first, there is no difficulty. The elements, out of which the power of coercing others is fabricated, are obvious to all. Of these we shall, therefore, not lengthen this article by any explanation.

All the difficult questions of Government relate to the means of restraining those, in whose hands are lodged the powers necessary for the protection of all, from making a bad use of it.

Whatever would be the temptations under which individuals would lie, if there was no Government, to take the objects of desire from others weaker than themselves, under the same temptations the members of Government lie, to take the objects of desire from the members of the community, if they are not prevented from doing so. Whatever, then, are the reasons for establishing Government, the very same exactly are the reasons for establishing securities, that those entrusted with the powers necessary for protecting others make use of them for that purpose solely, and not for the purpose of taking from the members of the community the objects of desire.

III.

That the requisite Securities against the Abuse of Power, are not found in any of the simple Forms of Government.

There are three modes in which it may be supposed that the powers for the protection of the community are capable of being exercised. The community may undertake the protection of itself, and of its members. The powers of protection may be placed in the hands of a few. And, lastly, they may be placed in the hands of an individual. The Many, The Few, The One; These varieties appear to exhaust the subject. It is not possible to conceive any hands, or combination of hands, in which the powers of protection can be lodged, which will not fall under one or other of those descriptions. And these varieties correspond to the three forms of Government, the Democratical, the Aristocratical, and the Monarchical.

It will be necessary to look somewhat closely at each of these forms in their order.

1. THE DEMOCRATICAL. – It is obviously impossible that the community in a body can be present to afford protection to each of its members. It must employ individuals for that purpose. Employing individuals, it must choose them; it must lay down the rules under which they are to act; and it must punish them, if they act in disconformity to those rules. In these functions are included the three great operations of Government – Administration, Legislation, and Judicature. The community, to perform any of these operations, must be assembled. This circumstance alone seems to form a conclusive objection against the democratical form. To assemble the whole of a community as often as the business of Government requires performance would almost preclude the existence of labour; hence that of property; and hence the existence of the community itself.

There is another objection, not less conclusive. A whole community would form a numerous assembly. But all numerous assemblies are essentially incapable of business. It is unnecessary to be tedious in the proof of this proposition. In an assembly, every thing

7

must be done by speaking and assenting. But where the assembly is numerous, so many persons desire to speak, and feelings, by mutual inflammation, become so violent, that calm and effectual deliberation is impossible.

It may be taken, therefore, as a position, from which there will be no dissent, that a community in mass is ill adapted for the business of Government. There is no principle more in conformity with the sentiments and the practice of the people than this. The management of the joint affairs of any considerable body of the people they never undertake for themselves. What they uniformly do is, to choose a certain number of themselves to be the actors in their stead. Even in the case of a common Benefit Club, the members choose a Committee of Management, and content themselves with a general controul.

2. THE ARISTOCRATICAL. – This term applies to all those cases, in which the powers of Government are held by any number of persons intermediate between a single person and the majority. When the number is small, it is common to call the Government an Oligarchy; when it is considerable, to call it an Aristocracy. The cases are essentially the same; because the motives which operate in both are the same. This is a proposition which carries, we think, its own evidence along with it. We, therefore, assume it as a point which will not be disputed.

The source of evil is radically different, in the case of Aristocracy, from what it is in that of Democracy.

The Community cannot have an interest opposite to its interest. To affirm this would be a contradiction in terms. The Community within itself, and with respect to itself, can have no sinister interest. One Community may intend the evil of another; never its own. This is an indubitable proposition, and one of great importance. The Community may act wrong from mistake. To suppose that it could from design, would be to suppose that human beings can wish their own misery.

The circumstances, from which the inaptitude of the community, as a body, for the business of Government, arises, namely, the inconvenience of assembling them, and the inconvenience of their numbers when assembled, do not necessarily exist in the case of Aristocracy. If the number of those who hold among them the powers of Government is so great, as to make it inconvenient to assemble them, or impossible for them to deliberate calmly when assembled, this is only an objection to so extended an Aristocracy, and has no application to an Aristocracy not too numerous, when assembled, for the best exercise of deliberation.

The question is, whether such an Aristrocracy may be trusted to make that use of the powers of Government which is most conducive to the end for which Government exists?

There may be a strong presumption that any Aristocracy, monopolizing the powers of Government, would not possess intellectual powers in any very high perfection. Intellectual powers are the offspring of labour. But an hereditary Aristrocracy are deprived of the strongest motives to labour. The greater part of them will, therefore, be defective in those mental powers. This is one objection, and an important one, though not the greatest.

We have already observed, that the reason for which Government exists is, that one man, if stronger than another, will take from him whatever that other possesses and he desires. But if one man will do this, so will several. And if powers are put into the hands of a comparatively small number, called an Aristocracy, powers which make them stronger than the rest of the community, they will take from the rest of the community as much as they please of the objects of desire. They will, thus, defeat the very end for which Government was instituted. The unfitness, therefore, of an Aristocracy to be entrusted with the powers of Government, rests on demonstration.

3. THE MONARCHICAL. – It will be seen, and therefore words to make it manifest are unnecessary, that, in most respects, the Monarchical form of Government agrees with the Aristocratical, and is liable to the same objections.

If Government is founded upon this, as a law of human nature, that a man, if able, will take from others any thing which they have and he desires, it is sufficiently evident that when a man is called a King, it does not change his nature; so that when he has got power to enable him to take from every man what he pleases, he will take whatever he pleases. To suppose that he will not, is to affirm that Government is unnecessary; and that human beings will abstain from injuring one another of their own accord.

It is very evident that this reasoning extends to every modification of the smaller number. Whenever the powers of Government are placed in any hands other than those of the community, whether those of one man, of a few, or of several, those principles of human nature which imply that Government is at all necessary, imply that those persons will make use of them to defeat the very end for which Government exists.

IV.
An Objection stated – and answered.

One observation, however, suggests itself. Allowing, it may be said, that this deduction is perfect, and the inference founded upon it indisputable, it is yet true, that if there were no Government, every man would be exposed to depredation from every man; but, under an Aristocracy, he is exposed to it only from a few; under a Monarchy, only from one.

This is a highly-important objection, and deserves to be minutely investigated.

It is sufficiently obvious, that, if every man is liable to be deprived of what he possesses at the will of every man stronger than himself, the existence of property is impossible; and, if the existence of property is impossible, so also is that of labour, of the means of subsistence for an enlarged community, and hence of the community itself. If the members of such a community are liable to deprivation by only a few hundred men, the members of an Aristocracy, it may not be impossible to satiate that limited number with a limited portion of the objects belonging to all. Allowing this view of the subject to be correct, it follows, that the smaller the number of hands into which the powers of Government are permitted to pass, the happier it will be for the community: that an Oligarchy, therefore, is better than an Aristocracy, and a Monarchy better than either.

This view of the subject deserves to be the more carefully considered, because the conclusion to which it leads is the same with that which has been adopted and promulgated, by some of the most profound and most benevolent investigators of human affairs. That Government by one man, altogether unlimited and uncontrolled, is better than Government by any modification of Aristocracy, is the celebrated opinion of Mr. Hobbes, and of the French *Economists*, supported on reasonings which it is not easy to controvert. Government by the many, they with reason considered an impossibility. They inferred, therefore, that, of all the possible forms of Government, absolute Monarchy is the best.

Experience, if we look only at the outside of the facts, appears to be divided on this subject. Absolute Monarchy, under Neros and Caligulas, under such men as Emperors of Morocco and Sultans of Turkey, is the scourge of human nature. On the other side, the people of Denmark, tired out with the oppression of an Aristocracy, resolved that their King should be absolute, and, under their absolute Monarch, are as well governed as any people in Europe. In Greece, notwithstanding the defects of Democracy, human nature ran a more brilliant career than it has ever done in any other age or country.

As the surface of history affords, therefore, no certain principle of decision, we must go beyond the surface, and penetrate to the springs within.

When it is said that one man, or a limited number of men, will soon be satiated with the objects of desire, and, when they have taken from the community what suffices to satiate them, will protect its members in the enjoyment of the remainder, an important element of the calculation is left out. Human beings are not a passive substance. If human beings, in respect to their rulers, were the same as sheep in respect to their shepherd; and if the King, or the Aristocracy, were as totally exempt from all fear of resistance from the people, and all chance of obtaining more obedience from severity, as the shepherd in the case of the sheep, it does appear that there would be a limit to the motive for taking to one's self the objects of desire. The case will be found to be very much altered when the idea is taken into the account, first, of the resistance to his will which one human being may expect from another; and secondly, of that perfection in obedience which fear alone can produce.

That one human being will desire to render the person and property of another subservient to his pleasures, notwithstanding the pain or loss of pleasure which it may occasion to that other individual, is the foundation of Government. The desire of the object implies the desire of the power necessary to accomplish the object. The desire, therefore, of that power which is necessary to render the persons and properties of human beings subservient to our pleasures, is a grand governing law of human nature.

What is implied in that desire of power; and what is the extent to which it carries the actions of men; are the questions which it is necessary to resolve, in order to discover the limit which nature has set to the desire on the part of a King, or an Aristocracy, to inflict evil upon the community for their own advantage.

Power is a means to an end. The end is every thing, without exception, which the human being calls pleasure, and the removal of pain. The grand instrument for attaining what a man likes is the actions of other men. Power, in its most appropriate signification, therefore, means security for the conformity between the will of one man and the acts of other men. This, we presume, is not a proposition which will be disputed. The master has power over his servant, because when he wills him to do so and so, – in other words, expresses a desire that he would do so and so, he possesses a kind of security that the actions of the man will correspond to his desire. The General commands his soldiers to perform certain operations, the King commands his subjects to act in a certain manner, and their power is complete or not complete, in proportion as the conformity is complete or not complete between the actions willed and the actions performed. The actions of other men, considered as means for the attainment of the objects of our desire, are perfect or imperfect, in proportion as they are or are not certainly and invariably correspondent to our will. There is no limit, therefore, to the demand of security for the perfection of that correspondence. A man is never satisfied with a smaller degree if he can obtain a greater. And as there is no man whatsoever, whose acts, in some degree or other, in some way or other, more immediately or more remotely, may not have some influence as means to our ends, there is no man, the conformity of whose acts to our will we would not give something to secure. The demand, therefore, of power over the acts of other men is really boundless. It is boundless in two ways; boundless in the number of persons to whom we would extend it, and boundless in its degree over the actions of each.

It would be nugatory to say, with a view to explain away this important principle, that some human beings may be so remotely connected with our interests as to make the desire of a conformity between our will and their actions evanescent. It is quite enough to assume, what nobody will deny, that our desire of that conformity is unlimited, in respect to all those men whose actions can be supposed to have any influence on our pains and pleasures. With respect to the rulers of a community, this at least is certain, that they have a desire for the uniformity between their will and the actions of every man in the community. And for our present purpose, this is as wide a field as we need to embrace.

With respect to the community, then, we deem it an established truth, that the rulers, one or a few, desire an exact conformity between their will and the acts of every member of the community. It remains for us to inquire to what description of acts it is the nature of this desire to give existence.

There are two classes of means by which the conformity between the will of one man and the acts of other men may be accomplished. The one is pleasure, the other pain.

With regard to securities of the pleasurable sort for obtaining a conformity between one man's will and the acts of other men, it is evident, from experience, that when a man possesses a command over the objects of desire, he may, by imparting those objects to other men, insure, to a great extent, conformity between his will and their actions. It follows, and is also matter of experience, that the greater the quantity of the objects of desire, which he may thus impart to other men, the greater is the number of men between whose actions and his own will he can insure a conformity. As it has been demonstrated that there is no limit to the number of men whose actions we desire to have conformable to our will, it follows, with equal evidence, that there is no limit to the command which we desire to possess over the objects which ensure this result.

It is, therefore, not true, that there is in the mind of a King, or in the minds of an Aristocracy, any point of saturation with the objects of desire. The opinion, in examination of which we have gone through the preceding analysis, that a King or an Aristocracy may be satiated with the objects of desire, and, after being satiated, leave to the members of the community the greater part of what belongs to them, is an opinion founded upon a partial and incomplete view of the laws of human nature.

We have next to consider the securities of the painful sort which may be employed for attaining conformity between the acts of one man and the will of another.

We are of the opinion, that the importance of this part of the subject has not been duly considered; and that the business of Government will be ill understood, till its numerous consequences have been fully developed.

Pleasure appears to be a feeble instrument of obedience in comparison with pain. It is much more easy to despise pleasure than pain. Above all, it is important to consider, that in this class of instruments is included the power of taking away life, and with it of taking away not only all the pleasures of reality, but, what goes so far beyond them, all the pleasures of hope. This class of securities is, therefore, incomparably the strongest. He who desires obedience, to a high degree of exactness, cannot be satisfied with the power of giving pleasure, he must have the power of inflicting pain. He who desires it, to the highest possible degree of exactness, must desire power of inflicting pain sufficient at least to insure that degree of exactness; that is, an unlimited power of inflicting pain; for, as there is no possible mark by which to distinguish what is sufficient and what is not, and as the human mind sets no bounds to its avidity for the securities of what it deems eminently good, it is sure to extend, beyond almost any limits, its desire of the power of giving pain to others.

It may, however, be said, that how inseparable a part soever of human nature it may appear to be, to desire to possess unlimited power of inflicting pain upon others, it does not follow, that those who possess it will have a desire to make use of it.

This is the next part of the inquiry upon which we have to enter; and we need not add that it merits all the attention of those who would possess correct ideas upon a subject which involves the greatest interests of mankind.

The chain of inference, in this case, is close and strong, to a most unusual degree. A man desires that the actions of other men shall be instantly and accurately correspondent to his will. He desires that the actions of the greatest possible number shall be so. Terror is the grand instrument. Terror can work only through assurance that evil will follow any want of conformity between the will and the actions willed. Every failure must, therefore, be punished. As there are no bounds to the mind's desire of its pleasure, there are of course no bounds to its desire of perfection in the instruments of that pleasure. There are, therefore, no bounds to its desire of exactness in the conformity between its will and the actions willed; and, by consequence, to the strength of that terror which is its procuring cause. Every, the most minute, failure, must be visited with the heaviest infliction: and, as failure in extreme exactness must frequently happen, the occasions of cruelty must be incessant.

We have thus arrived at several conclusions of the highest possible importance. We have seen, that the very principle of human nature upon which the necessity of Government is founded, the propensity of one man to possess himself of the objects of desire at the cost of another, leads on, by infallible sequence, where power over a community is attained, and nothing checks, not only to that degree of plunder which leaves the members (excepting always the recipients and instruments of the plunder) the bare means of subsistence, but to that degree of cruelty which is necessary to keep in existence the most intense terror.

The world affords some decisive experiments upon human nature, in exact conformity with these conclusions. An English Gentleman may be taken as a favourable specimen of civilization, of knowledge, of humanity, of all the qualities, in short, that make human nature estimable. The degree in which he desires to possess power over his fellow-creatures, and the degree of oppression to which he finds motives for carrying the exercise of that power, will afford a standard from which, assuredly, there can be no appeal. Wherever the same motives exist, the same conduct, as that displayed by the English Gentleman, may be expected to follow, in all men not farther advanced in human excellence than him. In the West Indies, before that vigilant attention of the English nation, which now, for thirty years, has imposed so great a check upon the masters of slaves, there was not a perfect absence of all check upon the dreadful propensities of power. But yet it is true, that these propensities led English Gentlemen, not only to deprive their slaves of property, and to make property of their fellow-creatures, but to treat them with a degree of cruelty, the very description of which froze the blood of their countrymen, who were placed in less unfavourable circumstances. The motives of this deplorable conduct are exactly those which we have described above, as arising out of the universal desire to render the actions of other men exactly conformable to our will. It is of great importance to remark, that not one item in the motives which had led

English Gentlemen to make slaves of their fellow-creatures, and to reduce them to the very worst condition in which the negroes have been found in the West Indies, can be shown to be wanting, or to be less strong in the set of motives, which universally operate upon the men who have power over their fellow-creatures. It is proved, therefore, by the closest deduction from the acknowledged laws of human nature, and by direct and decisive experiments, that the ruling One, or the ruling Few, would, if checks did not operate in the way of prevention, reduce the great mass of the people subject to their power, at least to the condition of negroes in the West Indies.*

We have thus seen, that of the forms of Government, which have been called the three simple forms, not one is adequate to the ends which Government is appointed to secure; that the community itself, which alone is free from motives opposite to those ends, is incapacitated by its numbers from performing the business of Government; and that whether Government is intrusted to one or a few, they have not only motives opposite to those ends, but motives which will carry them, if unchecked, to inflict the greatest evils.

These conclusions are so conformable to ordinary conceptions, that it would hardly have been necessary, if the development had not been of importance for some of our subsequent investigations, to have taken any pains with the proof of them. In this country, at least, it will be remarked, in conformity with so many writers, that the imperfection of the three simple forms of Government is apparent; that the ends of Government can be attained in perfection only, as under the British Constitution, by an union of all the three.

---

*An acute sense of this important truth is expressed by the President Montesquieu: "C'est une experience eternelle, que tout homme qui a du pouvoir est porte a en abuser; il va jusqu'a ce qu'il trouve de limites." – *Esp. de Loix*, II. 4.

V.

That the requisite Securities are not found in a Union of the Three simple Forms of Government; – Doctrine of the Constitutional Balance.

The doctrine of the union of the three simple forms of Government is the next part of this important subject which we are called upon to examine.

The first thing which it is obvious to remark upon it, is, that it has been customary, in regard to this part of the inquiry, to beg the question. The good effects which have been ascribed to the union of the three simple forms of Government, have been *supposed*; and the supposition has commonly been allowed. No proof has been adduced; or if any thing have the appearance of proof, it has only been a reference to the British Constitution. The British Constitution, it has been said, is an union of the three simple forms of Government; and the British Government is excellent. To render the instance of the British Government in any degree a proof of the doctrine in question, it is evident that three points must be established; 1st, That the British Government is not in show, but in substance, an union of the three simple forms; 2dly, That it has peculiar excellence; and, 3dly, That its excellence arises from the union so supposed, and not from any other cause. As these points have always been taken for granted without examination, the question with respect to the effects of an union of the three simple forms of Government may be considered as yet unsolved.

The positions which we have already established with regard to human nature, and which we assume as foundations, are these: That the actions of men are governed by their wills, and their wills by their desires: That their desires are directed to pleasure and relief from pain as *ends*, and to wealth and power as the principal means: That to the desire of these means there is no limit; and that the actions which flow from this unlimited desire are the constituents whereof bad Government is made. Reasoning correctly from these acknowledged laws of human nature, we shall presently discover what opinion, with respect to the mixture of the different species of Government, it will be incumbent upon us to adopt.

The theory in question implies, that of the powers of Government, one portion is held by the King, one by the Aristocracy, and one by the people. It also implies, that there is on the part of each of them a certain unity of will, otherwise they would not act as three separate powers. This being understood, we proceed to the inquiry.

From the principles which we have already laid down, it follows, That of the objects of human desire – and, speaking more definitely, of the means to the ends of human desire, namely, wealth and power – each of the three parties will endeavour to obtain as much as possible.

After what has been said, it is not suspected that any reader will deny this proposition; but it is of importance that he keep in his mind a very clear conception of it.

If any expedient presents itself to any of the supposed parties, effectual to said end, and not opposed to any preferred object of pursuit, we may infer, with certainty, that it will be adopted. One effectual expedient is not more effectual than obvious. Any two of the parties, by combining, may swallow up the third. That such combination will take place, appears to be as certain as any thing which depends upon human will; because there are strong motives in favour of it, and none that can be conceived in opposition to it. Whether the portions of power, as originally distributed to the parties, be supposed to be equal or unequal, the mixture of three of the kinds of Government, it is thus evident, cannot possibly exist.

This proposition appears to be so perfectly proved, that we do not think it necessary to dwell here upon the subject. As a part, however, of this doctrine, of the mixture of the simple forms of Government, it may be proper to inquire, whether an union may not be possible of two of them.

Three varieties of this union may be conceived; the union of the Monarchy with Aristocracy, or the union of either with Democracy.

Let us first suppose that Monarchy is united with Aristocracy. Their power is equal or not equal. If it is not equal, it follows, as a necessary consequence, from the principles which we have already established, that the stronger will take from the weaker, till it engrosses the whole. The only question, therefore, is, What will happen when the power is equal.

In the first place, it seems impossible that such equality should ever exist. How is it to be established? Or by what criterion is it to be ascertained? If there is no such criterion, it must, in all cases, be the result of chance. If so, the chances against it are as infinite to one. The idea, therefore, is wholly chimerical and absurd.

Besides, A disposition to overrate one's own advantages, and underrate those of other men, is a known law of human nature. Suppose, what would be little less than miraculous, that equality were established, this propensity would lead each of the parties to conceive itself the strongest. The consequence would be that they would go to war, and contend till one or other was subdued. Either those laws of human nature, upon which all reasoning with respect to Government proceeds, must be denied, and then the utility of Government itself may be denied, or this conclusion is demonstrated. Again, if this equality were established, is there a human being who can suppose that it would last? If any thing be known about human affairs it is this, that they are in perpetual change. If nothing else interfered, the difference of men in respect of talents, would abundantly produce the effect. Suppose your equality to be established at the time when your King is a man of talents, and suppose his successor to be the reverse; your equality no longer exists. The moment one of the parties is superior, it begins to profit by its superiority, and the inequality is daily increased. It is unnecessary to extend the investigation to the remaining cases, the union of democracy with either of the other two kinds of Government. It is very evident that the same reasoning would lead to the same results.

In this doctrine of the mixture of the simple forms of Government, is included the celebrated theory of the Balance among the component parts of a Government. By this, it is supposed, that, when a Government is composed of Monarchy, Aristocracy, and Democracy, they balance one another, and by mutual checks produce good government. A few words will suffice to show, that, if any theory deserve the epithets of "wild, visionary, chimerical," it is that of the Balance. If there are three powers, how is it possible to prevent two of them from combining to swallow up the third?

The analysis which we have already performed, will enable us to trace rapidly the concatenation of causes and effects in this imagined case.

We have already seen that the interest of the community, considered in the aggregate, or in the democratical point of view, is, that each individual should receive protection, and that the powers which are consitituted for that purpose should be employed exclusively for that purpose. As this is a proposition wholly indisputable, it is also one to which all correct reasoning upon matters of Government must have a perpetual reference.

We have also seen that the interest of the King, and of the governing Aristocracy, is directly the reverse; it is to have unlimited power over the rest of the community, and to use it for their own advantage. In the supposed case of the balance of the Monarchical, Aristocratical, and Democratical powers, it cannot be for the interest of either the Monarchy or the Aristocracy to combine with the Democracy; because it is the interest of the Democracy, or community at large, that neither the King nor the Aristocracy should have one particle of power, or one particle of the wealth of the community, for their own advantage.

The Democracy or Community have all possible motives to endeavour to prevent the Monarchy and Aristocracy from exercising power, or obtaining the wealth of the community, for their own advantage: The Monarchy and Aristocracy have all possible motives for endeavouring to obtain unlimited power over the persons and property of the community: The consequence is inevitable; they have all possible motives for combining to obtain that power, and unless the people have power enough to be a match for both, they have no protection. The balance, therefore, is a thing, the existence of which, upon the best possible evidence, is to be regarded as impossible. The appearances which have given colour to the supposition are altogether delusive.

VI.

In the Representative System alone the Securities for good Government are to be found.

What then is to be done? For, according to this reasoning, we may be told that good Government appears to be impossible. The people, as a body, cannot perform the business of Government for themselves. If the powers of Government are entrusted to one man, or a few men, and a Monarchy, or governing Aristocracy, is formed, the results are fatal: And it appears that a combination of the simple forms is impossible.

Notwithstanding the truth of these propositions, it is not yet proved that good Government is impossible. For though the people, who cannot exercise the powers of Government themselves, must entrust them to some one individual or set of individuals, and such individuals will infallibly have the strongest motives to make a bad use of them, it is possible that checks may be found sufficient to prevent them. The next subject of inquiry, then, is the doctrine of checks. It is sufficiently conformable to the established and fashionable opinions to say, that, upon the right constitution of checks, all goodness of Government depends. To this proposition we fully subscribe. Nothing, therefore, can exceed the importance of correct conclusions upon this subject. After the developments already made, it is hoped that the inquiry will be neither intricate nor unsatisfactory.

In the grand discovery of modern times, the system of representation, the solution of all the difficulties, both speculative and practical, will perhaps be found. If it cannot, we seem to be forced upon the extraordinary conclusion, that good Government is impossible. For as there is no individual, or combination of individuals, except the community itself, who would not have an interest in bad Government, if entrusted with its powers; and as the community itself is incapable of exercising those powers, and must entrust them to some individual or combination of individuals, the conclusion is obvious: The Community itself must check those individuals, else they will follow their interest, and produce bad Government.

But how is it the Community can check? The community can act only when assembled: And then it is incapable of acting.

The community, however, can chuse Representatives: And the question is, whether the Representatives of the Community can operate as a check?

VII.
What is required in a Representative Body to make it a Security for good Government?

We may begin by laying down two propositions, which appear to involve a great portion of the inquiry; and about which it is unlikely that there will be any dispute.

I. The checking body must have a degree of power sufficient for the business of checking.

II. It must have an identity of interest with the community; otherwise it will make a mischievous use of its power.

I. To measure the degree of power which is requisite upon any occasion, we must consider the degree of power which is necessary to be overcome. Just as much as suffices for that purpose is requisite, and no more. We have then to inquire what power it is which the Representatives of the community, acting as a check, need power to overcome. The answer here is easily given. It is all that power, wheresoever lodged, which they, in whose hands it is lodged, have an interest in misusing. We have already seen, that to whomsoever the community entrusts the powers of Government, whether one, or a few, they have an interest in misusing them. All the power, therefore, which the one or the few, or which the one and the few combined, can apply to insure the accomplishment of their sinister ends, the checking body must have power to overcome, otherwise its check will be unavailing. In other words, there will be no check.

This is so exceedingly evident, that we hardly think it necessary to say another word in illustration of it. If a King is prompted by the inherent principles of human nature to seek the gratification of his will; and if he finds an obstacle in that pursuit, he removes it, of course, if he can. If any man, or any set of men, oppose him, he overcomes them, if he is able; and to prevent him, they must, at the least, have equal power with himself.

The same is the case with an Aristocracy. To oppose them with success in pursuing their interest at the expense of the community, the checking body must have power successfully to resist whatever power they possess. If there is both a King and an Aristocracy, and if they would combine to put down the checking force, and to pursue their mutual interest at the expense of the community, the checking body must have sufficient power successfully to resist the united power of both King and Aristocracy.

These conclusions are not only indisputable, but the very theory of the British Constitution is erected upon them. The House of Commons, according to that theory, is the checking body. It is also an admitted doctrine, that if the King had the power of bearing down any opposition to his will that could be made by the House of Commons; or if the King and the House of Lords combined had the power of bearing down its opposition to their joint will, it would cease to have the power of checking them; it must, therefore, have a power sufficient to overcome the united power of both.

II. All the questions which relate to the degree of power necessary to be given to that checking body, on the perfection of whose operations all the goodness of Government depends, are thus pretty easily solved. The grand difficulty consists in finding the means of constituting a checking body, whose powers shall not be turned against the community for whose protection it is created.

There can be no doubt, that if power is granted to a body of men, called Representatives, they, like any other men, will use their power, not for the advantage of the community, but for their own advantage, if they can. The only question is, therefore, how they can be prevented? in other words, how are the interests of the Representatives to be identified with those of the community?

Each Representative may be considered in two capacities; in his capacity of Representative, in which he has the exercise of power over others, and in his capacity of Member of the Community, in which others have the exercise of power over him.

If things were so arranged, that, in his capacity of Representative, it would be impossible for him to do himself so much good by misgovernment, as he would do himself harm in his capacity of member of the community, the object would be accomplished. We have already seen, that the amount of power assigned to the checking body cannot be diminished beyond a certain amount. It must be sufficient to overcome all resistance on the part of all those in whose hands the powers of Government are lodged. But if the power assigned to the Representative cannot be diminished in amount, there is only one other way in which it can be diminished, and that is, in duration.

This, then, is the instrument; lessening of duration is the instrument, by which, if by any thing, the object is to be attained. The smaller the period of time during which any man retains his capacity of Representative, as compared with the time in which he is simply a member of the community, the more difficult it will be to compensate the sacrifice of the interests of the longer period, by the profits of misgovernment during the shorter.

This is an old and approved method of identifying as nearly as possible the interests of those who rule with the interests of those who are ruled. It is in pursuance of this advantage, that the Members of the British House of Commons have always been chosen for a limited period. If the Members were hereditary, or even if they were chosen for life, every inquirer would immediately pronounce that they would employ, for their own advantage, the powers entrusted to them; and that they would go just as far in abusing the persons and properties of the people, as their estimate of the powers and spirit of the people to resist them would allow them to contemplate as safe.

As it thus appears, by the consent of all men, from the time when the Romans made their Consuls annual, down to the present day, that the end is to be attained by limiting the duration, either of the acting, or (which is better) of the checking power, the next question is, to what degree should the limitation proceed?

The general answer is plain. It should proceed, till met by over-balancing inconveniences on the other side. What then are the inconveniences which are likely to flow from a too limited duration?

They are of two sorts; those which affect the performance of the service, for which the individuals are chosen, and those which arise from the trouble of election. It is sufficiently obvious, that the business of Government requires time to perform it. The matter must be proposed, deliberated upon, a resolution must be taken, and executed. If the powers of Government were to be shifted from one set of hands to another every day, the business of Government could not proceed. Two conclusions, then, we may adopt with perfect certainty; that whatsoever time is necessary to perform the periodical round of the stated operations of Government, this should be allotted to those who are invested with the checking powers; and secondly, that no time, which is not necessary for that purpose, should by any means be allotted to them. With respect to the inconvenience arising from frequency of election, though, it is evident, that the trouble of election, which is always something, should not be repeated oftener than is necessary, no great allowance will need to be made for it, because it may easily be reduced to an inconsiderable amount.

As it thus appears, that limiting the duration of their power is a security against the sinister interest of the people's Representatives, so it appears that it is the only security of which the nature of the case admits. The only other means which could be employed to that end, would be punishment on account of abuse. It is easy, however, to see, that punishment could not be effectually applied. In order for punishment, definition is required of the punishable acts; and proof must be established of the commission. But abuses of power may be carried to a great extent, without allowing the means of proving a determinate offence. No part of political experience is more perfect than this.

If the limiting of duration be the only security, it is unnecessary to speak of the importance which ought to be attached to it.

In the principle of limiting the duration of the power delegated to the Representatives of the people, is not included the idea of changing them. The same individual may be chosen any number of times. The check of the short period, for which he is chosen, and during which he can promote his sinister interest, is the same upon the man who has been chosen and re-chosen twenty times, as upon the man who has been chosen for the first time. And there is good reason for always re-electing the man who has done his duty, because the longer he serves, the better acquainted he becomes with the business of the service. Upon this principle of rechoosing, or of the permanency of the individual, united with the power of change, has been recommended the plan of permanent service with perpetual power of removal. This, it has been said, reduces the period within which the Representative can promote his sinister interest to the narrowest possible limits; because the moment when his Constituents begin to suspect him, that moment they may turn him out. On the other hand, if he continues faithful, the trouble of election is performed once for all, and the man serves as long as he lives. Some disadvantages, on the other hand, would accompany this plan. The present, however, is not the occasion on which the balance of different plans is capable of being compared.

VIII.

What is required in the Elective Body to secure the requisite Properties in the Representative Body.

Having considered the means which are capable of being employed for identifying the interest of the Representatives, when chosen, with that of the persons who choose them, it remains that we endeavour to bring to view the principles which ought to guide in determining who the persons are by whom the act of choosing ought to be performed.

It is most evident, that, upon this question, every thing depends. It can be of no consequence to insure, by shortness of duration, a conformity between the conduct of the Representatives and the will of those who appoint them, if those who appoint them have an interest opposite to that of the community; because those who choose will, according to the principles of human nature, make choice of such persons as will act according to their wishes. As this is a direct inference from the very principle on which Government itself is founded, we assume it as indisputable.

We have seen already, that if one man has power over others placed in his hands, he will make use of it for an evil purpose; for the purpose of rendering those other men the abject instruments of his will. If we, then, suppose, that one man has the power of choosing the Representatives of the people, it follows, that he will choose men who will use their power as Representatives for the promotion of this his sinister interest.

We have likewise seen, that when a few men have power given them over others, they will make use of it exactly for the same ends, and to the same extent, as the one man. It equally follows, that, if a small number of men have the choice of the Representatives, such Representatives will be chosen as will promote the interests of that small number, by reducing, if possible, the rest of the community to be the abject and helpless slaves of their will.

In all these cases, it is obvious and indisputable, that all the benefits of the Representative system are lost. The Representative system is, in that case, only an operose and clumsy machinery for doing that which might as well be done without it; reducing the community to subjection, under the One, or the Few.

When we say the Few, it is seen that, in this case, it is of no importance whether we mean a few hundreds, or a few thousands, or even many thousands. The operation of the sinister interest is the same; and the fate is the same of all that part of the community over whom the power is exercised. A numerous Aristocracy has never been found to be less oppressive than an Aristocracy confined to a few.

The general conclusion, therefore, which is evidently established is this; that the benefits of the Representative system are lost, in all cases in which the interests of the choosing body are not the same with those of the community.

It is very evident, that if the community itself were the choosing body, the interest of the community and that of the choosing body would be the same. The question is, whether that of any portion of the community, if erected into the choosing body, would remain the same?

One thing is pretty clear, that all those individuals whose interests are indisputably included in those of other individuals, may be struck off without inconvenience. In this light may be viewed all children, up to a certain age, whose interests are involved in those of their parents. In this light, also, women may be regarded, the interest of almost all of whom is involved either in that of their fathers or in that of their husbands.

Having ascertained that an interest identical with that of the whole community, is to be found in the aggregate males, of an age to be regarded as *sui juris*, who may be regarded as the natural Representatives of the whole population, we have to go on, and inquire, whether this requisite quality may not be found in some less number, some aliquot part of that body.

As degrees of mental qualities are not easily ascertained, outward and visible signs must be taken to distinguish, for this purpose, one part of these males from another. Applicable signs of this description appear to be three; Years, Property, Profession or Mode of Life.

According to the first of these means of distinction, a portion of the males, to any degree limited, may be taken, by prescribing an advanced period of life at which the power of voting for a Representative should commence. According to the second, the elective body may be limited, by allowing a vote to those only who possess a certain amount of property or of income. According to the third, they may be limited, by allowing a vote only to such persons as belong to certain professions, or certain connexions and interests. What we have to inquire is, if the interest of the number, limited and set apart, upon any of those principles, as the organ of choice for a body of Representatives, will be the same with the interest of the community?

With respect to the first principle of selection, that of age, it would appear that a considerable latitude may be taken without inconvenience. Suppose the age of forty were prescribed, as that at which the right of Suffrage should commence; scarcely any laws could be made for the benefit of all the men of forty which would not be laws for the benefit of all the rest of the community.

The great principle of security here is, that the men of forty have a deep interest in the welfare of the younger men; for otherwise it might be objected, with perfect truth, that, if decisive power were placed in the hands of men of forty years of age, they would have an interest, just as any other detached portion of the community, in pursuing that career which we have already described, for reducing the rest of the community to the state of abject slaves. But the great majority of old men have sons, whose interest they regard as an essential part of their own. This is a law of human nature. There is, therefore, no great danger that, in such an arrangement as this, the interests of the young would be greatly sacrificed to those of the old.

We come next to the inquiry, whether the interest of a body of electors, constituted by the possession of a certain amount of property or income, would be the same with the interest of the community?

It will not be disputed, that, if the qualification were raised so high that only a few hundreds possessed it, the case would be exactly the same with that of the consignment of the Electoral Suffrage to an Aristocracy. This we have already considered, and have seen that it differs in form rather than substance from a simple Aristocracy. We have likewise seen, that it alters not the case in regard to the community, whether the Aristocracy be some hundreds or many thousands. One thing is, therefore, completely ascertained, that a pecuniary qualification, unless it were very low, would only create an

Aristocratical Government, and produce all the evils which we have shown to belong to that organ of misrule.

This question, however, deserves to be a little more minutely considered. Let us next take the opposite extreme. Let us suppose that the qualification is very low, so low as to include the great majority of the people. It would not be easy for the people who have very little property, to separate their interests from those of the people who have none. It is not the interest of those who have little property to give undue advantages to the possession of property, which those who have the great portions of it would turn against themselves.

It may, therefore, be said, that there would be no evil in a low qualification. It can hardly be said, however, on the other hand, that there would be any good; for if the whole mass of the people who have some property would make a good choice, it will hardly be pretended that, added to them, the comparatively small number of those who have none, and whose minds are naturally and almost necessarily governed by the minds of those who have, would be able to make the choice a bad one.

We have ascertained, therefore, two points. We have ascertained that a very low qualification is of no use, as affording no security for a good choice beyond that which would exist if no pecuniary qualification was required. We have likewise ascertained, that a qualification so high as to constitute an Aristocracy of wealth, though it were a very numerous one, would leave the community without protection, and exposed to all the evils of unbridled power. The only question, therefore, is, whether, between these extremes, there is any qualification which would remove the right of Suffrage from the people of small, or of no property, and yet constitute an elective body, the interest of which would be identical with that of the community?

It is not easy to find any satisfactory principle to guide us in our researches, and to tell us where we should fix. The qualification must either be such as to embrace the majority of the population, or some thing less than the majority. Suppose, in the first place, that it embraces the majority, the question is, whether the majority would have an interest in oppressing those who, upon this supposition, would be deprived of political power? If we reduce the calculation to its elements, we shall see that the interest which they would have, of this deplorable kind, though it would be something, would not be very great. Each man of the majority, if the majority were constituted the governing body, would have something less than the benefit of oppressing a single man. If the majority were twice as great as the minority, each man of the majority would only have one-half the benefit of oppressing a single man. In that case, the benefits of good Government, accruing to all, might be expected to over-balance to the several members of such an elective body the benefits of misrule peculiar to themselves. Good Government, would, therefore, have a tolerable security. Suppose, in the second place, that the qualification did not admit a body of electors so large as the majority, in that case, taking again the calculation in its elements, we shall see that each man would have a benefit equal to that derived from the oppression of more than one man; and that, in proportion as the elective body constituted a smaller and smaller minority, the benefit of misrule to the elective body would be increased, and bad Government would be insured.

It seems hardly necessary to carry the analysis of the pecuniary qualification, as the principle for choosing an elective body, any farther.

We have only remaining the third plan for constituting an elective body. According to the scheme in question, the best elective body is that which consists of certain classes, professions, or fraternities. The notion is, that when these fraternities or bodies are represented, the community itself is represented. The way in which, according to the patrons of this theory, the effect is brought about, is this. Though it is perfectly true, that each of these fraternities would profit by misrule, and have the strongest interest in promoting it; yet, if three or four such fraternities are appointed to act in conjunction, they will not profit by misrule, and will have an interest in nothing but good Government.

This theory of Representation we shall not attempt to trace farther back than the year 1793. In the debate on the motion of Mr. (now Earl) Grey, for a Reform in the System of Representation, on the 6th of May, of that year, Mr. Jenkinson, the present Earl of Liverpool, brought forward this theory of Representation, and urged it in opposition to all idea of Reform in the British House of Commons, in terms as clear and distinct as those in which it has recently been clothed by leading men on both sides of that House. We shall transcribe the passage from the speech of Mr. Jenkinson, omitting, for the sake of abbreviation, all those expressions which are unnecessary for conveying a knowledge of the plan, and of the reasons upon which it was founded.

"Supposing it agreed," he said, "that the House of Commons is meant to be a legislative body, representing all descriptions of men in the country, he supposed every person would agree, that the landed interest ought to have the preponderant weight. The landed interest was, in fact, the *stamina* of the country. In the second place, in a commercial country like this, the manufacturing and commercial interest ought to have a considerable weight, secondary to the landed interest, but secondary to the landed interest only. But was this all that was necessary? There were other descriptions of people, which, to distinguish them from those already mentioned, he should style professional people, and whom he considered as absolutely necessary to the composition of a House of Commons. By professional people, he meant those Members of the House of Commons who wished to raise themselves to the great offices of the State; those that were in the army, those that were in the navy, those that were in the law." He then, as a reason for desiring to have those whom he calls "professional people" in the composition of the House of Commons, gives it as a fact, that country Gentlemen and Merchants seldom desire, and seldom have motives for desiring, to be Ministers and other great Officers of State. These Ministers and Officers, however, ought to be made out of the House of Commons. Therefore, you ought to have "professional people" of whom to make them. Nor was this all. "There was another reason why these persons were absolutely necessary. We were constantly in the habit of discussing in that House all the important concerns of the State. It was necessary, therefore, that there should be persons in the practice of debating such questions." "There was a third reason, which, to his mind, was stronger than all the rest. Suppose that in that House there were only country Gentlemen, they would not then be the Representatives of the nation, but of the landholders. Suppose there were in that House only commercial persons, they would not be the Representatives of the nation, but of the commercial interest of the nation. Suppose the landed and commercial interest could both find their way into the House. The landed interest would be able, if it had nothing but the commercial interest to combat with, to prevent that interest from having its due weight in the Constitution. All descriptions of persons in the country would thus, in fact, be at the mercy of the landholders." He adds, "the professional persons are, then, what makes this House the Representatives of the people. They have collectively no *esprit de corps*, and prevent any *esprit de corps* from affecting the proceedings of the House. Neither the landed nor commercial interest can materially affect each other, and the interests of the different professions of the country are fairly considered. The Honourable Gentleman (Mr. Grey), and the petition on this table, rather proposed uniformity of election. His ideas were the reverse – that the modes of election ought to be as varied as possible, because, if there was but one mode of election, there would, generally speaking, be but one description of persons in that House, and by a varied mode of election only could that variety be secured."

There is great vagueness undoubtedly in the language here employed; and abundant wavering and uncertainty in the ideas. But the ideas regarding this theory, appear in the same half-formed state in every speech and writing in which we have seen it adduced. The mist, indeed, by which it has been kept surrounded, alone creates the difficulty; because it cannot be known precisely how any thing is good or bad, till it is precisely known what it is.

According to the ideas of Lord Liverpool, the landholders ought to be represented; the merchants and manufacturers ought to be represented; the officers of the army and navy ought to be represented; and the practitioners of the law ought to be represented. Other patrons of the scheme have added, that literary men ought to be represented. And these, we believe, are almost all the fraternities which have been named for this purpose by any of the advocates of representation by clubs. To insure the choice of Representatives of the landholders, landholders must be the choosers; to insure the choice of Representatives of the merchants and manufacturers, merchants and manufacturers must be the choosers; and so with respect to the other fraternities, whether few or many. Thus it must be at least in *substance*; whatever the *form*, under which the visible acts may be performed. According to the scheme in question, these several fraternities are represented *directly*, the rest of the community is *not* represented directly; but it will be said by the patrons of that scheme, that it is represented *virtually*, which, in this case, answers the same purpose.

From what has already been ascertained, it will appear certain, that each of these fraternities has its sinister interest, and will be led to seek the benefit of misrule, if it is able to obtain it. This is frankly and distinctly avowed by Lord Liverpool. And by those by whom it is not avowed, it seems impossible to suppose that it should be disputed.

Let us now, then, observe the very principle upon which this theory must be supported. Three, or four, or five, or more clubs of men, have unlimited power over the whole community put into their hands. These clubs have, each, and all of them, an interest, an interest the same with that which governs all other rulers, in misgovernment, in converting the persons and properties of the rest of the community wholly to their own benefit. Having this interest, says the theory, they will not make use of it, but will use all their powers for the benefit of the community. Unless this proposition can be supported, the theory is one of the shallowest by which the pretenders to political wisdom have ever exposed themselves.

Let us resume the proposition. Three, or four, or five fraternities of men, composing a small part of the community, have all the powers of government placed in their hands. If they oppose and contend with one another, they will be unable to convert these powers to their own benefit. If they agree they will be able to convert them wholly to their own benefit, and to do with the rest of the community just what they please. The patrons of this system of Representation assume, that these fraternities will be sure to take that course which is *contrary* to their interest. The course which is *according* to their interest, appears as if it had never presented itself to their imaginations!

There being two courses which the clubs may pursue, one contrary to their interest, the other agreeable to it, the patrons of the club system must prove, they must place it beyond all doubt, that the clubs will follow the first course, and not follow the second: if not, the world will laugh at a theory which is founded upon a direct contradiction of one of the fundamental principles of human nature.

In supposing that clubs or societies of men are governed, like men individually, by their interests, we are surely following a pretty complete experience. In the idea that a certain number of those clubs can unite to pursue a common interest, there is surely nothing more extraordinary, than that as many individuals should unite to pursue a common interest. Lord Liverpool talks of an *esprit de corps* belonging to a class of landholders, made up of the different bodies of landholders in every county in the kingdom. He talks of an *esprit de corps* in a class of merchants and manufacturers, made up of the different bodies of merchants and manufacturers in the several great towns and manufacturing districts in the kingdom. What, then, is meant by an *esprit de corps?* Nothing else but a union for the pursuit of a common interest. To the several clubs supposed in the present theory, a common interest is created by the very circumstance of their composing the representing and represented bodies. Unless the patrons of this theory can prove to us, contrary to all experience, that a common interest cannot create an *esprit de corps* in men in combinations, as well as in men individually, we are under the necessity of believing, that an *esprit de corps* would be formed in the classes separated from the rest of the community for the purposes of Representation; that they would pursue their common interest; and inflict all the evils upon the rest of the community to which the pursuit of that interest would lead.

It is not included in the idea of this union for the pursuit of a common interest, that the clubs or sets of persons appropriated to the business of Representation should totally harmonize. There would, no doubt, be a great mixture of agreement and disagreement among them. But there would, if experience is any guide, or if the general laws of human nature have any power, be sufficient agreement to prevent their losing sight of the common interest; in other words, for insuring all that abuse of power which is useful to the parties by whom it is exercised.

The real effect of this motley Representation, therefore, would only be to create a motley Aristocracy; and, of course, to insure that kind of misgovernment which it is the nature of Aristocracy to produce, and to produce equally, whether it is a uniform, or a variegated Aristocracy; whether an Aristocracy all of landowners; or an Aristocracy in part landowners, in part merchants and manufacturers, in part officers of the army and navy, and in part lawyers.

We have now, therefore, examined the principles of the Representative system, and have found in it all that is necessary to constitute a security for good government: We have seen in what manner it is possible to prevent in the Representatives the rise of an interest different from that of the parties who choose them, namely, by giving them little time, not dependent upon the will of those parties: We have likewise seen in what manner identity of interest may be insured between the electoral body and the rest of the community: We have, therefore, discovered the means by which identity of interest may be insured between the Representatives and the community at large. We have, by consequence, obtained an organ of Government which possesses that quality, without which there can be no good Government.

IX.

I. Objection: That a perfect Representative System, if established, would destroy the Monarchy, and the House of Lords.

The question remains, Whether this organ is competent to the performance of the whole of the business of Government? And it may be certainly answered, that it is not. It may be competent to the making of laws, and it may watch over their execution: but to the executive functions themselves, operations in detail, to be performed by individuals, it is manifestly not competent. The executive functions of Government consist of two parts, the administrative and the judicial. The administrative, in this country, belong to the King; and it will appear indubitable, that, if the best mode of disposing of the administrative powers of Government be to place them in the hands of one great functionary, not elective, but hereditary; a King, such as ours, instead of being inconsistent with the Representative system, in its highest state of perfection, would be an indispensable branch of a good Government; and, even if it did not previously exist, would be established by a Representative body whose interests were identified, as above, with those of the nation.

The same reasoning will apply exactly to our House of Lords. Suppose it true, that, for the perfect performance of the business of Legislation, and of watching over the execution of the laws, a second deliberative Assembly is necessary; and that an Assembly, such as the British House of Lords, composed of the proprietors of the greatest landed estates, with dignities and privileges, is the best adapted to the end: it follows, that a body of Representatives, whose interests were identified with those of the nation, would establish such an Assembly, if it did not previously exist: for the best of all possible reasons; that they would have motives for, and none at all against it.

Those parties, therefore, who reason against any measures necessary for identifying the interests of the Representative body with those of the nation, under the pleas that such a Representative body would abolish the King and the House of Lords, are wholly inconsistent with themselves. They maintain that a King and a House of Lords, such as ours, are important and necessary branches of a good Government. It is demonstratively certain that a Representative body, the interests of which were identified with those of the nation, would have no motive to abolish them, if they were not causes of bad government. Those persons, therefore, who affirm that it would certainly abolish them, affirm implicitly that they are causes of bad, and not necessary to good government. This oversight of theirs is truly surprising.

The whole of this chain of deduction is dependent, as we stated at the beginning, upon the principle that the acts of men will be conformable to their interests. Upon this principle, we conceive that the chain is complete and irrefragable. The principle, also, appears to stand upon a strong foundation. It is indisputable that the acts of men follow their will; that their will follows their desires; and that their desires are generated by their apprehensions of good or evil; in other words, by their interests.

X.

II. Objection: That the People are not capable of acting agreeably to their Interest.

The apprehensions of the people, respecting good and evil, may be just, or they may be erroneous. If just, their actions will be agreeable to their real interests. If erroneous, they will not be agreeable to their real interests, but to a false supposition of interest.

We have seen, that, unless the Representative Body are chosen by a portion of the community the interest of which cannot be made to differ from that of the community, the interest of the community will infallibly be sacrificed to the interest of the rulers.

The whole of that party of reasoners who support Aristocratical power affirm, that a portion of the community, the interest of whom cannot be made to differ from that of the community, will not act according to their interest, but contrary to their interest. All their pleas are grounded upon this assumption. Because, if a portion of the community whose interest is the same with that of the community, would act agreeably to their own interest, they would act agreeably to the interest of the community, and the end of Government would be obtained.

If this assumption of theirs is true, the prospect of mankind is deplorable. To the evils of misgovernment they are subject by inexorable destiny. If the powers of Government are placed in the hands of persons whose interests are not identified with those of the community, the interests of the community are wholly sacrificed to those of the rulers. If so much as a checking power is held by the community, or by any part of the community, where the interests are the same as those of the community, the holders of that checking power will not, according to the assumption in question, make use of it in a way agreeable, but in a way contrary to their own interest. According to this theory, the choice is placed between the evils which will be produced by design, the design of those who have the power of oppressing the rest of the community, and an interest in doing it; and the evils which may be produced by mistake, the mistake of those who, if they acted agreeably to their own interest, would act well.

Supposing that this theory were true, it would still be a question, between these two sets of evils, whether the evils arising from the design of those who have motives to employ the powers of Government for the purpose of reducing the community to the state of abject slaves of their will, or the evils arising from the misconduct of those who never produce evil but when they mistake their own interest, are the greatest evils.

Upon the most general and summary view of this question, it appears that the proper answer cannot be doubtful. They who have a fixed, invariable interest in acting ill, will act ill invariably. They who act ill from mistake, will often act well, sometimes even by accident, and in every case in which they are enabled to understand their interest, by design.

There is another, and a still more important ground of preference. The evils which are the produce of interest and power united, the evils on the one side, are altogether incurable: the effects are certain while that conjunction which is the cause of them remains. The evils which arise from mistake are not incurable; for, if the parties who act contrary to their interest had a proper knowledge of that interest, they would act well. What is necessary, then, is knowledge. Knowledge, on the part of those whose interests are the same as those of the community, would be an adequate remedy. But knowledge is a thing which is capable of being increased: and the more it is increased the more the evils on this side of the case would be reduced.

Supposing, then, the theory of will opposed to interest to be correct, the practical conclusion would be, as there is something of a remedy to the evils arising from this source, none whatever to the evils arising from the conjunction of power and sinister interest, to adopt the side which has the remedy, and to do whatever is necessary for obtaining the remedy in its greatest possible strength, and for applying it with the greatest possible efficacy.

It is no longer deniable that a high degree of knowledge is capable of being conveyed to such a portion of the community, as would have interests the same with those of the community. This being the only resource for good government, those who say that it is not yet attained stand in this dilemma; either they do not desire good government, which is the case with all those who derive advantage from bad; or they will be seen employing their utmost exertions to increase the quantity of knowledge in the body of the community.

The practical conclusion, then, is actually the same, whether we embrace or reject the assumption that the community are little capable of acting according to their own interest.

That assumption, however, deserves to be considered. And it would need a more minute consideration than the space to which we are confined will enable us to bestow upon it.

One caution, first of all, we should take along with us; and it is this, That all those persons who hold the powers of Government, without having an identity of interests with the community, and all those persons who share in the profits which are made by the abuse of those powers, and all those persons whom the example and representations of the two first classes influence, will be sure to represent the community, or a part having an identity of interest with the community, as incapable in the highest degree, of acting according to their own interest; it being clear that they who have not an identity of interest with the community, ought to hold the power of Government no longer, if those who have that identity of interest could be expected to act in any tolerable conformity with their interest. All representations from that quarter, therefore, of their incapability so to act, are to be received with suspicion. They come from interested parties, they come from parties who have the strongest possible interest to deceive themselves, and to endeavour to deceive others.

It is impossible that the interested endeavours of all those parties should not propagate, and for a long time successfully uphold, such an opinion, to whatever degree it might be found, upon accurate inquiry, to be without foundation.

A parallel case may be given. It was the interest of the priesthood, when the people of Europe were all of one religion, that the laity should take their opinions exclusively from them; because, in that case, the laity might be rendered subservient to the will of the Clergy, to any possible extent; and as all opinions were to be derived professedly from the Bible, they withdrew from the laity the privilege of reading it. When the opinions which produced the Reformation, and all the blessings which may be traced to it, began to ferment, the privilege of the Bible was demanded. The demand was resisted by the Clergy, upon the very same assumption which we have now under contemplation. "The people did not understand their own interest. They would be sure to make a bad use of the Bible. They would derive from it not right opinions, but all sorts of wrong opinions."*

There can be no doubt that the assumption, in the religious case, was borne out by still stronger appearance of evidence, than it is in the political. The majority of the people may be supposed less capable of deriving correct opinions from the Bible, than of judging who is the best man to act as a Representative.

Experience has fully displayed the nature of the assumption in regard to religion. The power bestowed upon the people, of judging for themselves, has been productive of good effects, to a degree which has totally altered the condition of human nature, and exalted man to what may be called a different stage of existence.

For what reason then, is it, we are called upon to believe, that, if a portion of the community, having an identity of interests with the whole community, have the power of choosing Representatives, they will act wholly contrary to their interests, and make a bad choice?

Experience, it will be said, establishes this conclusion. We see that

---

*A most instructive display of these and similar artifices for the preservation of mischievous power, after the spirit of the times is felt to be hostile to it, may be seen in Father Paul's *History of the Council of Trent*.

the people do not act according to their interests, but very often in opposition to them.

The question is between a portion of the community, which, if entrusted with power, would have an interest in making a bad use of it, and a portion which, though entrusted with power, would not have an interest in making a bad use of it. The former are any small number whatsoever; who, by the circumstance of being entrusted with power, are constituted an Aristocracy.

From the frequency, however great, with which those who compose the mass of the community act in opposition to their interests, no conclusion can, in this case, be drawn, without a comparison of the frequency with which those, who are placed in contrast with them, act in opposition to theirs. Now, it may with great confidence be affirmed, that as great a proportion of those who compose the Aristocratical body of any country, as of those who compose the rest of the community, are distinguished for a conduct unfavourable for their interests. Prudence is a more general characteristic of the people who are without the advantages of fortune, than of the people who have been thoroughly subject to their corruptive operation. It may surely be said, that if the powers of Government must be entrusted to persons incapable of good conduct, they were better entrusted to incapables who have an interest in good government, than to incapables who have an interest in bad.

It will be said that a conclusion ought not to be drawn from the unthinking conduct of the great majority of an Aristocratical body, against the capability of such a body for acting wisely in the management of public affairs; because the body will always contain a certain proportion of wise men, and the rest will be governed by them. Nothing but this can be said with pertinency. And, under certain modifications, this may be said with truth. The wise and good in any class of men do, to all general purposes, govern the rest. The comparison, however, must go on. Of that body, whose interests are identified with those of the community, it may also be said, that if one portion of them are unthinking, there is another portion wise; and that, in matters of state, the less wise would be governed by the more wise, not less certainly than in that body, whose interests, if they were entrusted with power, could not be identified with those of the community.

If we compare in each of these two contrasted bodies the two descriptions of persons, we shall not find that the foolish part of the Democratical body are more foolish than that of the Aristocratical, nor the wise part less wise.

Though, according to the opinions which fashion has propagated, it may appear a little paradoxical, we shall probably find the very reverse.

That there is not only as great a proportion of wise men in that part of the community which is not the Aristocracy, as in that which is; but that, under the present state of education, and the diffusion of knowledge, there is a much greater, we presume, there are few persons who will be disposed to dispute. It is to be observed, that the class which is universally described as both the most wise and the most virtuous part of the community, the middle rank, are wholly included in that part of the community which is not the Aristocratical. It is also not disputed, that in Great Britain the middle rank are numerous, and form a large proportion of the whole body of the people. Another proposition may be stated, with a perfect confidence of the concurrence of all those men who have attentively considered the formation of opinions in the great body of society, or, indeed, the principles of human nature in general. It is, that the opinions of that class of the people, who are below the middle rank, are formed, and their minds are directed by that intelligent and virtuous rank, who come the most immediately in contact with them, who are in the constant habit of intimate communication with them, to whom they fly for advice and assistance in all their numerous difficulties, upon whom they feel an immediate and daily dependence, in health and in sickness, in infancy and in old age; to whom their children look up as models for their imitation, whose opinions they hear daily repeated, and account it their honour to adopt. There can be no doubt that the middle rank, which gives to science, to art, and to legislation itself, their most distinguished ornaments, the chief source of all that has exalted and refined human nature, is that portion of the community of which, if the basis of Representation were ever so far extended, the opinion would ultimately decide. Of the people beneath them, a vast majority would be sure to be guided by their advice and example.

The incidents which have been urged as exceptions to this general rule, and even as reasons for rejecting it, may be considered as contributing to its proof. What signify the irregularities of a mob, more than half composed, in the greater number of instances, of boys and women, and disturbing, for a few hours or days, a particular town? What signifies the occasional turbulence of a manufacturing district, peculiarly unhappy from a very great deficiency of a middle rank, as there the population almost wholly consists of rich manufacturers and poor workmen; with whose minds no pains are taken by anybody; with whose afflictions there is no virtuous family of the middle rank to sympathize; whose children have no good example of such a family to see and to admire; and who are placed in the highly unfavourable situation of fluctuating between very high wages in one year, and very low wages in another? It is altogether futile with regard to the foundation of good government to say that this or the other portion of the people, may at this, or the other time, depart from the wisdom of the middle rank. It is enough that the great majority of the people never cease to be guided by that rank; and we may, with some confidence, challenge the adversaries of the people to produce a single instance to the contrary in the history of the world.

JURISPRUDENCE.

I.

The end of Jurisprudence, viz. the Protection
of Rights. – Importance of the Inquiry, as
involving Human Happiness. – Confusion in
the vulgar uses of the word Right. – Use of the
term Right, in the Science of Jurisprudence. –
The principal ideas involved in the
Jurisprudential sense of the word Right. – All
Rights respect Objects desired; and desired as
means to an end. – The Objects of Rights are
twofold, viz. either Persons or Things. –
Rights, when closely inspected, mean *Powers* –
legalized Powers. – Powers over Persons, and
Powers over Things. – Every Right imports a
corresponding Obligation. – No Creation of
Good, by Rights, without the Creation of Evil.

The object and end of the science which is distinguished by the name
of Jurisprudence, is the protection of rights.

The business of the present discourse is, therefore, to ascertain the
means which are best calculated for the attainment of that end.

What we desire to accomplish is, The protection of rights: What we
have to inquire is, The means by which protection may be afforded.

That rights have hitherto been very ill protected, even in the most enlightened countries, is matter of universal acknowledgment and complaint. That men are susceptible of happiness, only in proportion as rights are protected, is a proposition, which, taken generally, it is unnecessary to prove. The importance of the inquiry, therefore, is evident.

It is requisite, as a preliminary, to fix, with some precision, what we denote by the expression *rights*. There is much confusion in the use of this term. That disorderly mass, the Roman law, changes the meaning of the word in stating its division of the subject, *Jura Personarum*, and *Jura Rerum*. In the first of these phrases, the word *Jura* means a title to enjoy; in the second, it must of necessity mean something else, because things cannot enjoy. Lawyers, whose nature it is to trudge, one after another, in the track which has been made for them; and to whose eyes, that which is, and that which ought to be, have seldom any mark of distinction, have translated the jargon into English, as well as into other modern languages.

This is not all the confusion which has been incurred in the use of the word *right*. It is sometimes employed in a very general way, to denote whatever ought to be; and in that sense is opposed to wrong. There are also persons – but these are philosophers, pushing on their abstractions – who go beyond the sense in which it is made to denote generally whatever ought to be, and who make it stand for the *founda-. tion* of whatever ought to be. These philosophers say, that there is a right and a wrong, original, fundamental; and that things ought to be, or ought not to be, according as they do, or do not, conform to that standard. If asked, whence we derive a knowledge of this right and wrong in the abstract, which is the foundation and standard of what we call right and wrong in the concrete, they speak dogmatically, and convey no clear ideas. In short, writers of this stamp give us to understand, that we must take this standard, like many other things which they have occasion for, upon their word. After all their explanations are given, this, we find, is what alone we are required, or rather commanded, to trust to. The standard exists, – Why? Because they say it exists; and it is at our peril if we refuse to admit the assertion. They assume a right, like other despots, to inflict punishment, for contumacy, or contempt of court. To be sure, hard words are the only instrument of tyranny which they have it in their power to employ. They employ them, accordingly; and there is scarcely an epithet, calculated to denote a vicious state of the intellectual, or moral part, of the human mind, which they do not employ to excite an unfavourable opinion of those who refuse subscription to their articles of faith.

With right, however, in this acceptation, we have at present, no farther concern than to distinguish it clearly from that sense in which the word is employed in the science of jurisprudence. To conceive more exactly the sense in which it is employed in that science, it is necessary to revert to what we established, in the article GOVERN-MENT, with regard to the end or object of the social union, for to that, every thing which is done in subservience to the social union, must of course bear a reference.

In that article it appeared, that, as every man desires to have for himself as many good things as possible, and as there is not a suf-ficiency of good things for all, the strong, if left to themselves, would take from the weak every thing, or at least as much as they pleased; that the weak, therefore, who are the greater number, have an interest in conspiring to protect themselves against the strong. It also appeared, that almost all the things, which man denominates good, are the fruit of human labour; and that the natural motive to labour is the enjoyment of its fruits.

That the object, then, of the social union, may be obtained; in other words, that the weak may not be deprived of their share of good things, it is necessary to fix, by some determination, what shall belong to each, and to make choice of certain marks by which the share of each may be distinguished. This is the origin of right. It is created by this sort of determination, which determination is either the act of the whole society, or of some part of the society which possesses the power of determining for the whole. Right, therefore, is factitious, and the creature of will. It exists, only because the society, or those who wield the powers of the society, will that it should exist; and before it was so willed, it had no existence.

It is easy to see what is the standard, in conformity with which the rights in question *ought* to be constituted; meaning by *ought*, that which perfect benevolence would desire. It is the greatest happiness of the greatest number. But whether rights are constituted, that is, whether the shares of good things are allotted to each, according to this standard, or not according to this standard, the allotment is still the act of the ruling power of the community; and the rights, about which the science of jurisprudence treats, have this alone for the cause of their existence.

In this complicated term, it is obvious that there is involved, on the one hand, the idea of the person to whom a share is allotted, and on the other hand, an idea of the things which are allotted. The one is the owner of the right, the person to whom it belongs; the other is the object of the right, namely, the person or thing over which certain powers are given.

All rights of course are rights to objects of human desire, – of nothing else need shares be allotted. All objects which men desire, are desired, either as the end, or as means. The pleasurable state of the mind is the end; consisting of the feelings of the mind. It would be absurd, however, to speak of giving a man a right to the feelings of his own mind. The objects of desire, therefore, which are the objects of right, are not the pleasurable feelings themselves, which are desired as the end, but the objects which are desired as the means to that end.

Objects of desire, as means to that end, may be divided into the class of persons and the class of things. Both may be the object of rights. In framing our language, therefore, we may say, that all rights are the rights *of* persons; but they may be rights *to*, either persons, or things.

All that men desire, either with persons or things, is to render them subservient to the end, for which they are desired as means. They are so rendered by certain powers over them. All rights, then, when the term is closely investigated, are found to mean powers; powers with respect to persons, and powers with respect to things. What any one means when he says that a thing is his property, is, that he has the power of using it in a certain way.

It is no part of the present inquiry to ascertain what rights *ought* to be constituted, or what rights perfect benevolence would choose to see constituted. That belongs to the question how government should be constituted; in other words, how the powers which are necessary for the general protection ought to be distributed, and the advantages of the union to be shared. At present our sole endeavour is to ascertain the most effectual means which the governing power of the state can employ for protecting the rights, whatever they are, which it has seen meet to create.

Rights, it must be remembered, always import obligations. This is a point of view, which, in the consideration of rights, has not, in general, attracted sufficient attention. If one man obtains a right to the services of another man, an obligation is, at the same time, laid upon this other to render those services. If a right is conferred upon one man to use and dispose of a horse, an obligation is laid upon other men to abstain from using him. It thus appears, that it is wholly impossible to create a right, without at the same time creating an obligation.

The consequences of this law of nature are in the highest degree important. Every right is a benefit; a command to a certain extent over the objects of desire. Every obligation is a burden; an interdiction from the objects of desire. The one is in itself a good; the other is in itself an evil. It would be desirable to increase the good as much as possible. But, by increasing the good, it necessarily happens that we increase the evil. And, if there be a certain point at which the evil begins to increase faster than the good, beyond that point all creation of rights is hostile to human welfare.

The end in view is a command over the objects of desire. If no rights are established, there is a general scramble, and every man seizes what he can. A man gets so much, and he is interdicted by the scramble from all the rest. If rights are established, he also gets so much, and is interdicted by his obligations from the rest. If what he obtains by his rights exceeds what he would have obtained by the scramble, he is a gainer by the obligations which he sustains.

If it is proposed to create rights in favour of all the members of a community, the limits are strict. You cannot give all your advantages to every one; you must share them out. If you do not give equal rights to all, you can only give more than an equal share to some, by diminishing the share of others, of whom, while you diminish the rights, you increase the obligations. This is the course which bad governments pursue; they increase the rights of the few, and diminish the rights of the many, till, in the case of governments virtually despotic, it is all right on the one side, all obligation on the other.

It may be necessary to say a word, to prevent misconstruction of the term "equal rights." Rights may truly be considered as equal, if all the sorts of obligation under which a man lies with respect to other men, they are placed under with respect to him: if all the abstinence which he is obliged to practise with respect to their property, they are obliged to practise with respect to his; if all the rules by which he is bound not to interfere with their actions bind them equally not to interfere with his. It is evident, that inequality of fortune is not excluded by equality of rights. It is also evident, that, from equality of rights must always be excepted those who are entrusted with the powers of the community for the purposes of government. They have peculiar rights, and the rest of the community are under corresponding obligations. It is equally evident, that those must be excepted who are not *sui juris*, as children in non-age, who must be under the guidance of others. Of two such classes of persons the relation to one another, that is, their reciprocal rights and obligations, need to be regulated by particular rules.

It is presumed that these illustrations will suffice to fix, in the minds of our readers, the exact meaning which is intended, in the present discourse, to be attached to the word *rights*. The sequel is to be occupied in discovering the means which are most proper to be employed for affording *protection* to those rights.

II.

Meaning of the Word Protection, in the Jurisprudential Phrase, Protection of Rights. – The first Requisite to the Protection of Rights is to make them capable of being known. – Definition of Rights, the first Instrument of Protection. – Definition of the Acts by which Rights are violated, and the Application of Preventive Motives, another Instrument of Protection. – Civil and Penal Codes, – What. – Code of Procedure, – What. – *Corpus Juris*, or Body of Law, – What.

In the term protection, it is hardly necessary to give notice, that we do not here mean protection against foreign enemies; that protection which is to be yielded by employing armies against invaders. The protection, of which it is the business of jurisprudence to find out and to describe the means, is that which is required by one member of the community against the other members. The members of the community, each of whom endeavours to have as much as possible of the objects of desire, will be disposed to take those objects one from another; to take them, either by force, or by fraud. The means of preservation must, therefore, be found. Certain members of the community, as organs of government, are furnished with powers for that purpose. The question is, what powers are required; and in what manner are they to be employed?

In proceeding to present what may be called a sort of skeleton-map of the ill-explored country of Jurisprudence, it is necessary to warn the reader, that he must supply, by his own attention, what the limits of the work did not permit to be done for him. The several topics are rather indicated, than expounded. It is hoped they are indicated so clearly, that there will be no difficulty in spreading out the ideas in detail. It is necessary, however, that the reader should do this for himself. As the writer has not been able to dwell upon the several topics, though of the utmost importance, long enough to stamp the due impression of them upon the mind; unless the reader takes time to do this, by reflection on each topic, as it arrives, he will pass to the succeeding ones without due preparation, and the whole will be perused without interest, and without profit.

That a man's rights may be effectually secured, it is obviously necessary, in the first place, that they should be made capable of being accurately known. This seems to be so undeniable, that it would answer little purpose to enlarge in its illustration. It is, however, exceedingly necessary that the importance of this requisite should be clearly and adequately conceived. How can a man's rights be protected from encroachment, if what are his rights be uncertain or unknown? If the boundary by which his rights are distinguished is clear and conspicuous, it is in itself a protection. It warns off invaders; it serves to strike them with awe; for it directs the eyes and indignation of mankind immediately and certainly to the offender. Where the boundary, on the other hand, is obscure and uncertain, so far scope is allowed for encroachment and invasion. When the question, to which of two men an article of property belongs, comes for decision to the judge, it is easy, if accurate marks are affixed, to point out and determine the rights of each. If no marks are attached, or such only as are obscure and variable, the decision must be arbitrary and uncertain. To that extent the benefit derived from the creation and existence of rights is diminished.

It is, therefore, demonstrable, and we may say demonstrated (the demonstration not being difficult), that, in the inquiry respecting the means of protecting rights, the *Definition of Rights* may be entered at the head of the list. Without this, as the ground-work, all other means are ineffectual. In proportion as rights can be ascertained, are the judicial functions, and judicial apparatus, capable of being employed to any beneficial purpose: in proportion to the facility with which they can be ascertained, is the extent of the benefit which the judicial functions are enabled to secure.

Such, then, is the first of the means necessary for the protection of rights: That they may receive the most perfect possible protection, they must be as accurately as possible defined.

In supposing that rights have need of protection, we suppose that there are acts by which rights are violated. With regard to those acts, the object is twofold; to redress the evil of the act when it has taken place; and to prevent the performance of such acts in future. To prevent the performance, two classes of means present themselves; to watch till the act is about to be committed, and then to interpose; or, to create motives which shall prevent the will to commit. It is but a small number of cases in which the first can be done; the latter is, therefore, the grand desideratum. From the view of these circumstances we discover two other articles in the catalogue of means. Those acts by which rights are violated require to be made accurately known; in other words to be defined; and the motives which are fitted to prevent them must be duly applied. Motives sufficient to that end can only be found in the painful class; and the act by which they are applied is denominated punishment. The definition, therefore, of offences, or of the acts by which rights are violated and which it is expedient to punish; and the definition of the penalties by which they are prevented, are equally necessary with the definition of rights themselves. The reasons which demonstrate this necessity are so nearly the same with those which demonstrate the necessity of the definition of rights, that we deem it superfluous to repeat them.

The definition of rights constitutes that part of law which has been generally denominated the *Civil Code*. The definition of offences and punishments constitutes that other part of law which has been generally denominated the criminal or *Penal Code*.

When rights are distributed, and the acts by which they may be violated are forbidden, an agency is required, by which that distribution may be maintained, and the violators of it punished. That agency is denominated judicature. The powers, by which that agency is constituted, require to be accurately defined; and the mode in which the agency itself is to be carried on must be fixed and pointed out by clear and determinate rules. These rules and definitions prescribe the form and practice of the courts, or mode in which the judicial functions are performed; and constitute that branch of law which has been called the *Code of Procedure*.

These three codes, the civil code, the penal code, and code of procedure, form together the whole subject of jurisprudence. Of the three, it sufficiently appears, that the last exists only for the sake of the other two. Courts and their operations are provided that the provisions of the civil and penal codes may not be without their effect. It is to be considered, therefore, as subordinate, and merely instrumental, in respect to the other two. They form the main body of the law; this is an accessary to the main body, though an accessary of indispensable use. It would be of great advantage to affix characteristic names to distinguish from one another the main and accessary parts of law. Unexceptionable names, however, it is not easy to find. Mr. Bentham, the great improver of this branch of knowledge, has called the civil and penal codes together, by the name of "substantive law," the code of procedure by that of "adjective law;" not, we may be satisfied, because he approved of those names, but because the language hardly afforded others to which equal objections would not apply. In the very sense in which either the term accessary, or the term adjective can be applied to the code of procedure, both may be applied to the penal code, as it respects the civil. The penal code exists purely for the sake of the civil; that the rights, which are ordained by the legislature, and marked out by the terms of the code, may be saved from infringement. The civil code is therefore the end and object of all the rest. The code of procedure, however, is auxiliary to each of the other two; the penal code to no more than one.

Having now explained the nature of the three codes which constitute the body of law necessary for the protection of rights, it remains that we illustrate, as much in detail as our limits will permit, what is required for the perfection of each.

III.

What is required for the perfection of the Civil Code. – Operations preliminary to the Definition of Rights. – Two Things necessary for the Definition of a Right: – First, a Description of its Extent; Secondly, a Description of the Facts which give it a Beginning and an End.

The grand object of the civil code is the definition of rights. Rights are sometimes more, sometimes less extensive. Thus the right of a man to a horse, may solely extend to use him in riding from one stage to another; it may extend to the power of doing with him as he pleases. In like manner, the rights of a man with respect to a person may extend only to some momentary service, or they may go the length of slavery. Even slavery itself does not imply rights always equally extensive. In some cases, it implies rights as extensive over the slave as over the inferior animals.

All rights, when the essence of them is spoken of, are powers; powers to an individual, which the government members of the community guarantee; powers, more or less extensive, of making either a person or a thing subservient to the gratification of his desires. To be made to gratify the desire of an individual, is to be made to render him a *service*. And the term *service* may, fortunately, be applied to both persons and things. A man receives a service from the field when it produces a crop, as well as from the servant and the horse who ploughed it. In one meaning of the word service, it implies only active service, or that rendered by the voluntary operations of sentient beings. In the present case, however, it is employed to denote both active and passive services. It is evident, that in every case in which any thing inanimate is rendered subservient to the gratification of a desire, the service is, properly speaking, a passive service. It is also evident, that even animate beings are rendered subservient to the gratification of desires in a way which may equally be called passive.

It is necessary to request attention to the explanation which is here given of the meaning in which the term *service* is to be employed; as both the English and the Roman lawyers use it in a very restricted sense. Here it is employed to denote the whole of that ministration to the gratification of our desires, which we are entitled, in consequence of rights, to derive either from persons or from things. Rights are powers, and the powers are means for the obtaining of services. We have now, therefore, a language, by the help of which we may speak with tolerable clearness.

Our object is to define rights, and rights are powers. But these powers can be defined, only by a reference to the services which they are the means of obtaining.

The first thing, therefore, to be done for the definition of rights is, to make out a list of all the kinds of services, which the legislature permits an individual to derive, first, from persons, and secondly, from things. This would not be a matter of very great difficulty. It would be right to begin with the most simple cases, and go on to the more complex. Thus, of the services derivable from a person, some are limited to a single species of act, and that within a limited time, and at a particular place. Others are services, consisting of various acts, limited or not limited in space and time. And lastly, are the whole services which a man is capable of rendering; without limitation as to either space or time. Considerable pains would be necessary to make the list complete; and not only considerable pains, but considerable logic would be necessary, to classify the services, in other words, make them up into lots, the most convenient for the purpose in question; and to fix the extent of each by an exact definition. It is obvious, that as soon as all the possible gradations, in the services which one human being can render to another, are exhibited by such enumeration and assortment, it is easy for the legislature to point out exactly whatever portion of these services it is its will to give any individual a right to.

The same considerations apply to the class of things. In being made subservient to the gratification of our desires, they also render services. In proportion as a man has the right to derive those services from them, they are said to be his property. The whole of the services, which are capable of being derived from them, may, without much difficulty, be enumerated and classified; and when they are so, those which it may be the pleasure of the legislature to make any one's property, may be very easily and distinctly pointed out.

We may take land for an example. All the different services which are capable of being derived from the land may be enumerated, and, being classed under convenient heads, may be referred to with perfect certainty; and any portion of them, which is made the property of any individual, may thus be accurately described. A man may have a right simply to pasture a field; to pasture it for a day, or a year, or a hundred years. He may have a right to crop it; and that either in a particular manner, or in any manner he pleases; for a year, or for any other time. He may have a right to use it for any purpose, and that during a limited time, or an unlimited time. The services which it is capable of rendering may belong to him in common with a number of other persons, or they may all belong to himself.

In illustration of this subject we may notice a classification of the services derivable from the land, made, though very rudely, by the English law. Blackstone, who, like other English lawyers, has, on this, as on all other occasions, no idea of any other classification, than that which is made by the technical terms of the English law, has distinguished certain lots of the services derivable from the land, under the name of "Estates therein; Estates with respect to, 1*st*, Quantity of interest; 2*dly*, Time of Enjoyment; 3*dly*, Number and connection of the tenants:" That is, estates in fee simple, comprehending the whole of the services which are capable of being derived from the land, unlimited in point of time; estates in fee tail, implying always limitation in point of time, and often a limitation in respect to some of the services; estates for years; estates at will; estates at sufferance; estates on condition; estates in remainder; estates in reversion; estates in jointenancy; estates in coparcenary; estates in common. The Roman law has made no enumeration or classification of the services derivable from any thing, not even from the land. It speaks of property in the abstract, and in two states; property in possession, and property in action. The English law does the same thing in regard to all other property but the land. "Property, in chattels personal, is either in possession or in action," says Blackstone. He does, indeed, add, "The property of chattels personal is liable to remainders, if created by will, to jointenancy, and to tenancy in common."

The services derivable from other articles of property than land, need not be divided under many heads. A piece of plate, for example, may render certain services without alteration of its form; it may be incapable of rendering other services till it has received an alteration of its form. It is chiefly, therefore, by limitation of time, that the various quantities of interest in such articles need to be determined. A man's right may extend to the use of a silver cup, for a day, or a year, or for his life. During this time the different services which it is capable of rendering have no occasion to be divided. They go naturally altogether. An unlimited right to its services implies the power of using it, either with or without alteration of its form, and without limitation of time. In most instances the limited right would be called loan, though, in the case of heirlooms and some others, there is a limited use to which the term loan is not customarily applied.

In speaking of the rights which a man may have to persons; as master, as father, as husband, and so on; there is one case so remarkable, that it requires a few words to be added in its explanation. It is that of one's own person. In this case the rights of the individual have no proper limitation beyond the obligations under which he is laid, in consequence either of the rights conferred upon others, or of the means which are thought necessary for protecting them.

If we have enabled our readers to form a tolerable conception of what we desire to be accomplished under the title of an enumeration and commodious classification of the services derivable from persons and things, we have performed what we proposed. The enumeration and classification, themselves, are evidently incommensurate with the design of an article in the present work. That they are practicable may be confidently taken for granted. In fact, they amount to nothing more than a description of the different degrees in which the property of a thing may be possessed; a point which is decided upon in every legal dispute. If this be done, from time to time, for one article after another, it may be done once for all.

We have already said, that rights are powers, powers for the obtaining of certain services. We have also said, that those powers can be defined only by a reference to the services which they are the means of obtaining. When those services are enumerated and classified, what remains is easy. A right to those services must begin; and it must end. The legislature has only to determine what fact shall be considered as giving a beginning to each right, and what shall be considered as putting an end to it, and then the whole business is accomplished.

It is evident that, for the definition of rights, two things are necessary. The first is, an exact description of the extent of the right; the second is, the description of the fact which gives birth to it. The extent of the right is described by reference to the lots of services, in the title to which services all rights consist. The facts, which the convenient enjoyment of rights has pointed out as the fittest for giving commencement to rights, have been pretty well ascertained from the earliest period of society; and there has, in fact, been a very great conformity with respect to them in the laws of all nations.

The following is an imperfect enumeration of them: – *An expression of the will of the legislature*, when it makes any disposition with regard to property; *Occupancy*, when a man takes what belongs to nobody; *Labour*; *Donation*; *Contract*; *Succession*. Of these six causes of the commencement of a right there is a remarkable distinction between the first three and the last three. The first three give commencement to a right in favour of one individual, without necessarily putting an end to a right enjoyed by any other individual. The last three give commencement to a right in favour of one individual, only by making the same right to cease in favour of another individual. When a man, by donation, gives a horse to another man, the horse ceases to be the property of the one man by the very same act by which he becomes the property of the other; so in the case of sale, or any other contract.

It is necessary for the legislature, in order that each man may know what are the objects of desire which he may enjoy, to fix, not only what are the facts which shall give commencement to a right, but what are the facts which shall put an end to it. In respect to these facts, also, there is a great harmony in the laws of all nations.

There is first the will of the legislature. When it confers a right, it may confer it, either for a limited, or for an unlimited time. In the term unlimited time, we include the power of tradition, or transfer, in all its shapes. If the time is limited, by the declaration of the legislature, either to a certain number of years, or the life of the party, the fact which terminates the right is obvious. If a man possesses a right, unlimited in point of time, the events are three by which it has been commonly fixed that it may be terminated; 1. some expression of his own will, in the way of gift or contract; 2. some act of delinquency; or 3. his death.

The possessor of a right, unlimited in point of time, may, in the way of gift or contract, transfer his right either for a limited or for an unlimited time. Thus the owner of a piece of land may lease it for a term of years. He may also, in this way, convey the whole of the services which it is capable of rendering, or only a part of them. In this transaction, one event gives birth to a right in favour of the man who receives the lease, and terminates a right which was possessed by the man who gives it; and another event, namely, the arrival of the period assigned for the termination of the lease, terminates the right of the man who had received the lease, and revives the former right of the man who gave it.

Acts of delinquency have been made to terminate rights, by the laws of most nations, in the various modes of forfeiture and pecuniary penalty.

The mode in which the event of death should terminate rights has been variously regulated. Sometimes it has been allowed to terminate them simply; and what a man left at his death was open to the first occupant. All but rude nations, however, have determined the persons to whom the rights which a man possessed without limitation of time shall pass at his death. The will of the former owner, when expressed, is commonly allowed to settle the matter. When that is not expressed, it has by most legislators been regulated, that his rights shall pass to his next of kin.

What is the extent of each right; by what event it shall receive its commencement; and by what event it shall be terminated; – this is all which is necessary to be pre-determined with respect to it. To do this is the duty of the legislature. When it is done, the inquiry of the judge is clear and simple. Does such a right belong to such a man? This question always resolves itself into two others. Did any of the events, which give commencement to a right, happen in this case? And did any of those events, which terminate a right, not happen in this case? These are questions of fact, as distinguished from law; and are to be determined by the production of evidence. If a man proves that an event which gives commencement to a right, happened in his case, and if another man cannot prove that an event which terminates a right happened subsequently in that case, the right of the first man is established.

If we have now ascertained the importance and practicability of a civil code, and have shown what is to be done in order to obtain the benefit of it, we shall conclude, with some confidence, that we have rendered a great service to mankind. We proceed to the consideration of the penal code. The object of that code is, the acts by which rights may be violated.

IV.

What is necessary to the Perfection of the Penal Code. – Acts meet for Punishment. – What is required to the Definition of an Offence.

In the term violation, we include all those acts by which the powers, conveyed by a right, are prevented from operating according to the will of the owner.

With respect to a part of such acts, all that it is found convenient to do, through the instrumentality of judicature, is, to remove the obstruction which prevents the enjoyment of the right, without inflicting any penalty for creating it. Thus, if a debt is not paid when due, the right is violated of the man who ought to receive it. Enough, however, is in this case supposed to be done, if the man who owes the debt is constrained to make payment. The act of secretly abstracting, with a view to appropriate, a property of perhaps less value, would be an act which the laws of all nations would punish as theft.

Of injurious acts, those alone, to the commission of which it has been deemed expedient that penalties should be annexed, are considered as the object of the penal code. Of injurious acts so perfect an analysis has been exhibited by Mr. Bentham; so perfectly, too, have the grounds been laid down upon which those acts which are destined for punishment should be selected from the rest; and so accurately have the principles, according to which punishment should be meted out, been established, by that great philosopher, that, on this part of the subject, the philosophy of law is not far from complete.

As acts are declared to be offences, and are made subject to punishment, solely for the protection of rights, it is evident, that all acts which enter into the penal code, are acts which infringe upon rights, either directly, or indirectly. Those which infringe upon rights *directly*, are those by which injury is done to some individual or individuals; a blow, for example, an act of theft, and so on. We include also, under this division, all acts the *effects* of which produce an immediate infringement of rights; destroying a mound, for example, to inundate the lands of another man; importation of infection, by which the health or lives of others may be destroyed. Those acts by means of which rights are affected *indirectly*, are those which bear immediately upon the means which the state has provided for the protection of rights. The means which the state has provided for the protection of rights, are the operations of government generally. All acts, therefore, meet for punishment, are acts which disturb either individuals in the enjoyment of their rights, or the operations required for the protection of those rights. The latter, though mediately, and not immediately hurtful, are apt to be more extensively mischievous than the former. An act which infringes upon a right immediately, is commonly injurious only to one individual, or a small number of individuals; an act which prevents any of the operations of government from proceeding in its natural course is injurious to all those individuals to whose protection the due course of that operation is useful. Permit acts which interrupt all the operations of government, and all rights are practically destroyed.

If, as it thus appears, acts are meet for punishment, only because they infringe upon a right, or because they interrupt the operations provided for the protection of rights, it is evident, that, in the definition of one set of those acts, must be included the specification of the right which is infringed; and, in the definition of the other, must be included the specification of the operation disturbed. Before, therefore, an accurate penal code can exist, there must exist an accurate civil code, and also what we may call a constitutional or political code; the latter consisting of an accurate definition of the powers created for the purposes of government, and of the limitations, applied to their exercise.

From what has been said, it may appear, that the definition of offences by which name we shall hereafter distinguish punishable acts, consists necessarily of two parts. The first part is the specification of the right infringed, or the operation of government disturbed; and the second part is the definition of the mode. Thus, for the definition of an act of theft, the right which the act has violated must be distinctly marked, and also the mode in which the violation has been committed. In the same class of offences, those against property for example, the mode in which the violation is performed is that chiefly which constitutes the difference between one offence and another. In a theft and a robbery, the right violated may be exactly the same; the mode in which the violation was effected constitutes the difference.

For several purposes of the penal code, it is useful, that, in the specification of the right violated, the value of what has been violated, in other words, the amount of the evil sustained, should sometimes be included. It is evident, that the value of rights can be judged of ultimately, only by a reference to human feelings. Of these feelings, however, certain outward marks must be taken as the standard. In offences which concern property the modes of valuation are familiarly known. In injuries to the person, those marks which denote injuries regarded by mankind in general as differing in magnitude; the size, for example, or position, of a wound; in injuries to reputation, the words used, and the occasion when, and so forth, are the only means of distinction which can be employed.

It may be necessary also to remark, that, in that part of the definition which relates to the mode, are to be distinguished the parties, when more than one, who engage in the same offence with different degrees of criminality; meaning, by different degrees of criminality, nothing more than demand for different degrees of punishment. The chief classes of such persons are those of principals and accessaries; and of accessaries both those before and those after the fact.

In the definition of the mode, the act is first to be described in its ordinary shape. The act, however, may be attended with aggravating circumstances on the one hand, or extenuating circumstances on the other; presenting a demand for increased punishment in the first case, and diminished punishment in the second. Mr. Bentham has logically remarked, that the circumstances which are to be regarded as aggravating, and the circumstances which are to be regarded as extenuating, being pretty nearly the same in all cases, they may be defined, in a separate chapter, once for all. This being done, the code proceeds in the following manner: – The definition is given of the offence in its ordinary shape, and the appropriate punishment is annexed; then immediately follows the same offence with aggravating circumstances; punishment so much the more severe: the same offence with extenuating circumstances; punishment so much the less.

Thus far we have spoken of the definition of offences, into which we have entered the less in detail, because we do not think there is much of controversy on the subject. Many persons, who doubt the possibility of framing a civil code, though, after the preceding exposition of the subject, it is a doubt which could not, we should imagine, very easily maintain itself, allow, that offences may all be defined; and that it is possible to prevent the monstrous iniquity of punishing men for acts as offences which they have not the means of knowing to be such.

V.
The Doctrine of Punishment. – Satisfaction.– Penalties.

After offences comes the consideration of the punishment to be annexed to them. This is a subject of considerable detail; it has been, however, so fully and admirably treated by Mr. Bentham, that only some of the more general considerations, necessary to mark out the place and importance of the topic, need here to be introduced.

When a right has been infringed, there are two things, it is evident, which ought to be done: The injury which has been sustained by the individual ought to be repaired: And means ought to be taken to prevent the occurrence of a like evil in future.

The doctrine of Satisfaction is not at all difficult, as far as regards the regulating principles; the complication is all in the detail. The greater number of injuries are those which concern property. A pecuniary value can generally be set upon injuries of this sort; though it is not very easy to determine the *pretium affectionis*, a matter of considerable importance, which the English law, so much made up of clumsiness in one part, and false refinement in another, wholly overlooks. For injuries to the person, also, it is most frequently in the pecuniary shape alone that any compensation can be made. In making these estimates, some general marks are all that can be conveniently defined by the law, and a considerable discretion must be left to the judge. Indeed, the question of damages is always a question of fact, which must be determined by the evidence adduced in each instance.

It accords with the feelings of every man to say, that he who has committed an injury, should be made to repair it. One part of punishment, therefore, ought, wherever special reason does not forbid, to consist in making satisfaction to the party injured. Pecuniary satisfaction, where the delinquent is rich, may be a small part of the due punishment; still, however, there is an obvious propriety, in making it a part so far as it can go. In the cases in which the delinquent has no property, there is the same propriety in making his labour subservient to that end. Hard labour, with the most economical fare, till the produce of the labour equals the amount of the satisfaction required, is, therefore, a species of punishment, recommended by the strongest considerations. It is not said that labour so limited would always be sufficient punishment, and there are many cases in which it would be too much; but even then, it should go as far as it can in the one case, and as far as it ought in the other.

When the injury is done to reputation, there is a manifest propriety in making the injurer contribute to the reparation, wherever it can be done. In many of the cases, too, the proper mode is abundantly obvious: all those, for example, where the publication of falsehood is the injurious act. The author of the injury may, in a way as public as that of the offence, and as well calculated as possible for the reparation of the injury, be obliged to declare that he has been solemnly adjudged to have propagated a falsehood, and is condemned to publish his own shame.

In the case of those offences which affect rights indirectly, namely, by affecting the securities provided for them, satisfaction seldom can have any place, because not any determinate individual or individuals have sustained an injury.

This may suffice, in exposition of the first thing which is desirable where an injury has been committed, namely, that reparation should be made. The second is, that measures should be adopted for preventing the future occurrence of similar events.

Acts are performed, only because there are motives to the performance of them. Of course injurious acts are performed, only because there are motives to the performance of them.

Corporal restraint being out of the question where all the members of the community are concerned, it is evident that only two means remain for preventing injurious acts; either, first, to take away the motives which provoke to them; or, secondly, to apply motives sufficient for the prevention of them.

From the very nature of many of the acts it is impossible to take away the motives which provoke to them. From property stolen it is impossible to detach the value of the property; from vengeance it is impossible to detach the hope of that relief which is sought by the blow that is aimed.

What is wanted, then, is a sufficiency of motive in each instance to counteract the motives which lead to the crime. Whatever the motives of the alluring kind which lead to an act, if you give stronger motives of the same kind to abstain from the act, the act will, of course, be prevented. The man who would steal from you 5*l*. will assuredly not do so, if he knows that he shall receive 6*l*. for abstaining.

The question may then be started, Why should not all crimes be prevented in this way, since reward is much more desirable and humane than punishment? The answer is most satisfactory, and is built upon a ground which ought to receive profound attention, on many occasions, on which it is treated with the most perfect disregard. No reward can be given to one man, or set of men, but at the expense of some other man or set of men. What is reward to one is therefore punishment to others. If 6*l*. be given to the man who would steal 5*l*., it must be taken from some one or more individuals of the community. If one man is elevated by any title or distinction, all the rest with regard to him are degraded and depressed. This is utterly unavoidable. The one event is necessarily included in the other. The giving of rewards, therefore, is a matter of serious import. It is not that simple act, that pure creation of good, which it is often so fraudulently given out to be, and so credulously and foolishly admitted to be.

Other reasons, which prove the insufficiency of rewards for preventing injurious acts, are too obvious to require to be mentioned. We shall not therefore dwell upon this topic. This at least is sufficiently evident, that to counteract the motives which lead to the commission of an act, we have but two methods. If we cannot apply motives, of the pleasurable sort, to induce the party to abstain from committing the act, we must apply such motives, of the painful sort, as will outweigh the motives which prompt to the performance. To prevent, by such means, a theft of 5*l*., it is absolutely necessary to affix to that act a degree of punishment which shall outweigh the advantage of possessing 5*l*.

We have now, it is evident, obtained the principle by which punishment ought to be regulated: We desire to prevent certain acts: That is our end, and the whole of our end: We shall assuredly prevent any acts, if we attach to them motives of the painful kind, sufficient to outweigh the motives of the opposite kind which lead to the perform-ance. If we apply a less quantity of evil than is sufficient for outweigh-ing those motives, the act will still be performed, and the evil will be inflicted to no purpose; it will be so much suffering in waste. If we apply a greater quantity of evil than is necessary, we incur a similar inconvenience; we create a quantity of evil which is absolutely useless; the act, which it is the tendency of the motives of the pleasurable kind to produce, will be prevented, if the motives of the painful kind outweigh them in the smallest degree, as certainly as if it outweigh them to any degree whatsoever. As soon, therefore, as the legislator has reached that point, he ought immediately to stop. Every atom of punishment which goes beyond is so much uncompensated evil, so much human misery created without any corresponding good. It is pure unmingled mischief.

As no exact measure, indeed, can be taken of the quantity of pain which will outweigh a supposed quantity of pleasure, it is sometimes necessary to risk going somewhat beyond the mark, in order to make sure of not falling short of it. And, in the case of acts of which the evil is very great; of the higher order of crimes, in short; it may be expedient to risk a considerable degree of excess in order to make sure of reaching the point of efficiency.

In estimating the quantity of evil which it may be necessary to create, in order to compensate the motive which leads to a mis-chievous act, two circumstances should be taken into the account. These are, certainty and proximity. It is of the less importance here to enter far into the illustration of these topics, because they are now pretty generally understood. It is well known that the prospect of an evil which is to happen within an hour, or two hours, produces a much greater uneasiness, than the prospect of the very same evil removed to the distance of years. Every man knows that he will die within a certain number of years; many are aware that they cannot live beyond a few years; and this knowledge produces no uneasiness. The effort, on the other hand, which enables a man to behave with tranquillity, on the prospect of immediate death, is supposed to be so difficult, that it is this which makes the hero. It is, therefore, of the greatest import-ance, that punishment should be immediate; because, in that case, a much smaller quantity of evil suffices. It is imperatively required, by the laws of benevolence, that, if evil is a necessary means to our end, every expedient should be used to reduce it to the smallest quantity possible. It is cruelty; it belongs only to a malignant nature; to apply evil in a way which demands a quantity of it greater than would otherwise have been required. Suppose a law, that no act of theft should be punished or challenged till twenty years after the commission, or till the life of the thief was supposed to be near its end. It is evident that all punishment, in this case; that death, in the greatest torture, would be nearly destitute of power. This is partly the ground of the complaint, of the little efficacy of religious punishment, though dreadful beyond expression in the degree.

The want of certainty is a defect of equal importance. If it is a matter of doubt, whether a threatened evil will take place, the imagination is prone to magnify the chance of its not happening; and, by indulgence, magnifies it to such a degree, that the opposite chance at last excites a comparatively feeble influence. This is a remarkable law of human nature, from the influence of which even the most wise and prudent of men are not exempt; and of which the influence is predominant in those inconsiderate minds which are the most apt to give way to the allurements of vice. To illustrate this law, the influence of the religious punishments affords the most instructive of all examples. The punishments themselves go far beyond what the imagination can conceive. It is the complaint of divines, and the observation of all the world, that, with the great body of men, the efficacy of them is exceedingly small. The reason is, that to the want of proximity is added the greatest uncertainty. If a man puts his finger in the candle, he knows that he will be punished, and immediately, by being burned. If a man commits even a heinous sin, he has no fear of receiving the religious punishment immediately, and he conceives that, in the mercy of his Judge, in repentance and faith, he has a chance of escaping it altogether. This chance his imagination exaggerates, and most men can, in this way, go on sinning with tranquillity, to the end of their days. If all punishments were as certain and immediate as that of putting a finger in the candle, the smallest quantity, it is evident, beyond what would form a counterbalance to the advantage of the forbidden act, would suffice for its prevention. If uncertainty is admitted, to any considerable degree, no quantity of evil will suffice. It is a fact, which experience has most fully established, and which is now recognized in the most vulgar legislation, that undue severity of punishment runs counter to its end. This it does by increasing uncertainty; because men are indisposed to be the instruments of inflicting evil by which their feelings are lacerated. That legislation, therefore, is bad, which does not take measures for the greatest possible degree of proximity and certainty in the punishments which it applies.

The sources are three, from which motives of the painful sort, applicable to the purposes of the legislator, are capable of being drawn: – 1. The physical; 2dly, The moral; and, 3dly, The religious.

I. Pains from the Physical Source may be communicated to a man through,

1. His person,
2. His connections,
3. His property.

Through his person, they may be communicated in four principal ways, – by death, disablement, restraint and constraint, simple pain.

A man's connections are either public or private; private, as spouse, parent, servant, master, &c.; public, as ruler, subject, teacher, scholar, and so on.

The modes in which a man is punished through his property need no explanation.

II. Pains, from the Moral Source, are the pains which are derived from the unfavourable sentiments of mankind. For the strength of the pains, derived from this source, we must refer to the writers who have treated of this part of human nature. It is sufficient here to advert to what is universally recognized, that these pains are capable of rising to a height, with which hardly any other pains, incident to our nature, can be compared; that there is a certain degree of unfavourableness in the sentiments of his fellow creatures, under which, hardly any man, not below the standard of humanity, can endure to live.

The importance of this powerful agency for the prevention of injurious acts, is too obvious to need to be illustrated. If sufficiently at command, it would almost supersede the use of other means. It is, therefore, one of the first objects to the legislator to know, in what manner he can employ the pains of the popular sanction with the greatest possible effect.

To know how to direct the unfavourable sentiments of mankind, it is necessary to know in as complete, that is, in as comprehensive a way as possible, what it is which gives them birth. Without entering into the metaphysics of the question, it is a sufficient practical answer, for the present purpose, to say, that the unfavourable sentiments of men are excited by every thing which hurts them. They love that which gives them pleasure; hate that which gives them pain. Those acts of other men which give them pleasure or save them from pain, acts of beneficence, acts of veracity, and so on, they love. Acts, on the other hand, which give them pain, mendacity, and so on, they hate. These sentiments, when the state of mind is contemplated out of which the acts are supposed to arise, are transformed into approbation and disapprobation, in all their stages and degrees; up to that of the highest veneration, down to that of the deepest abhorrence and contempt.

The unfavourable sentiments, which the legislator would excite towards forbidden acts, must, therefore, in each man, arise from his conception of the mischievousness of those acts. That conception depends upon three circumstances; 1*st*, The view which he himself takes of the act; 2*dly*, The view which appears to be taken by other people; 3*dly*, Every thing which operates to render more or less permanently present to his mind his own and other men's conception of its mischievousness. From these circumstances, the practical rules for applying this great power, as an instrument of the legislator for the prevention of mischievous acts, are easily deduced. 1. Let the best measures be taken for giving the people a correct view of the mischievousness of the act; and then their unfavourable sentiments will be duly excited. 2. Let proper pains be taken that the people shall know every mischievous act that is committed, and know its author; that, so, no evil act may, by concealment, escape the punishment which their unfavourable sentiments imply. 3. Let the legislature, as the leading section of the public, make publication of its own unfavourable sentiments; let it brand the act with infamy. 4. Let the same publication of his own unfavourable sentiments be made by the judge in the shape of reprimand and other declarations. 5. The legislature may increase the effect of these declarations, where the case requires it, by symbolical marks; or, 6, by personal exposure. 7. The legislature may so order matters in certain cases, that the mischievous act can be done only through another act already infamous; as when it is more infamous to break a vow to God than to make false declarations to men, a witness may be made to swear that he will tell the truth. 8. As the favourable sentiments of mankind are so power-fully excited towards wealth, a man suffers through the popular sanc-tion when his property is so diminished as to lessen his rank.

III. In pointing and proportioning the apprehension of divine punish-ment, the legislator can do three things:

1. He can declare his own apprehension, and the measure of it, which should be as exactly proportioned as possible to the mis-chievousness of the acts:

2*dly*, He can hire other people to declare similar apprehensions, and to make the most of the means which are available for their propagation:

3*dly*, He may discountenance the pointing of religious apprehen-sions to any acts which are not mischievous; or the pointing of them more strongly to acts which are slightly, than to acts which are deeply mischievous. Whatever power of restraining from mischievous acts may be lodged in religious apprehensions, is commonly misapplied and wasted. It would be worth the cost, therefore, of pretty forcible means to prevent such a misapplication and waste of religious fears.*

In drawing from one, or more, of all these sources, a lot of punish-ment adapted to each particular case, the following properties, desir-able in a lot of punishment, ought to be steadily borne in view. Every lot of punishment ought, as much as possible, to be,

1. Susceptible of graduation, so as to be applied in different degrees.

2. Measurable, that the difference of degrees may be duly ascertained.

3. Equable, that is, calculated to operate with uniform intensity upon all persons.

---

*Nothing which can in any degree interfere with the rights of conscience, including whatever interpretation any man may put upon the words of Scripture, is here under-stood. It is the object of the legislator to encourage acts which are useful, prevent acts which are hurtful, to society. But religious hopes and fears are often applied, not to promote acts which are useful, prevent acts which are hurtful, to society; in which way, alone, they are capable of conducing to the views of the legislator; but to mere ceremonies. And cases are not wanting in which they are applied to produce acts that are hurtful, prevent those that are useful, to society. As far as religious motives are attached to the useful, instead of the useless or hurtful objects, society is benefited. It is this benefit which it is recommended to the legislator to pursue.

4. Such, that the thought of the punishment may naturally excite the thought of the crime.
5. Such, that the conception of it may be naturally vivid and intense.
6. Public, addressed to the senses.
7. Reformative.
8. Disabling; viz. from crime.
9. Remediable; viz. if afterwards found to be undeserved.
10. Compensative; viz. to the party injured.
11. Productive; viz. to the community, as labour.

Of all the instruments of punishment which have yet occurred to the ingenuity of man, there is none which unites these desirable qualities in any thing like an equal degree with the *Panopticon Penitentiary*, as devised and described by Mr. Bentham.†

One general rule applies, in the case of all the lots of punishment. It is this: That the private good which has operated as the motive to the injurious action, should, in all possible cases, be cut off, and the expected enjoyment prevented. Where this can be done completely, all the additional punishment necessary is only that which would suffice to compensate the want of certainty and proximity in the act of deprivation; for no man would commit a crime which he was sure he could not profit by; no man would steal, if he knew that the property stolen would that minute be taken from him. The interests which are capable of being promoted by a criminal act, may be summed up under the following titles:

1. Money, or money's worth.
2. Power.
3. Revenge.
4. Vanity, emulation.
5. Sensual pleasure, chiefly venereal.
6. Safety in respect to legal punishment.

With respect to four of these interests, viz. money, power, vanity, and safety in respect to legal punishment, the contemplated benefit is capable, in many cases, of being completely intercepted.

In the case in which revenge has operated through the degradation

† [Mill describes Bentham's Panopticon in *Prisons and Prison Discipline*, reprinted below (see *infra*, p. 199). – Ed.]

of the party suffering, the evil doer may be disappointed by re-exaltation of the degraded party.

Sensual pleasure, having been enjoyed, is beyond the reach of this operation.

It is highly worthy of observation, that, among the advantages constituting the motives to crime, those which can be cut off, and from the enjoyment of which the offender can be precluded, constitute by far the most frequent incentives to crime.

This must suffice as a summary of what should be said on the mode of applying pain most usefully for the prevention of certain acts. It only remains to add, that the following are the cases in which it may be pronounced unfit that pain should be employed for that purpose:

1. Where the evil to the community does not overbalance the good to the individual.
2. Where the evil necessary for the punishment would outweigh the evil of the act.
3. Where the evil created is not calculated to prevent the act.
4. Where the end could be obtained by other means.

VI.
The Code of Procedure. – First stage of the Judicial Business. – Second stage of the Judicial Business.

We have now, therefore, stated, what the limits of this discourse enable us to adduce, on the subject of the main body of the law; the enactments of the legislature with respect to rights, and with respect to those acts by which rights are violated. It remains that we consider that subsidiary branch of law, by which an agency is constituted for the purpose of carrying those enactments into effect. The inquiry here is, 1. what are the operations essential to that agency; 2. by what agents are they most likely to be well performed; and 3. what are the best securities that can be taken for the good conduct of these agents.

It most significantly illustrates the manner in which ignorance gropes its way in the dark, to observe, that the agency, the sole end of which is to carry into execution the civil and penal laws, was created first, and was in operation for ages, before the idea of the other branches of law was even tolerably framed. It is also worthy of remark, that the men, whose wisdom rules our affairs, are in the habit of calling the mode in which ignorance gropes its way in the dark, by the name of experience; the mode of acting upon a plan, and with foresight, by the names of theory and speculation.

There is instruction, in observing the mode, in which this inverted course of law-making was pursued. Men disputed; and their disputes were attended with the most destructive consequences. Originally, the king, at the head of the military force, and his subordinates, each at the head of a section of that force, interfered in those disputes. After a time, the king appointed functionaries, under the name of judges, for that particular service. These judges decided, without any rule, by their own discretion. The feelings of the community, grounded upon their experience of what tended to good and evil upon the whole, pointed vaguely to certain things as right, to other things as wrong; and to these the judge, as often as he was in *bona fides*, conformed his decision. The mode was similar both in arbitrating, and in punishing.

As punishing, especially in the severer cases, was an act which made a vivid impression upon the mind, the mode in which that act had been performed in previous cases was apt to be remembered: of the several modes, that which was most approved by the public would naturally be followed the most frequently, and at last there would be a species of scandal, if it was unnecessarily departed from. In this way a uniformity, more or less perfect, was established, in punishing the more heinous offences; and in regard to them custom first established what had some feeble portion of the attributes of a law.

In those cases in which, without a call for punishment, the authoritative termination of a dispute was all that was required, the experience of what was necessary, not only for any degree of mutual comfort, but even for the means of subsistence, soon established a few leading points of uniformity. Thus, when a man had cultivated a piece of ground, which belonged to nobody more peculiarly than to himself, it was evidently necessary that the crop should be considered as belonging to him; otherwise, no crops would be raised, and the community would be deprived of the means of subsistence.

These general feelings, with the remembrance, more or less perfect, of what had been done in similar cases, were the only guide; and it is surprising to what an extent, over the surface of the whole globe, law has, in all ages, remained in that state of imperfect existence, if, indeed, with any propriety, it can be called a state of existence. In every part of Asia, and in all ages, law has remained in that state of existence, or non-existence. In Europe, where, at a pretty early period, it became the practice to record in writing the proceedings of the judges, the natural propensity of referring to the past as a rule for the present, begat in time a species of obligation of being directed by the examples which had already been set. This created a uniformity and certainty, which, however imperfect, afforded something better than the arbitrary proceedings of Asiatic judges. Yet this was a benefit which had a dreadful alloy. A body, not of law, but of decisions, out of which, on each particular occasion, a law for that particular occasion, as out of the crude ore, was to be smelted, hammered, and wire-drawn, was the natural material out of which to manufacture a system of chicane. How accurately the system of law, in the several nations of Europe, has conformed to the character of a system of chicane, is matter of present and lamentable experience. The uncertainty, the delay, the vexation and expence, and that immorality of the worst species with which they inundate the community, are not the only evils, great as they are, of laws constructed upon such a plan. A system of laws, so constructed, becomes an instrument of conversation for the barbarous customs and ideas of the times in which they were engendered; and infests society with the evils of an age, which it has left behind.

To conceive the operations which are necessary to give effect to the enactments of the legislature, it is necessary to conceive the occasions which call for them.

When the legislature has established rights, so long as there is no dispute about those rights, and so long as there is no complaint of any violation of them, so long there is no occasion for any agency to give to the enactments of the legislature their effect. The moment, however, one person says, the right to that object is mine, and another person says no, but the right to that object is mine; or the moment any man complains that such or such a right belonging to him another man has violated, that moment occasion for the agency in question begins.

It is evident, also, that the operations necessary to give effect to the enactments of the legislature are confined to those two occasions;

namely, that on which a right is disputed, and that on which it has been violated. On the occasions on which a right is disputed, it is requisite to determine to whom it belongs. On the occasions on which a right has been violated, it is sometimes only required to compel reparation to the injured party; sometimes it is necessary, besides, to inflict punishment upon the offender. The question is, What are the operations required for these several results?

Where a right is disputed, all possible cases may be resolved into that of A who affirms, and B who denies. That right is mine, says A, it is not yours, says B.

If no such fact is affirmed, the right does not exist. If some such fact is affirmed, it may be met by the opponent in one of two ways. B either may deny the fact, and affirm that the right never had a commencement; or he may allow the fact, and admit that the right had a commencement, but affirm that there had subsequently happened one of those facts which put an end to rights: admitting that A bought the horse, and had a right to him in the month of July, he might affirm that A sold him again in August, and by that transaction put an end to his right.

When B meets the affirmation of A in the first way, that is, by denying the commencement of the right, he may do it in either of two ways. He may deny the investitive fact which A affirms, or not denying the fact, he may affirm some antecedent fact which deprived it of its investitive power. Thus, if A affirmed that he got the property by occupancy, B may affirm that it was not open to occupancy, but the property of another person. If A affirmed that he got the property by succession to his father, B may allow the fact of the succession, but affirm that the property did not belong to the father of A at the time of his death.

Whenever the legislature has accurately determined what are the facts which shall give commencement, and what those which shall give termination to a right, the whole confused and intricate mass of what in English law is called *Pleading*, reduces itself to these clear and simple elements. A begins, by affirming some one of the facts which gives commencement to a right. B may deny this fact directly: A affirms contract for example, B denies it; and then, of course, comes the evidence: Or, instead of denying it, B may affirm an antecedent fact which deprived the fact affirmed by A of its investitive force; or he may affirm a subsequent fact, which put an end to the right. In those two cases, in which B affirms a new fact, A must be called upon for a reply, in other words, asked whether he admits or denies it. If he admits, there is an end, of course, to the claim of A. If he denies, then again we have affirmation and denial upon a matter of fact, which is to be determined by the production of evidence.

This is the first part of the proceeding, neither intricate nor obscure. The next is, the adduction of evidence. A fact is disputed; affirmed on the one side, denied on the other. A produces evidence to prove the fact, B produces evidence to disprove it. The decision is on the one side or the other, and the dispute is at an end.

If both parties obey the decision, there is no occasion for another act. If the losing party disobeys, force is necessary to compel obedience. This is called execution, and terminates the agency required.

It is needless to particularize a penal proceeding; all the possible varieties of which fall under one or other of the cases illustrated.

Thus, when a man is charged with a crime, the prosecutor affirms one of the acts violating rights, to which punishment is annexed by the legislator. The defendant can meet this affirmation in one of only two ways. First, he may deny the act, and then the second stage of proceeding, the adduction of evidence, immediately takes place. Or, not denying the act, he may affirm some previous act, which prevented it from having the effect of violating a right. Not denying the fact of taking the horse out of the field with a view to appropriate him, he may affirm a previous purchase, gift, &c. The adduction of evidence has nothing peculiar in the case of a penal proceeding at law. In the last stage, that of execution, the peculiar act of inflicting punishment is required.

Having thus a view, though very summary, of the operations required, we shall be the better able to judge of the agents necessary for the performance.

The stages, we have observed, are three. The *first* is that in which the plaintiff adduces the fact on which he relies, and is met by the defendant either with a denial of the fact, or the affirmation of another fact, which, to maintain the suit, the plaintiff must deny. The *second* is that in which evidence, to prove or disprove the fact on which the affirmation and denial of the parties ultimately rests, is adduced and decided upon. The *third* is that in which the operations are performed necessary for giving effect to the sentence of the judge.

What is desirable in the operations of the first stage is, 1*st,* That the affirmations and negations with respect to the facts should be true; and, 2*dly,* That the facts themselves should be such as really to have the quality ascribed to them. For the first of these purposes, all the securities, which the nature of the case admits of, should be taken, for the veracity of the parties. There is the same sort of reason that the parties should speak truly, as that the witnesses should speak truly. They should speak, therefore, under all the sanctions and penalties of a witness. They cannot, indeed, in many cases swear to the existence or non-existence of the fact; which may not have been within their cognizance. But they can always swear to the state of their belief with respect to it. For the second of the above purposes, namely, that it may be known whether the facts affirmed and denied are such as to possess the quality ascribed to them, two things are necessary; the first is, that all investitive and divestitive facts and acts by which rights are violated should have been clearly predetermined by the legislature, in other words, that there should be a well-made code; the second is, that the affirmations and denials with respect to them should be made in the presence of somebody capable of telling exactly whether they have the quality ascribed to them or not. The judge is a person with this knowledge, and to him alone can the power of deciding on matters so essential to the result of the inquiry be entrusted.

To have this important part of the business done, then, in the best possible way, it is necessary that the parties should meet in the very first instance in the presence of the judge. A is asked, upon his oath, to mention the fact which he believes confers upon him or has violated his right. If it is not a fact capable of having that effect, he is told so, and his claim is at an end. If it is a fact capable of having that effect, B is asked whether he denies it; or whether he affirms another fact, either one of those, which, happening previously, would prevent it from having its imputed effect, or in a civil case one of those which, happening subsequently, would put an end to the right to which the previous fact gave commencement. If he affirmed only a fact which could have neither of these effects, the pretension of B would be without foundation.

Done in this manner, the clearness, the quickness, and the certainty of the whole proceeding are demonstrated. Remarkable it is, that every one of the rules for doing it in the best possible manner, is departed from by the English law, and that to the greatest possible extent. No security whatsoever is taken that the parties shall speak the truth; they are left with perfect impunity, aptly by Mr. Bentham denominated the *mendacity-licence*, to tell as many lies as they please. The legislature has never enumerated and defined the facts which give commencement, or put a period to or violate rights; the subject, therefore, remains in a state of confusion, obscurity, and uncertainty. And, lastly, the parties do not make their affirmations and negations before the judge, who would tell them whether the facts which they allege could or could not have the virtue ascribed to them; they make them in secret, and in writing, each along with his attorney, who has a motive to make them not in the way most conducive to the interests of his client, but in the way most conducive to his own interests, and those of his confederates, from the bottom to the top of the profession. First, A, the plaintiff, writes what is called the declaration, an instrument for the most part full of irrelevant absurdity and lies; and this he deposits in an office, where the attorney of B, the defendant, obtains a copy of it, on paying a fee. Next B, the defendant, meets the declaration of A, by what is called a plea, the form of which is not less absurd than that of the declaration. The plea is written and put into the same office, out of which the attorney of the opposite party obtains a copy of it on similar terms. The plea may be of two sorts; either, 1*st*, a dilatory plea, as it is called; or, 2*dly*, a plea to the action. To this plea the plaintiff may make a *replication*, proceeding through the same process. To the replication the defendant may put in a *rejoinder*. The plaintiff may answer the rejoinder by a *sur-rejoinder*. This, again, the defendant may oppose by a *rebutter*, and the plaintiff may answer him by a *sur-rebutter*.

All this takes place without being once seen or heard of by the judge; and no sooner has it come before him, than some flaw is perhaps discovered in it, whereupon he quashes the whole, and sends it to be performed again from the beginning.

This mischievous mess, which exists in defiance and mockery of reason, English lawyers inform us, is a strict, and pure, and beautiful exemplification of the rules of logic. This is a common language of theirs. It is a language which clearly demonstrates the state of their minds. All that they see in the system of pleading is the mode of performing it. What they know of logic is little more than the name.

The agency necessary for the performance of this portion of the business, is some person, who, when he hears a fact affirmed and denied, can tell whether it is one of those facts to which the legislature has attached the power of giving commencement or of putting a period to rights. It is evident, that on such occasion, any one person, with the requisite knowledge, attention, and probity, is as competent to the task as a hundred. If he is single, the attention and probity is likely to be the greatest, as responsibility is not weakened merely, it is almost annihilated by being shared. There should be one judge, therefore, and not more, to superintend that branch of procedure which consists of pleading.

The agency best adapted to the business of the second stage of judicature, is that which next demands our attention. It is the business of taking evidence; in other words, the doing all that is necessary to ascertain whether the disputed fact happened or did not happen.

The subject of evidence is a matter of complexity in the detail. And where any thing complex is to be stated in words, there is always difficulty in the expression, how plain soever the ideas. Such general considerations, however, as we can even here adduce, will, we hope, throw sufficient light upon the subject, to leave no doubt with respect to the conclusions which we have it in view to establish. This is one of the topics, connected with law, which Mr. Bentham has exhausted, though a small part only of what he has written upon it has yet seen the light.*

With respect to all facts, legally operative, that is, which give or take away rights, it is desirable that evidence, amounting to proof, should, if possible, always exist. With respect to a great proportion of them, it is in the power of the legislature to take measures, that evidence of them shall be collected at the moment of their happening, and shall be preserved. This is the case with all those of which an evidentiary writing can be made and preserved by registration; all contracts, births, deaths, marriages, and so on. The proportion is really very great of the whole number of facts, legally operative, in regard to which a legislature, by proper means, might secure the existence of evidence, and to that extent might either prevent disputes, or render the decision of them easy. That so little of this most important and obvious work has any where been done, only shows how ill the

*We are happy to say, there are hopes that this part of Mr. Bentham's writings will soon be presented to the public by M. Dumont, the first of translators and redacteurs, in that happy form which he has given to other portions of that philosopher's manuscripts.

legislatures of the world have hitherto performed their duty. It is in the power of the legislature, by a proper classification, to have an accurate formulary, for the different species of *contracts*, *wills*, and other *evidentiary writings*. Those formularies properly made and printed with blanks to fill up, would render the business of *Conveyancing*, which, in England, is a boundless, trackless, and almost impenetrable jungle, abounding with expence, with delay and vexation to parties, with wealth and almost boundless power over the fortunes of other men to lawyers, a thing of the greatest simplicity, certainty and ease.

Into the question of what might be, and ought to be done by the legislature, for making and preserving evidence of the principal facts by which rights are made to begin or to end, we cannot enter at length, on the present occasion. The great importance which belongs to the subject, is evident from what we have thus shortly advanced.

The business of him, who is only called upon to determine whether a disputed fact did or did not happen is, to make the best use of all the evidence which exists, whether it were, or were not desirable, that more had been made to exist. For the best use of that which exists, three things are necessary:

1*st*, That the whole of it should be made to bear, that is, should be taken, and applied.

2*dly*, That it should be taken in those circumstances which are most conducive to trust-worthiness.

3*dly*, That the proper value should be set upon each article, and upon the whole.

1. That the evidence may be taken as completely as possible, two things are necessary. The first is, that the judge should have power to send for, and to compel the attendance of, all persons and things which may be capable of affording evidence. The second is, that the evidence should all be taken, and nothing be omitted or lost.

It is not necessary here to enter into any details with respect to the first of those requisites. The necessity of the powers is obvious, and the end to be attained is so precise and perspicuous, that there can be no difficulty in conceiving the mode of putting together and applying the means. There is no limit, it is obvious, to the physical power which should be placed at the disposal of the judge. He ought to have the right of calling upon every man, upon the whole community, to aid him in any act which is necessary to the performance of any part of his judicial duty; because any force, opposed to the performance of that duty, there ought to be a force sufficient promptly to overcome. It is convenient, however, to the community, instead of being liable to be called upon, individually, for the performance of the ordinary services auxiliary to the business of the judge, to provide him with a proper number of officers, paid for attending to execute his commands. Their principal business, as regards this stage of the judicial proceedings, is, to serve notice upon any persons whose own presence, or that of any writing or other thing which they may possess, is required by the judge. Persons or things, subjected immediately to the operations of judicature, have a particular name in English. They are said to be *forthcoming*, a word which has an exact equivalent in few other languages, and is exceedingly appropriate and useful. It is of the greatest convenience, when a concrete term, the use of which is very frequent, has an abstract term corresponding to it; as good, has goodness; hard, hardness, and so on. There was not any word in the language corresponding in this way to *forthcoming*. Mr. Bentham, perceiving the great need of it, made the term *forthcomingness*; not exceptionable on the score either of harshness or obscurity. The small wits thought proper to laugh at him. We shall, nevertheless – sorry at the same time that we cannot supply a defect in the language without offending them, make use of the word; in which we find great appropriateness and great convenience. This particular branch, therefore, of the judicial agency is that which relates to *forthcomingness*; and forthcomingness is required for two purposes, both for evidence and for justiciability; for evidence, that a true decision may be passed; for justiciability, that the sentence of the judge may not fail of its intended effect.

So much with respect to the forthcomingness of evidence. The second condition, required to give the decision the benefit of all existing evidence is, that the whole should be taken, and that not any part of it which can be taken without preponderant inconvenience should be excluded and lost.

Of the several articles of evidence, some will always be of more importance, some of less; and some may be of very little importance; but whether of little or of much, it is always desirable that all should be taken, and every the smallest portion counted for what it is worth.

The discovery of truth is promoted by taking advantage of every thing which tends to throw light upon the subject of dispute.

These propositions, it may appear to be useless, indeed impertinent, formally to state. They are too evident, it may be said, to be disputed, and too important to be overlooked. Important as they are, and undisputed by all the rest of the world, they are not only disputed, but trampled upon by lawyers, especially English lawyers. They have unhappily established a set of rules in direct opposition to them. These rules they applaud in all forms of expression, and celebrate as guards and fences of all that is dear to mankind.

In all causes, they have determined, that persons so and so situated, things so and so situated, though apt to be pregnant with information beyond all other persons and things, shall not be admitted as sources of evidence. Thus, in English law, we have incompetency of witnesses, that is, exclusion of them, 1*st*, From want of understanding; 2*dly*, From defect of religious principle; 3*dly*, From infamy of character; 4*thly*, From interest. These are undisguised modes of exclusion; besides which, there is an extensive assortment of disguised modes. Under this title comes the rule, that only the best evidence be given which the nature of the case admits of; according to which, it often happens that the only evidence which can be had is excluded. Under this title also falls the rule, making certain kinds of evidence conclusive, by which proceeding, all other evidence is excluded. To the same list belongs the rule, that hearsay evidence is not admissible. The rules, so extensive in their application, by which writings are wholly rejected, only because they want certain formularies, are rules of exclusion; and so are the limitations with respect to time, and to number of witnesses. Into the very extensive subject, however, of the absurdity and mischievousness of the rules of evidence in English law, we cannot pretend so much as to enter. A remarkable exemplification of them was afforded on the trial of Warren Hastings, to which, for this purpose, the reader may be referred. (See Mill's *History of British India*, Book VI. Chap. ii.)

The only conceivable reasons for the exclusion of evidence are three:

1. Irrelevancy.
2. Inconvenience in obtaining and producing.
3. Danger of deception.

With regard to irrelevancy the decision is clear. What has no tendency either to prove or disprove the point in question, it would be loss of time to receive.

With regard to inconvenience, it is no doubt liable to happen, that when all the good which can be expected from the obtaining of a lot of evidence is compared with the evil of the delay, cost, and vexation, inseparable from the obtaining of it, the evil may be more than an overmatch for the good. In all such cases, it is expedient that the lot of evidence should be foregone.

As a guard against the danger of deception, it is equally certain that no evidence ought ever to be excluded. An account of all the reasons by which the absurdity is demonstrated of exclusion on this ground, and of the wide and deplorable mischief which, in the vulgar systems, is produced by it, would be far too extensive for the contracted limits of the present discourse. Reasons, however, decisive of the question, present themselves so obviously, that hardly any man, with an ordinary understanding, not fettered by prejudice, can look at the subject without perceiving them.

If evidence is to be received from no source from which evidence, liable to produce deception, is capable of coming, evidence must not be received at all. Evidence must be received from sources whence false evidence, as well as true, is liable to flow. To refuse all information from such sources, is not the way by which a knowledge of the truth can be obtained. This is the way to make sure of not having that knowledge. The means of obtaining it are, to receive evidence from every possible source, and to separate the bad from the good, under all those securities, and by the guidance of all those marks, of which understanding and attention know how to avail themselves.

It is not enough to say, we will receive information from those sources only which are least likely to yield deceptious evidence, refuse to receive it from those which are most likely. You are obliged to receive it from sources differing in almost all possible degrees of likelihood. Where are you to draw the line of separation? Is not the same discernment which guards you against the danger of false information from the sources which you deem the least likely to yield it, sufficient to guard you against it from those sources which you deem the most likely to do so? In fact, it will be still more sufficient; because in this case you will be much more apt to be upon your guard. The very best information is, in truth, liable to be derived from the very worst of sources, – from a man who, you know, would not tell you one word of truth, if he could help it.

The securities that a man will give true information, independently of those artificial securities which the legislature can apply equally to all, are, 1*st*, Intelligence, 2*dly*, Probity, 3*dly*, Freedom from interest. Suppose that one, or two, or all of these securities are wanting; it only follows, that what he states should be heard with a proportional distrust. It may still be of the utmost importance to the discovery of the truth that he should be heard. Hear him with the proper allowances, and it must always be less favourable to that great end, that, he should not be heard at all. His testimony may appear, when heard, to be utterly unworthy of credence. But that could not be known till it was heard and examined. It might so have been, that it was not only worthy of credence, but completed the proof of a fact of the greatest possible importance. That a man should not be heard as a witness, on account of his religious creed, is an absurdity which we cannot descend to notice.

2. The second of the three things which we found necessary, as above, for making the best use judicially of whatever evidence, to the fact in question, exists, was, that it should be taken under those circumstances, which are most conducive to trust-worthiness. Those circumstances are constituted by the artificial securities, which arrangements can be made to apply. The following enumeration of them has been made by Mr. Bentham (*Introduction to the Rationale of Evidence*, p. 54), and appears to be complete.

1. Punishment.
2. Shame.
3. Interrogation, including counter-interrogation.
4. Counter evidence, – admission of.
5. Writing, – use made of it for giving permanence, &c. to evidence.
6. Publicity, – to most purposes and on most occasions.
7. Privacy, – to some purposes, and on some occasions.

For developing the import of these several securities, we can afford to say nothing. The principal operation of the judicial functionary in this part of the business is, to preside over the interrogation; to see that it is properly and completely performed. The question, then, what is the sort of agency best adapted for the performance of this part of the task of taking evidence is not difficult to answer. There is nothing in it which one man, with the proper intellectual and moral qualifications, is not as capable of performing, as any number of men.

3. All the existing evidence being collected and received, it only remains that the proper value should be attached to the several portions, and a corresponding decision pronounced.

It is sufficiently evident that, for the performance of this duty, no very precise instructions can be laid down. The value which belongs to an article of evidence often depends on minute and almost indescribable circumstances; and the result must be left to the sagacity and conscience of the judge.

At the same time, however, service to this end, and of the greatest importance, may be, and, of course, ought to be, rendered by the legislature. The different marks of trust-worthiness may, to a certain extent of particularity, be very correctly described. This being done, the difference between the value of any two lots of evidence, to which those marks attach, may be very exactly ascertained. One has a certain number of the marks of trust-worthiness, as laid down by the legislature; another has all these and so many more; the result is clear. It is evident, that as far, in this respect, as experience and foresight can go, nothing should be left undone by the legislature.

Another important service can be rendered by the legislature; and that is, to provide an accurate language for the judge; a language in which he can express precisely the degree of value which he allots to each article of evidence, and to the whole. Various expedients may be adopted for this purpose. A very obvious one is, to fix upon some particular, well known, article of evidence, the value of which all men appreciate equally; the clear testimony, for example, of a man of the ordinary degree of intelligence and probity, as a standard. Is the value to be expressed, which the judge attaches to any other article of evidence? If inferior to the standard, it falls below it by so many degrees, one, two, three, four: If superior, it rises above it by so many.

Having provided an accurate language, the legislature should take security that it be used; and admit of no vague and general expressions in the account of the value which the judge attaches to each article of the evidence on which he grounds his decision.

At the same time that the legislature insists upon the use of precise language in stating the value of evidence, it should insist upon reasons; upon receiving from the judge a precise statement of the grounds upon which he attaches such a value, and no other, to each and every article of evidence; that is, upon receiving a reference, as exact as language can give, to each of the circumstances which contributed to suggest to him that particular estimate which he says he has formed.

Of the importance of all these expedients we presume that no illustration is required.

We come now to the third and last stage of the business of judicature; when all that remains is to carry into effect the sentence of the judge.

When they, upon whom the sentence operates, are willing to obey, all that is necessary is, to afford them notice of what it requires them to perform. In well ordered countries, all but a very insignificant number will be found to be cases of this description. When opposition is to be overcome, a physical force must be provided, sufficient for the purpose. As there seems nothing mysterious in determining how this should be formed, and under what rules it should act, to secure the ends for which it is provided, with the smallest possible amount of collateral evil, we shall here take leave of the subject.

VII.

The Judicial Establishment; or Inquiry what is the best form of the Agency required for giving effect to the Laws. – Securities for the intellectual Endowments of the Judge. – Securities for the moral Qualities of the Judge.

We have now seen the whole of the operations to be performed. The parties are received to state before the judge the investitive or divestitive facts on which they rely. If they state, for this purpose, a fact which is not possessed of those qualities, they are immediately told that it is not possessed of them, and not calculated to support their claim. They come, by two or three steps, at the longest, to a fact upon which the question ultimately turns; and which is either contested, or not contested. In a great many cases it would not be contested. When the subject was stript of disguise, the party who had no right, would generally see that he had no hope, and would acquiesce. The suit would thus be terminated without the adduction of evidence. When it was not, the cases would be frequent in which it might be terminated by the evidence which the parties brought along with them. In these cases, also, the first hearing would suffice. A vast majority of the whole number of suits would be included in these two sets of cases. For the decision of a vast majority, therefore, of the whole number of suits, a few minutes would suffice. When all the evidence could not be forthcoming at the first hearing, and only then, would a second hearing be required. In this mode of proceeding, justice would be, that without which it is not justice, expeditious and cheap.

In all this there is nothing which one man, with the appropriate intellectual and moral qualities, is not as competent to perform as any number of men. As one man is cheaper than any greater number, that is one reason why no more than one judge should be allowed to one tribunal.

The next object of inquiry is, to ascertain what securities can be provided that those who are entrusted with the business of judicature shall possess the requisite intellectual and moral endowments.

The intellectual endowments depend upon those who have the power of choosing and of dismissing the judges: and who do or do not appoint men whose knowledge and capacity are ascertained. The moral behaviour of the judges depends upon the interests which act upon them in the situation in which they are placed.

Into the question, who should have the appointment of the judges, we do not intend to enter. The answer would be different under different forms of government; and this is not the place to compare the different forms of government, either for this or any other of the ends of its institution. One thing only we shall state, because it carries its evidence along with it. Those who appoint the judges ought to have no interest contrary to the best administration of justice.

As the uprightness of the judge is assailed by interests inseparable from his situation; viz. the profit which he may derive from misdecision, it is necessary to counterbalance them by opposite interests, assuming the character of securities. Several of the securities, which we have already seen applying to the situation of witness, apply also to the situation of judge: Some are peculiar to each. The following is the list of those which apply to the situation of judge.

1. Punishment.
2. Shame.
3. Publicity.
4. Writing, for the sake of accuracy and permanence.
5. Singleness of the functionary.
6. Appeal.

For the *Punishment* of the several kinds of judicial offences, provision ought to be made in the penal code.

In the case of the judge there is particular occasion to point accurately, and to strengthen to the utmost, the operation of *Shame*; for in the situation of judge it is possible to be guilty of offences very numerous and very serious, without permitting so much of evidence to attach to any definite act, as would suffice to form a ground for punishment.

The great instrument for the application of shame is *Publicity*. The importance of publicity, therefore, is paramount. It is not only the great instrument for creating and applying the moral sanction, the approbation and disapprobation of mankind; but it is of essential service towards the application of punishment, by making known the occasions on which it is deserved. It is not only a great security in itself, but it is the principle of life and strength to all other securities.

All other publicity is feeble and of little worth compared with that of the *Press*. Not only, therefore, ought this to be allowed to operate with its utmost force upon the judge, but effectual provision ought to be made to cause it to operate upon him with its utmost force. Not only ought the judgment hall to be rendered as convenient as possible for the reception of the public; not only ought the greatest freedom to be enjoyed in publishing the proceedings of the judge; and in publishing all manner of observations upon them, favourable or unfavourable; but measures ought to be taken to make a public, and to produce publication, where there is any chance that a voluntary public, and voluntary publication, would be wanting. For this purpose, unless other very important considerations intervene, the judgment seat should always be in that place, within the district to which it belongs, where the most numerous and intelligent public, and the best means of publication, are to be had.

In England, where there is no definition of libel, and where the judges, therefore, are allowed to punish, under the name of libel, whatever writing they do not like, the publishing of unfavourable observations on the conduct of a judge – nay, in some instances, and these the highest in importance, the simple report of his proceedings – is treated as one of the most heinous of all possible offences. No wonder! Allow judges, or allow any men, to frame laws, and they will frame them, if they can, to answer their own purposes. Who would not, if he could, make a law to protect himself from censure? More especially if he were a man disposed to act in such a way as to deserve censure?

Would you allow falsehood to be published against the judge? The word falsehood is here ambiguous. It means both erroneous opinions, and false statements with regard to fact. Erroneous opinions we would undoubtedly permit, because we know no standard for ascertaining them, other than that which is afforded by public discussion; and because this is an adequate remedy for all the evil which erroneous opinions have any tendency to produce. Affirmation of facts injurious to the judge, if false, and made without reasonable grounds for having been believed to be true, we would prevent.

Allow facts, injurious to the judge, to be published, even when true; allow comments, unfavourable to the judge, to be made upon his actions, you discredit the administration of justice. Discredit the administration of justice, to which the people are resorting every day for the greatest of all possible benefits, protection from injury! As well talk of discrediting the business of a bread-baker, a meat-seller, if the fraudulent dealer is exposed to the censures of the public! Discredit the administration of justice, indeed, by taking measures of security against the vices of judges, indispensable for its perfection!

The importance of *recording, in permanent characters*, what takes place before the judge, we must content ourselves with assuming. We may do so, it is presumed, with propriety, on account of the facility with which the reasons present themselves. We must also leave it to our readers to draw the line of distinction between the occasions on which it is requisite, and the occasions on which it may be dispensed with; the occasions, for example, where every thing is simple and clear, and all parties are satisfied.

It is a great security, both for diligent and for upright conduct in the judge, that he occupy *singly* the judgment seat. When a man knows that the whole credit and reward of what is done well; the whole punishment and disgrace of what is done ill, will belong to himself, the motive to good conduct is exceedingly increased. When a man hopes that he can shuffle off the blame of negligence, the blame of unfairness, or fix a part of it on another, the uncertainty of the punishment operates, as we have already seen, to the diminution, and almost to the extinction, of its preventive force. Certain common, and even proverbial expressions, mark the general experience of that indifference, with which a duty, that belongs in common to many, is apt to be performed. What is every body's business is nobody's. This is as true in the family as in the state; as true in judicature as in ordinary life. Much remains to be said upon this topic, which is one of great importance; but we must pass to the next.

Of the use of *appeal*, as a security against the misconduct of the judge, there is the less occasion to adduce any proof, because it seems to be fully recognized by the practice of nations.

One thing, however, which is not recognized by that practice, is, that, if it is necessary in any one sort of causes, so it is in every other, without exception. Not a single reason can be given why it should exist in one set of cases, which is not equally strong to prove that it should exist in any other.

It is instructive to observe the cases in which it has been supposed that it ought to exist, and the cases in which it has been supposed that it might be omitted. The cases in which it has been thought necessary, are those which concern property of considerable value. Those in which it has been dispensed with are those which concern property of inconsiderable value. The first set of cases are those which are of importance to the aristocratical class; the second are those which are of no importance to that class. It is the aristocratical class who have made the laws; they have accordingly declared that the suits which were important to them should have the benefit of appeal; the suits not important to them should not have the benefit of appeal.

We recognize only one standard of importance; namely, influence upon human happiness and misery. The small sum of money for which the suit of the poor man is instituted is commonly of much greater importance to him, than the larger sum for which the suit of the rich man is instituted is to the rich. Again, for one rich man there are thousands and thousands of poor. In the calculation, then, of perfect benevolence, the suits for the small sums are not, as in the calculation of perfect aristocracy, those of the least, or rather no importance; they are of ten thousand times greater importance than the suits for the largest sums.

If an appeal ought to be had, how many *stages* should there be of appeal? This question, we imagine, is easily answered. If you go for a second judgment, you should, if possible, go to the very best source: and if you go at once to the best source, why go any farther?

What is required to be done, in the case of an appeal, is the first thing which deserves to be ascertained. An appeal takes place in consequence of a complaint against the previous judge. Where no complaint, there is no appeal, nor place for appeal.

A complaint against the judge must relate to his conduct, either at the first, the second, or the third stage, of the judicial operations.

If to his conduct at the first stage, it must be a complaint of his having permitted a party to rest upon a fact which had not the investitive or divestitive quality ascribed to it; and this implies either a mistake with respect to the law, or that he allowed the decision to turn upon a fact which did not embrace the merits of the question. It is evident, that for the decision of this question, all that is necessary is an exact transcription of *the pleadings*, and transmission of them to the court of appeal.

If the complaint relates to his conduct at the second stage, it must turn upon one of two points; either that he did not take all the evidence, or that he did not properly determine its value.

If he did not take the evidence properly, by a failure either in assembling the sources of it, or in extracting it from them when assembled, the proper remedy is to send back the cause to him, with an order to him to supply the omission; or, if he be suspected of having failed wilfully, to send it to the judge of one of the neighbouring districts, to retake the evidence and decide.

If the complaint relates to a wrong estimate of the evidence, the statement of it, transmitted to the court of appeal, with the reasons assigned by the judge for the value affixed to every portion of it, will enable the appellate court to decide.

With regard to the third stage, the only complaint there can be is, that the judge has not taken measures to execute his own sentence. If any inquiry is in this case to be made, the proper course is, that the appellate court refer it to one of the neighbouring judges. When a simple act is to be done, the proper order is to be dispatched, and the proper penalties for non-performance exacted.

It thus appears, that for every thing which is required to be done by the appellate judicature, nothing whatsoever is required, as a foundation, but certain papers. The presence is not required, either of parties or of witnesses.

As it is of no great consequence, in a country in which the means of communication are tolerably provided, whether papers have to be transmitted 50 or 500 miles, the distance, even though considerable, of the seat of the appellate jurisdiction is a matter of very little importance. The object, then, is to get the best seat; that is, the best public. The best public, generally speaking, is in the capital. The capital, then, is the proper seat of all appellate jurisdiction. And that there should be one judge, and one judge only, in each court of appeal, is proved by exactly the same reasons, as those which apply to the courts of primary jurisdiction.

The question how many courts there should be, as well of primary as of appellate jurisdiction, is to be determined by one thing, and one thing only; namely, the need there is for them. The number of the courts of primary jurisdiction must be determined, in some instances, by the number of suits; in some, by local extent. To render justice sufficiently accessible, the distance from the seat of judicature must not be great, though the number of accruing suits, either from the paucity or from the good conduct of the people, should be ever so small.

As the judgment seat should never be empty, for the need of staying injustice is not confined to times and seasons, and as one judge may be sometimes ill, sometimes called to a distance even by the duties of his office, provision ought to be made for supplying his place. For this purpose the proper expedient is a deputy. That the deputy should well perform his duty, the best security is, that he should be chosen and employed by the judge, the judge being responsible for the acts of the deputy, as his own. Whatever it be, which the judge cannot do, or cannot conveniently do, in that he may employ his deputy. If there is a great influx of causes, the deputy may be employed in some of the least complex and difficult. If there is any business, not of first-rate importance, requiring the presence of the judge at a distance, the delegation of the deputy or deputies is the proper resource.

Besides the judge and his deputy, there are two adjuncts to every tribunal, which are of the utmost importance; indispensable, indeed, to the due administration of justice. These are, a *pursuer-general*, and a *defender-general*. The business of both pursuer-general, and defender-general is, to reclaim the execution of all laws in the execution of which the nation has a peculiar interest, though individuals may not. The peculiar business of the pursuer-general is, to act on behalf of the administrative authority, in its character of plaintiff, and on behalf of every plaintiff who is without the means of engaging another advocate; to obviate any prejudice he sees likely to arise to justice from the conduct of plaintiffs, whether in civil matters or penal; and to perform, in the case of all offences, where no private prosecutor appears, the office of prosecutor. The peculiar duty of the defender-general is, to act on behalf of the administrative authority in its capacity of defendant, and on behalf of every defendant who has not the means of engaging another advocate, and to obviate any prejudice he sees likely to result to justice from want of skill or other causes on the part of a defendant who pleads his own cause, or on the part of the advocate who pleads it for him.

The courts of appeal, though all seated in the metropolis, ought to be as numerous as the speedy hearing of all the appeals which come to them requires. The judges of appeal ought all to be chosen from the judges of primary jurisdiction, not only on account of the education and the experience received, but as a step of promotion, and a proper motive to acquire the requisite education, and to merit approbation in the inferior employment. There is the same propriety, and for the same reason, in choosing the judges of primary jurisdiction from the deputies.

LIBERTY OF THE PRESS.

I.
Nature and Objects of the Inquiry.

The task of pointing out which of the acts, capable of being committed by the press, it would be expedient to prohibit under penalties, we trust will be found to be greatly diminished, by what we have already established in the articles GOVERNMENT and JURISPRUDENCE.

There is scarcely a right, for the violation of which, scarcely an operation of government, for the disturbance of which the press may not be employed as an instrument. The offences capable of being committed by the press are indeed nearly co-extensive with the whole field of delinquency.

It is not, however, necessary to give a separate definition of every such violation or disturbance, when committed by the press; for that would be to write the penal code a second time; first describing each offence as it appears in ordinary cases; and then describing it anew for the case in which the press is the particular instrument.

If, for the prevention of the violation of rights, it were necessary to give a separate definition, on account of every instrument which might be employed as a means of producing the several violations, the penal code would be endless. In general, the instrument or means is an immaterial circumstance. The violation itself, and the degree of alarm which may attend it, are the principle objects of consideration. If a man is put in fear of his life, and robbed of his purse, it is of no consequence whether he is threatened with a pistol or with a sword. In the definition of a theft, of a fraud, or a murder, it is not necessary

97

to include an account of all the sorts of means by which these injuries may be perpetrated. It is sufficient if the injury itself is accurately described. The object is to prevent the injury, not merely when produced by one sort of means or another sort of means, but by any means.

From these illustrations, it sufficiently appears, that, if an accurate penal code were composed, defining the violations of rights, and the disturbances of the operations of government, to which penalties were to be annexed, every offence, capable of being committed by the press, would be defined without mentioning the press. It is no less evident, that if we include in the term *libel*, as, to the great encouragement of confusion, is generally done, all the offences capable of being committed by the press, we include in the definition of libel all the definitions of the penal code.

As far as Persons and Property are concerned, the general definition of the acts by which rights are liable to be violated, has always been held sufficient; and has been regarded as including not less the cases in which the instrumentality of the press has been employed, than those in which any other means have been employed to the same end. Nobody ever thought of a particular law for restraining the press on account of the cases in which it may have been rendered subservient to the perpetration of a murder or a theft. It is enough that a law is made to punish him who has been guilty of the murder or theft, whether he has employed the press or any thing else as the means for accomplishing his end.

There can be no doubt, however, that the press is an instrument peculiarly adapted for the commission of injuries against Reputation, and for effecting disturbance to the operations of Government, while it has no peculiar adaptation for the commission of other offences. Here, too, there is the greatest disposition to restrain the press within improper limits. It is demanded of us, therefore, upon this part of the subject, to enter into greater detail.

We are then to inquire, in the first place, what are the acts of the press with respect to *private reputation?* and next, what are the acts with respect to *government*, which it is desirable that punishment should be employed to restrain?

II.
Offences of the Press with respect to Private Rights.

Agreeably to the principles which have been already considered in the article JURISPRUDENCE, no act can be regarded as an offence with respect to an individual, which is not a violation of some of his rights.*

In considering the rights which ought to be established with respect to reputation, one proposition may be assumed; That every man should be considered as having a right to the character which he deserves; that is, to be spoken of according to his actions.

Such Offences should be defined.

In what manner the definition of this right, which would form a part of the civil code, should be expressed, is not now the question; it is evident there is no peculiar difficulty in the matter. As words, not thoughts, are the object of legal cognizance, the right can only have respect to security against certain words; words, imputing to the individual, actions which he has not performed, or a disposition to certain actions, without evidence that such a disposition exists.

Suppose that one man has instituted a suit against another, for the offence of having violated, through the press, his right to some part of the reputation which he deserves. In his ground of complaint he must affirm that the man has imputed to him either the performance of actions which he did not commit, or a disposition to certain actions, where no evidence of such disposition can be given.

The words are produced; and the first question is, whether they do or do not impute the actions which, in the complaint, or bill of accusation, they are alleged to impute?

It is to be observed, that they who oppose the attempt to define the offences, which, for shortness, we call the offences of the press, make

---

*In the description which follows of that violation of rights which is most liable to be committed by the press, and of the mode in which it ought to be treated, the developments presented in the article JURISPRUDENCE are understood to be in the mind of the reader; if they are not, the very brief exposition here given will not be understood. [Mill's *Jurisprudence* is reprinted in the present collection. – Ed.]

use of such occasions, as this, to raise their objections. How, they ask, can all the forms of expression be defined, by which the imputation of such and such actions may be, either more openly, or more covertly, conveyed?

It is very evident that the question, on such an occasion, whether the words do or do not impute such or such actions, is a question of fact. The law says, that such and such actions shall not be imputed, defining the actions. Whether such and such a man has imputed such actions, and whether by one set of words, or another set of words, are questions of fact.

The law, when it said that such and such acts should not be imputed to a man, could not determine whether A, who is accused by B, of having imputed to him one of those acts, did so, or not. That is to be determined by evidence, bearing upon the point. One, and in general the main article of that evidence, are the words which have been used. What is the import of these words; or, which comes to the same thing, what is the degree of proof involved in them, is to be determined, as all questions respecting the weight of evidence are, in each instance, to be determined, by the tribunal before which the accusation is brought. The interpretation of words rests upon the same footing in this, as in all other cases, that, for example, of a Will. The law determines, that whatsoever disposition a man has made with respect to his property, shall take effect after his death. But whether A has left his manor of Dale to B, is a matter of fact to be determined by evidence applying to that particular point; principally by that arising from the words of the will.

It may still be argued, by persons who do not easily renounce an opinion to which they have once given their support, that the actions, the imputation of which, the legislature means to prohibit, cannot be defined.

But this is a position which cannot long be maintained.

It is hurtful to a man, if he is believed to have committed some actions, or to have a disposition to commit them; it is not hurtful in the case of others. Evidently it is by imputation of the first sort alone, that any right with respect to reputation can be infringed.

The acts, which a man receives injury from being believed to have committed, or to be disposed to commit, are either those to which the law has annexed penalties, or those to which the penalties of public disrepute and dislike are annexed.

With respect to those acts to which the law has annexed penalties, as theft, murder, perjury, and so on, it will not be pretended that there is any difficulty; the law has already defined them, or ought to define them, and they may be marked with perfect precision by a few words.

Those acts which it is hurtful to a man, solely on account of the disrepute and dislike which they produce, to have it believed that he has committed them, may also be with sufficient accuracy determined.

Compensation should be made to the individual for injuries sustained by Offences of the Press.

The ends to be attained by punishment are, Reparation to the individual to whom injury has been done, and Prevention of similar acts in future.

In the idea of all punishment, effectual reparation to the injured individual is a necessary and essential ingredient. Suppose, then, it were declared by the legislature, that every imputation to a man of acts which bring the evil of dislike and disrepute upon him who has committed them, that is, every false imputation, shall be punished at least by reparation to be made to the party injured; the term *evil* is to this purpose perfectly precise. It would remain with the complainant to show what kind and degree of injury he had received; which is a matter of fact, to be estimated, in each instance, from the evidence adduced, by the tribunal before which the question is brought. If the injury sustained is a pecuniary injury, the question coincides exactly with the question of damages, decided regularly, in English courts, as a question of fact, by the jury.

Injuries of the kind which we are now considering can affect a man only in two ways; either, by lessening the pecuniary value which he might otherwise have enjoyed; or, by lessening the marks of respect and affection which he would otherwise have received. What the loss is, in this latter instance, is also evidently a question of fact. It has nothing, therefore, to do with the legal definition of the offence, the business of the legislature. It is a question, which, like all other questions of fact, must of necessity be determined upon evidence by the tribunal before which it is brought. It is no doubt a question of delicacy, and considerable difficulty, because the evidence must often consist of very fine and minute circumstances, which can seldom be precisely ascertained. But this is not the only class of judicial questions, the determination of which depends upon such evidence as it is very difficult accurately to collect and to weigh. What is of greatest importance, on this occasion, to remark is, that all the difficulty lies in the matter of fact. There is no doubt or obscurity in the law, which says, that whatsoever hurt a man has sustained through actions or dispositions falsely imputed to him, he shall receive compensation for. Difficulties, however, arising either from the complexity of the matter of fact, or the obscurity of the evidence, no legislative enactments can prevent. These are confided to the skill and integrity of the judge.

The compensation which ought to be made to a man for the diminution of those marks of respect and affection which he would otherwise have received, is a question for the legislature. Let us suppose that a soldier has been accused of cowardice, in such a manner as to create a general belief of the truth of the accusation; that a man of honour has been accused of mendacity, or of some of those irregular propensities to which the horror of the public is attached; it is evident that money is not, in such cases, an appropriate compensation.

When a man, through the offence of another, has been deprived of a certain amount of money, or of money's worth, we say that he has received compensation, when he is placed in the same situation in which he would have been, if the offence had never taken place.

According to this idea of compensation, a man, against whom an unfavourable opinion has been created, by the act of another man, has received compensation, when he is placed in the same situation with regard to the opinion of those with whom he is connected, as if that act had not taken place. This, therefore, is the object which it ought to be the endeavour of the legislature to effect.

One expedient is perfectly appropriate. It is, that the man who has falsely propagated an unfavourable opinion with respect to another, should be made to do whatever is in his power to remove the impression he has made. To this end, he should publish the sentence of the judge, declaring that the action, or disposition which he had imputed to the individual injured, he had imputed to him falsely. He should at least be made to publish it in every way in which he had published the imputation. Frequently a more extensive publication might be required.

In most cases, it will be allowed, that thus much would suffice. It may, however, be affirmed, that often the impression would be too profoundly struck, to be effaced by a mere knowledge of the sentence of the judge. In such cases, something more in the way of compensation would be required. On this, it is of importance to be observed, that if the impression produced by an imputation, which, after solemn inquiry, the judge has declared to be false, should not, by that declaration, be completely effaced, it implies necessarily one of two things; either that the public have evidence of the truth of the accusation, which was not adduced to the judge, and then the remaining impression is not owing to the imputation which the judge has condemned, but to the evidence; or, secondly, that the public mind is in a state of gross ignorance and imbecility, capable of forming opinions, even on the clearest subjects, not only not according to evidence, but in opposition to it. If the public mind, however, is in such a deplorable condition, it is the fault of the legislature; and for the rectification of this evil, the best course undoubtedly is, to take effectual measures for the instruction of the people, which instruction would soon place them beyond the danger of such delusions. In the mean time, if something more than the publication of the sentence of the judge were necessary to restore a man to that degree of consideration, of which the false imputation had deprived him, governments have numerous ways of raising the consequence of individuals; and no legislature would be at a loss for a gradation of expedients suited to the scale of demand.

Means which should be used for preventing the violation of Rights by the Press.

We have now illustrated that part of this question which regards compensation to the injured individual. It remains to inquire what is best to be done in this case, for the attainment of the other object of punishment, namely, the prevention of similar offences in time to come.

To devise a punishment sufficient to prevent an offence, is to provide a motive sufficient to counteract the motive which leads to the offence. We have hence to consider what are the motives by which men are incited to make false imputations on the characters of others.

These motives may be of three different sorts. A man may derive *pecuniary profit*, he may derive *comparative distinction*, or he may satisfy his desire of *vengeance*, by blackening the character of his neighbour.

In the case in which a man has by calumny wrongfully intercepted the pecuniary receipts of his neighbour, the obligation of making satisfaction to the party injured would, it is obvious, alone suffice, provided the machinery of the laws were sufficiently perfect, to render the execution of them certain. Seldom would any man calumniate his neighbour, for the sake of placing £20 in his own pocket, if he were sure that, next day, or next week, he would have to restore it, with all the profit which might have been made by the use of it, and with the disgrace besides of having committed an action which other men abhor.

Sometimes, however, a man may derive pecuniary profit from calumniating persons whom he has not by that means deprived of any pecuniary advantage; by the sale, for example, of a slanderous publication; when the satisfaction due to the individual may not be of a nature to counteract the motive which leads to the offence. The expedient in this case, also, is sufficiently obvious, and sufficiently simple. It is necessary to ascertain the whole of the gain which has been made by the offender, and to take it away from him. This, together with the satisfaction which he ought to make to the injured individual, would, if it were certain, create a surplus of motive to abstain from the injurious act.

In both of these cases, if the execution of the law is uncertain, an additional punishment may be necessary, sufficient to compensate for the chance of escape. The allowance to be made on this score must depend upon the imperfection of the laws; while one important fact is to be kept in remembrance, that as a severity of punishment, beyond a certain point, is increased, certainty of execution is diminished. The true expedient, therefore, is to render the machinery of the laws so perfect, that the penalties which they denounce may always be sure of execution; and then hardly any thing beyond compensation to the individual, and the abstraction of any additional gain which might have been made by the propagation of slander, would be necessary to repress all offences against the reputation of others, to which the motive was constituted by pecuniary gain.

The two remaining cases are still more simple. If a man propagates a falsehood, for the sake of injuring the character of a man by whom his own consideration is eclipsed, it is only when he expects to obtain by that means a permanent advantage. If he knows that immediately the law will take its hold upon him; that he will be compelled to re-elevate the character of his neighbour, and to proclaim his own disgrace, he will see that, to attempt depressing the character of another man by calumny, is the very worst of all expedients, for giving a comparative elevation to his own. The same is the result in the case where vengeance constitutes the motive to injure the reputation of another. To render this proposition manifest, the most obvious illustration will suffice. No man, to gratify his malignity to another person, would kill his ox or his ass, provided he were sure that immediately he would be obliged to make him full satisfaction; and instead of injuring the man whom he hated, to injure only himself. No, the rudeness and inefficacy of the law, holding out a chance of escaping the duty of making reparation, is the sole origin and cause of all offences of this description; and if the law were placed in a state but approaching perfection, hardly any thing beside the obligation of making satisfaction would be necessary to repress the whole of this order of crimes.

Whether any Imputation by which Truth is not violated, should be considered an Offence by the Press.

We have now made considerable progress in this important inquiry. We have ascertained, we think, with sufficient evidence, all that is necessary to be done for preventing injuries to the reputation of individuals; provided the rights of reputation are, by the civil code, not made to extend beyond the boundaries of truth. Whether or not they ought to extend farther, and individuals ought to be protected from the disclosure of acts which they may have committed, is, we confess, a question highly worthy of solution; upon which, therefore, before we proceed to any of the subsequent topics, we shall offer the following reflections.

There can be no doubt that the feelings of the individual may be as painful, where actions of a disreputable nature are, truly, as where they are falsely, imputed to him. It is equally certain, that no painful feelings ought to be wilfully excited in any man, where no good, sufficient to overbalance that evil, is its natural consequence.

We have already shown, that reputation is injured by the imputation of acts of two different descriptions; first, those to which the law annexes penalties; secondly, those to which disrepute and the dislike of others are annexed.

With respect to those acts to which the law annexes penalties, there is no room for uncertainty or dispute. Unless the law is a bad law, which ought to be repealed (this, we confess, constitutes an exception, and one, which, in very imperfect codes, extends a great way), the law ought not to be disappointed of its execution. The man who gives information against a murderer, or a thief, by the press, or without the press, renders a public service, and deserves not punishment but reward.

It appears, therefore, that the question, whether a man ought to be protected from the imputation of actions which he has really committed, refers solely to those acts which, without being punishable by the law, are attended with disrepute; acts, in other words, which the members of the society disapprove and dislike.

The prospect of the immediate and public exposure of all acts of this description, would be a most effectual expedient to prevent their being committed. Men would obtain the habit of abstaining from them, and would feel it as little painful to abstain, as at present it is to any well educated person to keep from theft, or those acts which constitute the ill manners of the vulgar. The fable of Momus has always been understood to carry an important moral. He found grievous fault that a window had not been placed in the breast of every man, by which, not his actions alone, but his thoughts, might have been known. The magnanimity of that Roman has been highly applauded, who not only placed his residence in such a situation that his fellow-citizens might see as much as possible of his actions, but declared a wish that he could open to all eyes his breast as well as his house.

If the hatred and contempt of the people, therefore, were always rightly directed, and rightly proportioned; if they never operated against any actions but those which were hurtful, either to the individual himself, or to others, and never, but in the degree in which they were hurtful, the case would be clear; the advantage which would be derived from the true exposure of any man's actions of any sort, would exceed beyond calculation the attendant evil. The great difficulty of insuring the practice of morality, in those numerous and highly important cases, to which the legal sanction, or the *security of pains and penalties* does not extend, consists in the want of a motive always present, and powerful enough to counteract the instant motive which urges to the instant offence. That motive almost every man would derive from the knowledge that he had the eyes upon him of all those, the good opinion of whom it was his interest to preserve; that no immoral act of his would escape their observation, and a proportionate share of their hatred and contempt. It is in this view that the aid of religion has been sometimes regarded as of importance to morality; suggesting the idea of a high and constant observer. All motives, however, are feeble, in proportion as the pains and pleasures upon which they depend are distant, vague, or uncertain. Divines agree with all other men in complaining of the trifling effect of religious motives upon the lives of the greater number of men. From the nature of the prospect on which these motives depend, they could not be less feeble than they have been thus described. The case is not the same with the motives arising from the sentiments which we know we shall inspire in the breasts of our fellow-creatures. It is a matter of daily and incontrovertible experience, that these are among the most powerful which operate upon the human mind. The soldier rushes upon death, and endures all the hardships and toils of his cruel profession, that he may enjoy the admiration, and escape the contempt of his fellow men. On what else is founded the greater part of all human pursuits? How few, even of those who toil at the meanest occupations, but exert themselves to have something for show, something to make an impression upon the eyes of those who surround them? The very subject of the present inquiry derives from this source the whole of its importance. The value of reputation is, indeed, but another name for the value which we attach to the favourable and unfavourable sentiments of our fellow men.

It is, however, true, that their unfavourable sentiments do not always fall where they ought, and this, we confess, is a consideration of the highest importance. It very often happens that men's antipathies are excited to actions from which no evil ensues, either to him who performs them, or to any body else. If any man derives a pleasure from such actions, it is to limit his sphere of innocent enjoyment, to debar him from them. And if the press exposes him to the antipathies, the hatred and contempt of his fellow-creatures, on account of those actions, it produces an evil, uncompensated by the smallest portion of good. To an Indian Brahmen, if he were known to have eaten, even when starving, a morsel of food which had been prepared by a Christian, the consequences would be dreadful. Where the Roman Catholic religion is in vigour, a man who should indulge himself in animal food on forbidden days would be regarded with horror. The use of wine, however moderate, would render a Mahomedan execrable to the whole of his tribe.

This misdirection of the favourable and unfavourable sentiments of mankind, in other words, this perversion and corruption of their moral sentiments, has, in by far the greater number of instances, been the work of priests, contriving the means of increasing their influence. In some very important instances, such, for example, as the prejudices of birth, at one time in Europe so powerful as to make men of low birth objects of the greatest contempt, men of elevated birth objects of the highest veneration, the perversion of the moral sentiments is evidently the work of the aristocratical class, securing to themselves a more easy dominion over the rest of their fellow-creatures.

It is, therefore, evident, that where antipathies, religious or aristocratical, should prevail, the press would be hurtfully employed in giving notoriety to the facts which would expose a man to the operation of either.

We have now ascertained the cases in which it would *not* be good that men should be protected from the declaration of truth by the press, and also the cases in which it *would* be good that they should be so protected.

What, upon this view of the subject, would be desirable, is sufficiently clear. It would be desirable that, in the one set of cases, the declaration should be allowed, in the other it should not be allowed. Are the two sets of cases, however, capable of being accurately distinguished?

If the comparison is made with any attention, it will not be difficult to determine that the evil to be incurred by the loss of truth in the set of cases in which the declaration of it would be useful, is much greater than that which would arise from permitting the declaration in the cases in which it would be hurtful.

In the first place, the set of cases in which the declaration would be useful are much more numerous, and much more important, than those in which, in any tolerably civilized state of society, it would be hurtful. Those in which it would be useful embrace the whole field of morality, all those acts, the performance of which, on account of their singular importance, has been elevated to the rank of virtues. Every body believes and proclaims, that the universal practice of the moral virtues would ensure the highest measure of human happiness; no one doubts that the misery which, to so deplorable a degree, overspreads the globe, while men injure men, and instead of helping and benefiting, supplant, defraud, mislead, pillage, and oppress, one another, would thus be nearly exterminated, and something better than the dreams of the golden age would be realized upon earth. Toward the attainment of this most desirable state of things, nothing in the world is capable of contributing so much as the full exercise of truth upon all immoral actions, – all actions, the practice of which is calculated to lessen the amount of human happiness. According to this view, the justice of which it is impossible to dispute, the evil incurred by forbidding the declaration of truth upon all immoral actions is incalculable. That which would be incurred by the antipathies of misguided minds against actions innocent in themselves, nobody, we should imagine, would so much as think of placing in comparison.

In our own country, for example, the classes of actions which, though they injure nobody, expose a man to the unfavourable sentiments of others, are not numerous. The number of persons who would be exposed to inconvenience on account of the declaration of truth, in regard to them, would be small in comparison with those who would benefit by its declaration, in the case of all really hurtful acts.

It is, indeed, important to be observed, that a comparative smallness of number is necessarily implied in the supposition of injury from any unfounded antipathy. Those who share in the antipathy, of course, abstain from the action. And unless the antipathy were so general as to include almost the whole of the society, it would lose its injurious effect. Besides, all the injury which can be done to the individuals against whom truth would in this manner operate injuriously, would be, to make them abstain from the acts which were thus condemned.

Another thing to be considered is, that the whole of the evil arising from the exercise of truth is dependent upon an accidental circumstance, capable of being removed; upon a mental disease, requiring to be cured, which, the legislature ought to be constantly endeavouring to cure, and toward the cure of which truth is likely to operate as the most effectual of all expedients. If any considerable inconvenience were experienced from exposure to unfounded antipathies, in consequence of the publication of truth, the groundlessness of these antipathies could not fail in this case to be so often canvassed, and made to appear, that at last it would become familiar to the multitude, and the antipathies would expire.

It clearly, therefore, appears, that, if the cases in which the declaration of truth would expose to unfounded prejudices could not be clearly defined, and separated from the cases in which the declaration would be salutary, the rule of permitting truth ought to be universal. But though we perceive, that, to a considerable extent, there are cases, in respect to which it would be vain to hope for agreement in drawing the line of distinction between what is hurtful and what is not, we are persuaded that principles might be laid down in which all would agree, and which would serve to mark out certain cases for exception with sufficient exactness. If any such cases could be separated, either of actions which, though injurious to nobody, excited antipathies, or of facts, as those of birth, for which, though a man was in no respect worse, he might be regarded as worse; the exercise of truth, with regard to them, might, on the express ground that they were actions innoxious, or facts which ought to be of no importance in the estimate of human worth, be forbidden, when injurious, under the penalty of at least making reparation for all the injury of which it had been the cause.

III.
Offences of the Press with respect to **Government**

We have now explained, we trust, with sufficient clearness for the present occasion, the principles upon which laws should be constructed for protecting the *rights of individuals* against violations committed by the press. the first part of this inquiry, therefore, we must consider as completed. In the second part we have to explain the principles upon which they should be constructed for protecting *the operations of government.*

Exhortations to obstruct the operations of Government in detail, should;
Exhortations to resist all the powers of Government at once should not,
be considered offences.

Unless a door is left open to resistance of the government, in the largest sense of the word, the doctrine of passive obedience is adopted; and the consequence is, the universal prevalence of mis-government, ensuring the misery and degradation of the people. On the other hand, unless the operations of government, instituted for the protection of rights, are secured from obstruction, the security of rights, and all the advantages dependent upon the existence of government, are at an end. Between these two securities, both necessary to obtain the benefits of good government, there appears to be such a contrariety, that the one can only be obtained by the sacrifice of the other.

As this difficulty, however, arises chiefly from the largeness of the terms, a close inspection of the cases which they involve, and which they have a tendency to confuse, will enable us to discover the course which it belongs to practical wisdom to pursue.

It is necessary, first of all, to ascertain what sort of obstructions are inconsistent, and what are not inconsistent, with those operations of government, which are necessary for the protection of rights.

The application of physical force, to resist the government in applying to the execution of the laws the physical power placed at its disposal by the law, is such an obstruction of the operations of government, as would, if frequent, render it inadequate to the ends which it is provided to secure. This application of force, therefore, must be treated as an offence; and any thing proceeding from the press, tending directly to produce it, as a similar offence.

This proposition requires to be illustrated. The application of physical force which is here described, and treated as an evil, is clearly distinguishable from that resistance of government which is the last security of the many against the misconduct of the few. This is an application of physical force to obstruct the operations of government in detail; the proceedings, for example, of a court of justice; the proceedings of the legislative organ, or the proceedings of any of the administrative functionaries, in the execution of the duties with which they are charged. This is not the species of resistance which is necessary, in the last resort, to secure the people against the abuse of the powers of government. This last is not a resistance to the operations of government in detail. It is a resistance to all the powers of government at once, either to withdraw them from the hands in which they have hitherto been deposited, or greatly to modify the terms upon which they are held.

Even this last species of resistance it may be necessary to punish, at least in a certain degree, whenever it is not successful; that society may not be disturbed by commotions which the majority of the people disapprove. This, however, is a question which belongs to the penal code in general, and does not concern the inquiry into the offences capable of being committed by the press: because we think it may be satisfactorily shown, that no operation of the press, however directly exhorting to this species of resistance, ought to be treated as an offence.

The reason is, that no such exhortation can have any immediate, or formidable effect; can, indeed, have any effect at all, except through such mediums as ought to be at all times perfectly free. Suppose that a work is published, exhorting the people in general to take arms against the government, for the purpose of altering it against the consent of its rulers. The people cannot take arms against the government without the certainty of being immediately crushed, unless there has been already created a general consent. If this consent exists in such perfection as to want nothing to begin action but an exhortation, nothing can prevent the exhortation; and forbidding it is useless. If the consent does not exist in nearly the last degree of perfection, a mere exhortation, read in print, can have no effect which is worth regarding. In all circumstances, therefore, it is useless, and consequently absurd, to treat this species of exhortation as an offence. If, on the other hand, it were clearly recognized, that every man had a licence to exhort the people to the general resistance of the government, all such exhortations would become ridiculous, unless on those rare and extreme occasions, on which no prohibitions, and no penalites, can or ought to prevent them. The doctrine of this paragraph, which will appear somewhat startling and paradoxical to minds accustomed only to a certain train of ideas, will receive illustration, and we trust will be amply confirmed, as we proceed.

Having mentioned this as a grand exception, we now return to the cases in which not only physical force applied to obstruct the operations of government, but the publishing of exhortations to that obstruction, ought to be treated as an offence. These relate solely, as above remarked, to the operations of government in detail. Obstructions, it is evident, may be offered to the operations in detail of a government which possesses and deserves the fullest confidence of the community at large; and the press may be employed in directly and efficiently exciting to these obstructions. A hand-bill, for example, distributed at a critical moment, and operating upon an inflamed state of mind, in a narrow district, may excite a mob to disturb the proceedings of a court of justice, to obstruct public officers in the execution of their duties, or even to disturb, on this or that occasion, the deliberations of the legislature itself.

These are clearly hurtful acts; they may be very accurately defined; and penalties, of moderate severity, would be sufficient to deter from the performance of them. Satisfaction by the party offending to the party injured, would often, in offences of this description, be out of the question; because there would be no definite party to whom an injury would be occasioned. It would only be necessary to ascertain the sorts of motives by which such offences would be liable to be produced, and to apply skilfully, as in other cases, motives of an opposite tendency, sufficient to counteract them. This would not be more difficult in this than in other cases, and it is not, therefore, necessary to explain at any length the mode of performing it.

One principle is to be carefully and most religiously observed, that of not imposing an atom of punishment for the purposes of *vengeance*. This is a principle, the justness and importance of which are so completely recognized, that we might have expected to be relieved ere now from the necessity of recommending attention to it. The fact, however, is, that so long as there are abuses in governments, so long will the men, who have the means of profiting by those abuses, exert themselves to multiply the list of offences against government, and to apply to them punishments of the greatest severity.

Punishments for contempt of court; punishments to vindicate the honour of the court, of the government, of the magistracy; punishments for the support of dignity; punishments severe in proportion as the dignity of the party offended is supposed to be high, and so on, are punishments almost always applied for purposes of vengeance, or the protection of the instruments of abuse. They are punishments, therefore, which will be rigidly excluded from a code which wisely and steadily pursues the general good.

*Of Exhortations to obstruct the Operations of Government, in detail,
there are two Sorts: 1. The Direct, 2. The Implied, or Constructive.*

What the *sort of acts* are, to which the exhortations of the press
ought not to be applied, has been so far ascertained. The next point is,
to determine with accuracy what *sort of exhortation* it is that ought to be
forbidden.

To all those who profit by the abuses of government, that is more
especially, to all those who, in a defective government, wield any of its
powers, it is of great importance to leave as undefined as possible the
sort of exhortation that ought to be forbidden. The point of greatest
importance to them is, to keep the people at large from complaining,
or from knowing or thinking that they have any ground of complaint.
If this object is fully attained, they may then, without anxiety, and
without trouble, riot in the pleasures of misrule: there is no limit to
the degree in which the few may pursue their own advantage at the
expence of the many.

There can be nothing, therefore, in which they have a greater
interest, than preventing the press from being employed in any such
way, as will lead the people to think that they have any thing, on the
part of their rulers, of which to complain. All artifices possible will be
sure to be employed to effect that prevention. And if it is enacted, that
exhortations to acts which obstruct the operations of government in
detail should be punished, *without defining accurately what sort of exhortations*, they will easily find expedients which, to a great extent, will
accomplish their purpose.

Under the sort of constructions which it will be their interest to
apply, every thing which can be done by the press, to make the people
know or believe that there is any thing in the system of their government, or the conduct of their rulers, of which they have to complain,
may be treated as an exhortation to obstruct the operations of government. Of these constructions, our experience affords innumerable
examples. Does not the imputing of defects to the government, or
misconduct to those who wield the powers of government, tend to
bring both "into hatred and contempt?" And if the people hate and
contemn the institutions and rulers of their country, will they not
oppose their operations? The imputing of these faults, therefore, is it
not, in essence and effect, an exhortation to oppose the operations of
government? And are we to be governed, in our legislature, by the

mere forms in which a set of words may appear, and not by our knowledge of their nature and consequences?

This is not only exceedingly plausible, but almost all the propositions which it involves are perfectly true. It is thus, therefore, the more easy to establish such a mode of interpreting an indefinite law of the press, as will prevent, or where the people cannot yet bear a total prevention, will go far towards preventing, whatever can lead the people to believe that any thing is amiss in the manner in which they are ruled.

There are two species of exhortations, one the explicit and direct, the other implied and constructive. In the one, a particular act is pointed out, and the party, or parties, addressed, are called upon to perform it. In the other, certain grounds are only laid, from which the opinion of the addresser, that the act ought to be performed, may, with more or less certainty, be inferred.

With respect to the first, there is no occasion for doubt. A direct and explicit exhortation to commit one of those acts, described above, as obstructing the operations of government in detail, should be treated as an offence. The precise question is, whether any exhortation, which is only implied and constructive, should be considered an offence? In the answer to this question, almost every thing which relates to the use of the press in matters of government, will be found to be involved.

Exhortations which are Implied and Constructive, ought not to be punished.

We have already divided the subject of resistance to government into two parts; first, that general resistance, the object of which is some great change in the government at large; and, secondly, resistance to this or that of its operations in detail.

We have already adduced an argument, which appears to us to be conclusive, to show, that no exhortation, whether explicit or implied, direct or indirect, the object or tendency of which is to produce the first species of resistance, ought to be subject to legal restraint.

It is necessary here to enter a little more fully into the grounds of that opinion.

We think it will appear, with sufficient evidence, that in the way of indirect exhortation to resistance, that is, in laying the grounds of dissatisfaction with the government, there is no medium between allowing every thing, and allowing nothing; that the end, in short, which is sought to be gained, by allowing any thing to be published in censure of the government, cannot be obtained, without leaving it perfectly free to publish every thing.

The end which is sought to be obtained, by allowing any thing to be said in censure of the government, is, to ensure the goodness of the government; the most important of all the objects, to the attainment of which, the wisdom of man can be applied. If the goodness of government could be ensured by any preferable means, it is evident that all censure of the government ought to be prohibited. All discontent with the government is only good, in so far as it is a means of removing *real cause* of discontent. If there is no cause, or if there is better means of removing the cause, the discontent is, of course, an evil, and that which produces it an evil.

So true it is, however, that the discontent of the people is the only means of removing the defects of vicious governments, that the freedom of the press, the main instrument of creating discontent, is, in all civilized countries, among all but the advocates of misgovernment, regarded as an indispensable security, and the greatest safeguard of the interests of mankind.

For what is meant by a vicious government? or wherein do the defects of government consist? Most assuredly they all consist in sacrificing the interests of the many to the interests of the few. The small number, in whose hands the powers of government are, in part directly, in part indirectly, placed, cannot fail, like other men, to have a greater regard for what is advantageous to themselves, than what is advantageous to other men. They pursue, therefore, their own advantage, in preference to that of the rest of the community. That is enough. Where there is nothing to check that propensity, all the evils of misgovernment, that is, in one word, the worst evils by which human nature is afflicted, are the inevitable consequence. (See the article GOVERNMENT.)*

There can be no adequate check without the freedom of the press. The evidence of this is irresistible. In all countries, the people either have a power legally and peaceably of removing their governors, or they have not that power. If they have not that power, they can only

---

* [Reprinted as the first essay in the present volume. – Ed.]

obtain very considerable ameliorations of their governments by resistance, by applying physical force to their rulers, or, at least, by threats so likely to be followed by performance, as may frighten their rulers into compliance. But resistance, to have this effect, must be general. To be general, it must spring from a general conformity of opinion, and a general knowledge of that conformity. How is this effect to be produced, but by some means, fully enjoyed by the people, of communicating their sentiments to one another? Unless where the people can all meet in general assembly, there is no other means, known to the world, of attaining this object, to be compared with the freedom of the press.

It is, no doubt, true, that in countries where the liberty of the press is unknown, evil governments are frequently overthrown. This is almost always accomplished by the military force, revenging some grievance of their own, or falling in with some heat and animosity of the people. But does it ever enable them to make a new government, in which any greater security is provided for their interests than there was before? In such cases, the people get rid of one set of rulers, whom they hate, only to obtain another set, with equal powers of doing them injury.

There are, however, we believe, some people who say, that though the liberty of the press is a necessary instrument to attain good government, yet, if it is fairly attained, and if legal and peaceable means are in the hands of the people of removing their governors for misconduct; – if the people of England, for example, really chose the members of the House of Commons, and renewed their choice so frequently, as to have the power of removal after a short experience of misconduct, the freedom of the press would be unnecessary.

So far is this from being true, that it is doubtful whether a power in the people of choosing their own rulers, without the liberty of the press, would be an advantage.

Freedom of Censure on the Conduct of their Rulers, is necessary for the good of the People.

It is perfectly clear, that all chance of advantage to the people, from having the choice of their rulers, depends upon their making a good choice. If they make a bad choice – if they elect people either incapable, or disinclined, to use well the power entrusted to them, they

incur the same evils to which they are doomed when they are deprived
of the due control over those by whom their affairs are administered.

We may then ask, if there are any possible means by which the
people can make a good choice, besides the *liberty of the press?* The
very foundation of a good choice is knowledge. The fuller and more
perfect the knowledge, the better the chance, where all sinister interest is absent, of a good choice. How can the people receive the most
perfect knowledge relative to the characters of those who present
themselves to their choice, but by information conveyed freely, and
without reserve, from one to another?

There is another use of the freedom of the press, no less deserving
the most profound attention, that of making known the conduct of the
individuals who have been chosen. This latter service is of so much
importance, that upon it the whole value of the former depends.

This is capable of being rigidly demonstrated. No benefit is
obtained by making choice of a man who is well qualified to serve the
people, and also well inclined to serve them, if you place him in a
situation in which he will have preponderant motives to serve himself
at their expence.

If any set of men are chosen to wield the powers of government,
while the people have not the means of knowing in what manner they
discharge their duties, they will have the means of serving themselves
at the expence of the people; and all the miseries of evil government
are the certain consequence.

Suppose the people to choose the members of the Legislative
Assembly, with power of rechoosing, or dismissing them, at short
intervals: To what desirable end could these powers be exercised,
without the liberty of the press? Suppose that any one of those whom
they have chosen has misconducted himself, or promoted, as far as
depended upon him, the ends of misgovernment; how are the people
to know that the powers with which they had entrusted him had been
treacherously employed?

If they do not know, they will rechoose him, and that as cordially as
the man who has served them with the greatest fidelity. This they are
under a deplorable necessity of doing, even to be just; for, as they
know no difference between him and the best, it would be on their
part iniquity to make any. The consequences would be fatal. If one
man saw that he might promote misrule for his own advantage, so
would another; so, of course, would they all. In these circumstances,

we see laid the foundation on which, in every country, bad government is reared. On this foundation it is impossible that it should not be reared. When the causes are the same, who can expect that the effects will be different? It is unnecessary to dwell upon these fundamental truths, because they have already been developed in the article GOVERNMENT.

Without the knowledge then, of what is done by their representatives, in the use of the powers entrusted to them, the people cannot profit by the power of choosing them, and the advantages of good government are unattainable. It will not surely cost many words to satisfy all classes of readers that, without the free and unrestrained use of the press, the requisite knowledge cannot be obtained.

That an accurate report of what is done by each of the representatives, a transcript of his speeches, and a statement of his propositions and votes, is necessary to be laid before the people, to enable them to judge of his conduct, nobody, we presume, will deny. This requires the use of the cheapest means of communication, and, we add, the free use of those means. Unless every man has the liberty of publishing the proceedings of the Legislative Assembly, the people can have no security that they are fairly published. If it is in the power of their rulers to permit one person, and forbid another, the people may be sure that a false report, – a report calculated to make them believe that they are well governed, when they are ill governed, will be often presented to them.

One thing more is necessary, and so necessary, that, if it is wanting, the other might as well be wanting also. The publication of the proceedings tells what is done. This, however, is useless, unless a correct judgment is passed upon what is done.

We have brought this inquiry, then, to an important point. In the article GOVERNMENT, we have seen that, unless the people hold in their own hands an effectual power of control on the acts of their government, the government will be inevitably vicious: We have now seen, that they cannot exercise this control to any beneficial purpose without the means of forming a correct judgment upon the conduct of their representatives: We have likewise seen, that one of the means necessary to enable them to judge correctly of the conduct of their representatives, is the liberty to every body of publishing reports of what they do. It remains to inquire, by what other acts the press can be made to contribute to the same desirable end.

What is wanted is, that all the people, or as many of them as possible, should estimate correctly the consequences of the acts proposed or done by their representatives, and also that they should know what acts might have been proposed, if the best were not proposed, from which better consequences would have followed. This end would be accomplished most effectually, if those who are sufficiently enlightened would point out to those who are in danger of mistakes, the true conclusions; and showing the weight of evidence to be in their favour, should obtain for them the universal assent.

How is this to be accomplished? In what manner are those wise men to be chosen? And who are to be the choosers? Directly the object cannot be attained. There are no distinct and indubitable marks by which wisdom, and less by which integrity, is to be known. And who is to be trusted with the privilege of pointing them out? They whose judgment requires to be directed are not well qualified to determine who shall direct them. And if the rulers are to choose, they will employ none but those who will act in conformity to their views, and enable them to benefit themselves by the pillage and oppression of the people.

As there is no possible organ of choice, no choice whatever ought to be made. If no choice is to be made, every man that pleases ought to be allowed. All this is indubitable. The consequences of denying any part of it are so obvious, that hardly any man, we suppose, will risk the imputations to which such a denial would justly expose him.

They who say that no choice ought to be made, say, in effect, that no limit whatsoever ought to be imposed upon the liberty of the press. The one of these propositions is involved in the other. To impose any restraint upon the liberty of the press, is undoubtedly to make a choice. If the restraint is imposed by the government, it is the government that chooses the directors of the public mind. If any government chooses the directors of the public mind, that government is despotic.

Suppose that, by the restraint imposed upon the liberty of the press, all censure of the government is forbidden, here is undoubtedly a choice. The government, in this case, virtually says, The people who might attempt the task of directing the public mind are of two sorts; one that of those who would censure; another that of those who would not censure; I choose the latter.

Suppose that not every censure, but only such and such kinds of censure, are forbidden; here, again, is still a choice, while confessedly there is no party to whom the power of choosing for the rest can with safety be given.

If not every censure, but only some censures, are to be forbidden, what are those to which the prohibition should extend? The answer to this question will elucidate nearly all that yet remains in any degree obscure, of the doctrine of the liberty of the press.

It will not be said that any censure which is just should be forbidden; because that would undoubtedly be to detract from the means of enabling the people to form correct judgments; and we have, we trust, rendered it indisputable that no source of benefit to society is at all to be compared with that of correct judgments, on their government and its functionaries, formed by the people, and determining their actions.

But what censures are just and what are unjust; in other words, what are the conclusions which ought to be formed respecting the properties and the acts of the government, is exactly the point to be determined. If you say that no man is to pass an unjust censure upon the government, who is to judge? It is surely unnecessary to repeat the proof of the proposition, that there is nobody who can safely be permitted to judge. The path of practical wisdom is as clear as day: All censures must be permitted, equally; just, and unjust.

Where various conclusions are formed among a number of men, upon a subject on which it would be unsafe, and therefore improper, to give any minor portion of them a power of determining for the rest, only one expedient remains. Fortunately, that is an expedient, the operation of which is powerful, and its effects beneficial in the highest degree. All the conclusions which have formed themselves in the minds of different individuals, should be openly adduced; and the power of comparison and choice should be granted to all. Where there is no motive to attach a man to error, it is natural to him to embrace the truth; especially if pains are taken to adapt the explanation to his capacity. Every man, possessed of reason, is accustomed to weigh evidence, and to be guided and determined by its preponderance. When various conclusions are, with their evidence, presented with equal care and with equal skill, there is a moral certainty, though some few may be misguided, that the greater number will judge aright, and that the greatest force of evidence, wherever it is, will produce the greatest impression.

As this is a proposition upon which every thing depends, it is happy that the evidence of it should be so very clear and striking. There is, indeed, hardly any law of human nature more generally recognized, wherever there is not a motive to deny its existence . . .

[A long string of quotations from other authors has been omitted. – Ed.]

We have then arrived at the following important conclusions, – that there is no safety to the people in allowing any body to choose opinions for them; that there are no marks by which it can be decided beforehand, what opinions are true and what are false; that there must, therefore, be equal freedom of declaring all opinions, both true and false; and that, when all opinions, true and false, are equally declared, the assent of the greater number, when their interests are not opposed to them, may always be expected to be given to the true. These principles, the foundation of which appears to be impregnable, suffice for the speedy determination of every practical question.

All censure thrown upon the government, all censure thrown either upon the institutions of the government, or upon the conduct of any of the functionaries of government, supreme or subordinate, has a tendency to produce resistance to the government.

Of the censures thrown upon government, some may have a tendency to produce resistance to the operations of government in detail; others that general resistance which has in view some great alteration in the government.

Of the first sort would be any such accusation of the conduct and disposition of a judge, as might excite the people, whose sympathies were roused in favour of the individual against whom his sentence was to operate, to rescue him from the officers of justice. We have already shown that such a rescue ought to be punished, and any direct exhortation to it ought to be punished. It will now be evident, we trust, that no censure on the judge, though capable of being treated as an indirect exhortation, ought to be punished.

The reason is conclusive. The people ought to know, if possible, the real qualities of the actions of those who are entrusted with any share in the management of their affairs. This they have no chance of knowing, without the unlimited power of censure upon those actions, both in gross and detail. To see the full force of these propositions, it is only necessary to apply the principles which have been already established.

If the people have not the means of knowing the actions of all public functionaries, they have no security for the good conduct even of their representatives. Suppose it is the duty of their representatives to watch the conduct of the judges, and secure the perfection of judicature, the people cannot know whether their representatives perform this duty, unless they know what the conduct of the judges is. Ignorance of this would of itself suffice to vitiate the government. A door would be left open, through which the rulers might benefit themselves at the expence of the people. All the profit to be made by an abuse of the power of justice, would thus become the profit of the representatives, by whom it would be allowed, and encouraged, as far as the knowledge, which they could not withhold from the people, would permit.

That the people ought, therefore, to know the conduct of their judges, and when we say judges we mean every other functionary, and the more perfectly the better, may be laid down as indubitable. They are deprived of all trust-worthy means of knowing, if any limit whatsoever is placed to the power of censure.

All censure consists in the delivery of an unfavourable opinion, with or without the grounds of it. This is the essence of censure. But if the conduct of the judge deserves that an unfavourable opinion should be entertained of it, the more perfectly that is known to the people, the better.

The conduct of the judge, on this occasion, says a defender, does not deserve an unfavourable opinion: A public expression of such an opinion ought, therefore, to be prohibited. But there are occasions on which the conduct of judges deserves an unfavourable opinion. When it is deserved, there is no security for good government, unless it is allowed to be made known. How can you allow an unfavourable opinion to be delivered in the one case, and not delivered in the other? To have the benefit of it in the one case, you must submit to the evil of it in the other.

In matters of Government, undeserved Praise as mischievous as undeserved Blame.

As the real point of importance is, to establish correct opinions in the minds of the people, it is as mischievous to inculcate a favourable opinion, when an unfavourable is deserved, as an unfavourable when a favourable is deserved; and, in the eye of reason, it is incontrovertible, that, if the one deserves to be prevented by punishment, so does the other.

But, if an unfavourable opinion is pronounced of any public functionary; of a judge, for example, would you have it left uncontradicted? Would you not grant the liberty of calling in question the truth of the allegations, and of supporting a different opinion? If not, the character of no public functionary would be safe, and any man, however deserving, might be made to appear the proper object of the most unfavourable sentiments. Why should not the two cases be treated equally? Why should not the favourable, as well as the unfavourable opinion be open to contradiction?

It is perfectly certain, that it is not in the power of law to mark out, by antecedent definition, any sort of men, of whom it can say, all opinions favourable to such men shall be punished. It can never be affirmed of any men beforehand that they will certainly perform such and such injurious actions. If they do perform them, all declarations conformable with the matter of fact are good. But the question is, whether they have performed them? One man, affirms that they have. Is that to be taken for granted? And is no man to be allowed to affirm the contrary, and to sift the grounds upon which the allegations of the other man are supported? It is by weighing well the evidence on both sides, that a well-founded opinion is capable of being formed. And it is certain, that the best security for having the evidence on both sides fully adduced, and the strength and weakness of it perfectly disclosed, is by permitting all those who are attached to different opinions to do what they can for the support of them.

If it is evident that it ought not to be permitted to speak evil of public functionaries without limit, while any limit is put to the power of speaking well of them; it is equally evident that, for the purpose of forming a correct opinion of their conduct, it ought not to be permitted to speak well of them, and oppose any limit whatsoever to the power of speaking ill of them.

It ought not to be permitted to speak evil of them without an equal liberty of speaking well; because, in that case, the evidence against them might be made to appear much stronger than it was. It ought not to be permitted to speak well of them without an equal liberty of speaking ill; because, in that case, the evidence in favour of them might be made to appear much greater than it really was. In either case, the people would be misguided, and defrauded of that moral knowledge of the conduct of their rulers, the paramount importance of which has so fully appeared.

It may be said (as by the short-sighted, if we did not anticipate them, it would be said), that if, by limiting the power of censure, the people are made to judge more favourably of their rulers than they deserve, the evil is small; but if they are permitted to form a very unfavourable opinion, the consequences are alarming.

We believe it may be rigidly demonstrated, that no evils are greater than those which result from a more favourable opinion of their rulers, on the part of the people, than their rulers deserve; because just as far as that undue favour extends, bad government is secured. By an opinion of their rulers more favourable than they deserve, is implied an ignorance on the part of the people of certain acts of their rulers by which the people suffer. All acts by which the rulers have any motive to make the people suffer, are acts by which the rulers profit. When the ignorance of the people extends to material points, all the evils of bad government are secured. These are the greatest of all possible evils. To this it will not be said that the ignorance of the people ought to extend. On all material points, it is admitted, then, that the freedom of censure ought to be complete. But if it is to be allowed on great points, on those where it is calculated to excite the greatest disapprobation; what can be thought of their consistency, who would restrain it on those where it is only calculated to excite a small? If it is proper to protect the people from great injuries at the hands of their rulers, by exciting a strong, it is good to protect them against small injuries, by exciting a weak disapprobation.

To public functionaries may be imputed either acts which they have not performed, or a want of certain qualifications, moral or intellectual, which they possess.

With respect to acts, and even dispositions, which do not, either directly or indirectly, concern their public function, the same protection may be safely extended to them as to private men.

Acts in their public capacity which they have not performed, may be imputed to them either by mere forgery, and without any appearance of ground, or they may be imputed with some appearance of ground. From permitting the former, no good can be derived. They ought, therefore, to be prevented, in the same way as false imputations, injurious to individuals in their private capacity. That there should be no restraint in imputing actions to any public functionary which he may appear to have done, flows immediately from the principles already established, and requires not that any thing should here be added to its proof. Any appearance sufficient to lay the foundation of the slightest suspicion, renders it useful to call the attention of the public to the suspected part, which can only be done by making the suspicion known. A man may, indeed, publish, as a matter of fact, what is supported by appearances which would only justify the slightest suspicion. In that case, he is sure of incurring the disgrace of temerity, if not of malignity; and this is all the penalty which needs or can safely be inflicted upon him.

In imputing inaptitude to a public functionary, on the score either of intellectual or moral qualities, scarcely any limitation would be safe. Every man ought to have liberty to declare upon this subject any opinion which he pleases, and support it by any evidence which he may think adapted to the end. If, in supporting his opinion of the inaptitude of any public functionary, he imputes to him actions which there is not even an appearance of his having performed, that limited prohibition, the propriety of which we have just recognized, will strictly apply. With this exception, freedom should be unimpaired.

We have now, therefore, explained, we hope sufficiently, in what manner the principles which we have established require, that the use of the press should be regulated in speaking of the action of public functionaries, and of their fitness for the duties which they are appointed to discharge, whether those functionaries are the immediate representatives of the people, or others whom it is the business of those representatives to control.

Freedom of Censure on the Institutions of Government is necessary for the good of the People.

We have next to inquire in what manner those principles require that the use of the press should be regulated in speaking of the *institutions* of government. The illustrations already adduced will supersede the use of many words upon this part of the subject.

Institutions of government are good in proportion as they save the people from evil, whether it be evil created by the government, or evil not prevented by the government. Institutions of government are bad in proportion as they are the cause of evil to the people, either by what they create, or what they fail in preventing.

According to this statement, which it is impossible to controvert, institutions of government may, in strict propriety of speech, be said to be the cause of all the evil which they do not save the people from, and from which the people would be saved by any other institutions.

It is therefore of the highest importance that the people should know what are the institutions which save from the greatest quantity of evil, and how much their own institutions want of being those best institutions.

Institutions of government are bad, either because those in whose hands the powers of government are placed do not know that they are bad, and though willing, cannot improve them; or they are bad, because those who have in their hands the powers of government do not wish that they should be improved.

Where the rulers are willing, but do not know how to improve the institutions of government; every thing which leads to a knowledge of their defects is desirable to both rulers and people. That which most certainly leads to such knowledge is, that every man who thinks he understands any thing of the subject, should produce his opinions, with the evidence on which they are supported, and that every man who disapproves of these opinions should state his objections. All the knowledge which all the individuals in the society possess upon the subject is thus brought, as it were, to a common stock or treasury; while every thing which has the appearance of being knowledge, but is only a counterfeit of knowledge, is assayed and rejected. Every subject has the best chance of becoming thoroughly understood, when, by the delivery of all opinions, it is presented in all points of view; when all the evidence upon both sides is brought forward, and all those who are most interested in showing the weakness of what is weak in it, and the strength of what is strong, are, by the freedom of the press, permitted, and by the warmth of discussion excited, to devote to it the keenest application of their faculties. False opinions will then be delivered. True; but when are we most secure against the influence of false opinions? Most assuredly when the grounds of these opinions are the most thoroughly searched. When are the grounds of opinions most thoroughly searched? When discussion upon the subject is the most general and the most intense; when the greatest number of qualified persons engage in the discussion, and are excited by all the warmth of competition, and all the interest of important consequences, to study the subject with the deepest attention. To give a body of rulers, or any other body of men, a power of choosing, for the rest, opinions upon government, without discussion, we have already seen, upon good evidence, is the way to secure the prevalence of the most destructive errors.

When institutions are bad, and the rulers would gladly change them if they knew they were bad, discussion, it will not be disputed, would be good for both parties, both rulers and ruled. There is, however, another case, and that by far the most common, where the rulers are attached to the bad institutions, and are disposed to do all in their power to prevent any alteration. This is the case with all institutions which leave it in the power of the men who are entrusted with the powers of government, to make use of them for their own advantage, to the detriment of the people; in other words, which enable them to do injury to the people, or prevent the people from good. This is the case with by far the greater number of those institutions by which the people suffer. They are institutions contrived for benefiting the few at the cost of the many.

With respect, therefore, to the greater number of defective institutions, it is the interest of the rulers that true opinions should not prevail. But with respect to these institutions, it is of still greater importance to the people that discussion should be free. Such institutions as the rulers would improve, if they knew that they were defective, will be improved as the rulers themselves become sensible of their defects. Such defective institutions as the rulers would not wish to see improved, will never be improved, unless the knowledge of these defects is diffused among the people, and excites among them a disapprobation which the rulers do not think it prudent to disregard.

That the prevalence of true opinions among the people, relative to those defects in their political institutions, by which the rulers profit at their expence, is of the utmost importance to the people, is therefore a proposition, which no improbity will dare openly to controvert. That freedom of discussion is the only security which the people can have for the prevalence of true opinions has already been proved. It is therefore proved, that freedom of discussion, in its utmost perfection, they ought to enjoy.

What is included in the term *freedom of discussion*, is evident from what has already been said.

Freedom of discussion means the power of presenting all opinions equally, relative to the subject of discussion; and of recommending them by any medium of persuasion which the author may think proper to employ. If any obstruction is given to the delivering of one sort of opinions, not given to the delivering of another; if any advantage is attached to the delivering of one sort of opinions, not attached to the delivering of another; so far equality of treatment is destroyed, and so far the freedom of discussion is infringed; so far truth is not left to the support of her own evidence; and so far, if the advantages are attached to the side of error, truth is deprived of her chance of prevailing.

To attach advantage to the delivering of one set of opinions, disadvantage to the delivering of another, is to make a choice. But we have already seen, that it is not safe for the people to let any body choose opinions for them. If it be said, that the people themselves might be the authors of this preference, what is this but to say, that the people can choose better before discussion than after; before they have obtained information than after it? No, if the people choose before discussion, before information, they cannot choose for themselves. They must follow blindly the impulse of certain individuals, who, therefore, choose for them. This is, therefore, a pretence, for the purpose of disguising the truth, and cheating the people of that choice, upon which all their security for good government depends.

If these deductions are as clear and incontrovertible as to us they appear to be, the inquiry respecting the principles which ought to regulate the use of the press is drawn pretty nearly to its close. We have shown, that as far as regards the violation of the rights of individuals, in respect to both persons and things, no definition on account of the press is required. We have shown in what manner the rights of individuals, in regard to reputation, should be defined by the civil code, and the violation of them prevented by the penal. We next proceeded to what may be considered as the main branch of the inquiry, namely, the use of the press in speaking of the institutions and functionaries of government. We have found, that in this respect the freedom of the press is of such importance, that there is no security for good government without it. We have also found, that the use of it, in respect to these subjects, admits but of two useful restrictions; – that of a direct exhortation to obstruct any of the operations of government in detail, and that of imputing to a functionary of government a criminal act, which there was no ground, nor even any appearance of ground, to impute to him. These restrictions, of course, it would be very easy to define in the criminal code, and to find appropriate motives to sanction. In all other respects, we have seen that the press ought to be free; that if there is any limit to the power of delivering unfavourable opinions, respecting either the functionaries, or the institutions of government, and of recommending those opinions by any media, with the single exception of false facts, under the circumstances mentioned above, the benefits which may be derived from the freedom of the press are so greatly infringed, that hardly any security for good government can remain.

IV.
Limitations to Freedom of Discussion, which involve its destruction.

In the administration of English law, or rather of what is called law, upon this subject, without being any thing better than the arbitrary will of the judges, it is said, that though discussion should be free, it should be "decent;" and that all "indecency" in discussion should be punished as a libel. It is not our object in this discourse to give an exposition of the manifold deformities of the English law of libel. If we have been successful in developing the true principles which ought to regulate the freedom of the press, every reader may, by an application of those principles, determine what he ought to think of the several particulars which there may attract his attention. We shall confine ourselves to a short notice of those *dicta*, or doctrines, which seem most likely to be pleaded in opposition to the principles which we have endeavoured to establish.

The question is, whether *indecent* discussion should be prohibited? To answer this question, we must, of course, inquire what is meant by indecent.

In English libel law, where this term holds so distinguished a place, is it not defined?

English legislators have not hitherto been good at defining; and English lawyers have always vehemently condemned, and grossly abused it. The word "indecent," therefore, has always been a term under which it was not difficult, on each occasion, for the judge to include whatever he did not like. "Decent," and "what the judge likes," have been pretty nearly synonymous.

Indecency of discussion cannot mean the delivery either of true or of false opinions, because discussion implies both. In all discussion there is supposed at least two parties, one who affirms, and one who denies. One of them must be in the wrong.

The delivery, though not of all true opinions, yet of some, may be said to be indecent. All opinions are either favourable or unfavourable. True opinions that are favourable to government and its functionaries will not be said to be indecent; nor will all opinions that are true and unfavourable be marked out for prohibition under that name. Opinions unfavourable may either be greatly unfavourable or slightly unfavourable. If any unfavourable opinions are exempted from the charge of indecency, it must be those which are slightly so. But observe what would be the consequence of prohibiting, as indecent, those which are greatly unfavourable. A true opinion, greatly unfavourable to a functionary, or institution of government, is an opinion that the functionary, or institution, is greatly hurtful to the people. You would permit the slight evil to be spoken of, and hence removed; you would not permit the great evil to be spoken of.

If no *true* opinion can be regarded as indecent, meaning by indecent, requiring *punishment*, we must inquire if any *false* opinion on matters of government ought to be treated as such. If all false opinions are indecent, all discussion is indecent. All false opinions, therefore, are not indecent. The English libel law does not treat any favourable opinions, how much soever false, as indecent. If all opinions that are false and unfavourable are said to be indecent, who is to judge if they are false? It has been already proved, that the people can confide the power of determining what opinions are true, what are false, to none but themselves. Nothing can resist the following argument. Either the people do know, or they do not know, that an opinion is false: if they do not know, they can permit nobody to judge for them, and must leave discussion its free course: if they do know, all infliction of evil for the delivery of an opinion which then can do no harm, would be purely mischievous and utterly absurd.

If all opinions, true and false, must be allowed to be delivered, so must all the media of proof. We need not examine minutely the truth of this inference, because it will probably be allowed. It will be said, however, that though all opinions may be delivered, and the grounds of them stated, it must be done in calm and gentle language. Vehement expressions, all words and phrases calculated to inflame, may justly be regarded as indecent, because they have a tendency rather to pervert than rectify the judgment.

To examine this proposition, it must be taken out of that state of vagueness in which so many things are left by the English law, and made, if possible, to speak a language, the meaning of which may be ascertained.

We have just decided, and as it appeared, on very substantial grounds, that the statement of no opinion, favourable or unfavourable, true or false, with its media of proof, ought to be forbidden. No language, necessary for that purpose, can be indecent, meaning here, as before, nothing by that term, as nothing can be meant, but simply *punishable* or proper for punishment.

But the only difference between delivering an opinion one way and another way is, that in the one case it is simply delivered, in the other it is delivered with indications of passion. The meaning of the phrase in question then must be, that an opinion must not be delivered with indications of passion.

What! not even a favourable one?

"Oh, yes! a favourable one. Merited *praise* ought to be delivered with warmth."

Here, then, is inequality, and therefore mischief, at once. An opinion, meaning here a true opinion, if it is favourable, you allow – if unfavourable, you do not allow – to be delivered in a certain way. Why? Because in that way, you say, it is calculated to make an undue impression. Opinions favourable, then, you wish to make an undue impression, and by that confess the wickedness of your intention. You desire that the people should think better of the institutions and functionaries of their government than they deserve; in other words, you wish the government to be bad.

If opinions, to what degree soever unfavourable, may be freely and fully delivered, there are two conclusive reasons why the terms in which they are delivered should not be liable to punishment. In the first place, the difference between one mode of delivery and another is of little consequence. In the second place, you cannot forbid the delivery in one set of terms, without giving a power of preventing it in almost all.

First, the difference is of little consequence. If I say barely that such a functionary of government, or such an institution of government, is the cause of great injury and suffering to the people, all that I can do more by any language is, to give intimation, that the conduct of such functionary, or the existence of such institution, excites in me great contempt, or great anger, or great hatred, and ought to excite them in others. But if I put this in the way of a direct proposition, I may do so, because then it will be a naked statement with regard to a matter of fact, and cannot be forbidden, without overthrowing the whole of the doctrine which we have already established.

If, then, I give indication of certain sentiments of mine, and of my opinion of what ought to be the sentiments of others *explicitly*, I ought, you say, to be held innocent; if *implicitly*, guilty. Implicitly, or explicitly, that is the difference, and the whole of the difference. If I say, that such a judge, on such an occasion, took a bribe, and pro-nounced an unjust decision, which ruined a meritorious man and his family, this is a simple declaration of opinion, and ought not, accord-ing to the doctrine already established, to meet with the smallest obstruction. If I also state the matter of fact with regard to myself, that this action has excited in me great compassion for the injured family, and great anger and hatred against the author of their wrongs, this must be fully allowed. I must further be allowed to express freely my opinion, that this action ought to excite similar sentiments in other members of the community, and that the judge ought to receive an appropriate punishment. Much of all this, however, I may say in another manner. I may say it much more shortly by implication. – Here, I may cry, is an act for the indignation of mankind! Here is a villain, who, invested with the most sacred of trusts, has prostituted it to the vilest of purposes! Why is he not an object of public execration? Why are not the vials of wrath already poured forth upon his odious head? – All this means nothing, but that he has committed the act; that I hate him for it, and commiserate the sufferers; that I think he ought to be punished; and that other people ought to feel as I do. It cannot be pretended, that between these two modes of expression, the difference, in point of real and ultimate effect, can be considerable. For a momentary warmth, the passionate language may have considerable power. The permanent opinion formed of the character of the man, as well as the punishment, which, under a tolerable administration of law, he can sustain, must depend wholly upon the real state of the facts; any peculiarity in the language in which the facts may have been originally announced soon loses its effect. If that language has expressed no more indignation than what was really due, it has done nothing more than what the knowledge of the facts themselves would have done. If it has expressed more indignation than what was due, the knowledge of the facts operates immediately to extinguish it, and, what is more, to excite an unfavourable opinion of him who had thus displayed his intemperance. No evil then is produced; or none but what is very slight and momentary. If there should be a short-lived excess of unfavourable feeling, we have next to consider what is the proper remedy. Punishment should never be applied where the end can be attained by more desirable means. To destroy any excess of unfavourable feeling, all that is necessary is, to show the precise state of the facts, and the real amount of the evil which they import. All excess of feeling arises from imputing to the facts a greater efficacy in the way of evil than belongs to them. Correct this opinion, and the remedy is complete.

Secondly, you cannot forbid the use of passionate language, without giving a power of obstructing the use of censorial language altogether. The reason exists in the very nature of language. You cannot speak of moral acts in language which does not imply approbation and disapprobation. All such language may be termed passionate language. How can you point out a line where passionate language begins, dispassionate ends? The effect of words upon the mind depends upon the associations which we have with them. But no two men have the same associations with the same words. A word which may excite strains of emotion in one breast, will excite none in another. A word may appear to one man a passionate word, which does not appear so to another. Suppose the legislature were to say, that all censure, conveyed in passionate language, shall be punished, hardly could the vices of either the functionaries or the institutions of government be spoken of in any language which the judges might not condemn as passionate language, and which they would not have an interest, in league with other functionaries, to prohibit by their condemnation. The evil, therefore, which must of necessity be incurred by a power to punish language to which the name of *passionate* could be applied, would be immense. The evil which is incurred by leaving it exempt from punishment is too insignificant to allow that almost any thing should be risked for preventing it.

Religion, in some of its shapes, has, in most countries, been placed on the footing of an institution of the state. Ought the freedom of the press to be as complete, in regard to this, as we have seen that it ought to be, in regard to all other institutions of the state? If any one says that it ought not, it is incumbent upon him to show wherein the principles, which are applicable to the other institutions, fail in their application to this.

We have seen, that, in regard to all other institutions, it is unsafe for the people to permit any but themselves to choose opinions for them. Nothing can be more certain, than that it is unsafe for them to permit any but themselves to choose for them in religion.

If they part with the power of choosing their own religious opinions, they part with every power. It is well known with what ease religious opinions can be made to embrace every thing upon which the unlimited power of rulers, and the utmost degradation of the people, depend. The doctrine of *passive obedience* and non-resistance was a *religious doctrine*. Permit any man, or any set of men, to say what shall, and what shall not, be religious opinions, you make them despotic immediately.

This is so obvious, that it requires neither illustration or proof.

But if the people here, too, must choose opinions for themselves, discussion must have its course; the same propositions which we have proved to be true in regard to other institutions, are true in regard to this; and no opinion ought to be impeded more than another, by any thing but the adduction of evidence on the opposite side.

EDUCATION

Introduction. – Extent of the Subject. – The different Questions which it involves

The end of Education is to render the individual, as much as possible, an instrument of happiness, first to himself, and next to other beings.

The properties, by which he is fitted to become an instrument to this end, are, partly, those of the body, and partly those of the mind.

Happiness depends upon the condition of the body, either immediately, as where the bodily powers are exerted for the attainment of some good; or mediately, through the mind, as where the condition of the body affects the qualities of the mind.

Education, in the sense in which it is usually taken, and in which it shall here be used, denotes the means which may be employed to render the *mind*, as far as possible, an operative cause of happiness. The mode in which the *body* may be rendered the most fit for operating as an instrument of happiness is generally considered as a different species of inquiry; belonging to physicians, and others, who study the means of perfecting the bodily powers.

Education, then, in the sense in which we are now using the term, may be defined, the best employment of all the means which can be made use of, by man, for rendering the human mind to the greatest possible degree the cause of human happiness. Every thing, therefore, which operates, from the first germ of existence, to the final extinction of life, in such a manner as to affect those qualities of the mind on which happiness in any degree depends, comes within the scope of the present inquiry. Not to turn every thing to account is here, if any where, bad economy, in the most emphatical sense of the phrase.

The field, it will easily be seen, is exceedingly comprehensive. It is everywhere, among enlightened men, a subject of the deepest complaint, that the business of education is ill performed; and that, in this, which might have been supposed the most interesting of all human concerns, the practical proceedings are far from corresponding with the progress of the human mind. It may be remarked, that, notwithstanding all that has been written on the subject, even the *theory* of education has not kept pace with philosophy; and it is unhappily true, that the *practice* remains to a prodigious distance behind the theory. One reason why the theory, or the combination of ideas which the present state of knowledge might afford for improving the business of education, remains so imperfect, probably is, that the writers have taken but a partial view of the subject; in other words, the greater number have mistaken a part of it for the whole. And another reason of not less importance is, that they have generally contented themselves with vague ideas of the object or end to which education is required as the means. One grand purpose of the present inquiry will be to obviate all those mistakes; and, if not to exhibit that comprehensive view, which we think is desirable, but to which our limits are wholly inadequate; at any rate, to conduct the reader into that train of thought which will lead him to observe for himself the boundaries of the subject. If a more accurate conception is formed of the end, a better estimate will be made of what is suitable as the means.

1. It has been remarked, that every thing, from the first germ of existence to the final extinction of life, which operates in such a manner as to affect those qualities of the mind on which happiness in any degree depends, comes within the scope of the present inquiry. Those circumstances may be all arranged, according to the hackneyed division, under two heads: They are either physical or moral; meaning by physical those of a material nature, which operate more immediately upon the material part of the frame; by moral those of a mental nature, which operate more immediately upon the mental part of the frame.

2. In order to know in what manner things operate upon the mind, it is necessary to know how the mind is constructed. *Quicquid recipitur, recipitur ad modum recipientis.* This is the old aphorism, and nowhere

more applicable than to the present case. If you attempt to act upon the mind, in ways not adapted to its nature, the least evil you incur is to lose your labour.

3. As happiness is the end, and the means ought to be nicely adapted to the end, it is necessary to inquire, What are the qualities of mind which chiefly conduce to happiness, – both the happiness of the individual himself, and the happiness of his fellow-creatures?

It appears to us, that this distribution includes the whole of the subject. Each of these divisions branches itself out into a great number of inquiries. And, it is manifest, that the complete development of any one of them would require a greater space than we can allow for the whole. It is, therefore, necessary for us, if we aim at a comprehensive view, to confine ourselves to a skeleton.

The first of these inquiries is the most practical, and, therefore, likely to be the most interesting. Under the Physical Head, it investigates the mode in which the qualities of the mind are affected by the health, the aliment, the air, the labour, &c. to which the individual is subject. Under the Moral Head it includes what may be called, 1. Domestic Education, or the mode in which the mind of the individual is liable to be formed by the conduct of the individuals composing the family in which he is born and bred: 2, Technical or scholastic education, including all those exercises upon which the individual is put, as means to the acquisition of habits, – habits either conducive to intellectual and moral excellence, or even to the practice of the manual arts: 3. Social education, or the mode in which the mind of the individual is acted upon by the nature of the political institutions under which he lives.

The two latter divisions comprehend what is more purely theoretical; and the discussion of them offers fewer attractions to that class of readers, unhappily numerous, to whom intellectual exercises have not by habit been rendered delightful. The inquiries, however, which are included under these divisions, are required as a foundation to those included under the first. The fact is, that good practice can, in no case, have any solid foundation but in sound theory. This proposition is not more important, than it is certain. For, What is theory? The *whole* of the knowledge, which we possess upon any subject, put into that order and form in which it is most easy to draw from it good practical rules. Let any one examine this definition, article by article, and show us that it fails in a single particular. To recommend the separation of practice from theory is, therefore, simply, to recommend bad practice.

SECTION I
Theory of the Human Mind. – Its Importance
in the Doctrine of Education

1. The first, then, of the inquiries, embraced by the great subject of education, is that which regards the nature of the human mind; and the business is, agreeably to the foregoing definition of theory, to put the knowledge which we possess respecting the human mind, into that order and form, which is most advantageous for drawing from it the practical rules of education. The question is, How the mind, with those properties which it possesses, can, through the operation of certain means, be rendered most conducive to a certain end? To answer this question, the whole of its properties must be known. The whole science of human nature is, therefore, but a branch of the science of education. Nor can education assume its most perfect form, till the science of the human mind has reached its highest point of improvement. Even an outline, however, of the philosophy of the human mind would exceed the bounds of the present article; we must, therefore, show what ought to be done, rather than attempt, in any degree, to execute so extensive a project.

With respect to the human mind, as with respect to every thing else, all that passes with us under the name of knowledge is either matter of experience, or, to carry on the analogy of expression, matter of guess. The first is real knowledge; the properties of the object correspond to it. The latter is supposititious knowledge, and the properties of the object do or do not correspond to it; most likely not. The first thing desirable is, to make an exact separation of those two kinds of knowledge; and, as much as possible, to confine ourselves to the first.

What, then, is it which we experience with regard to the human mind? And what is it which we guess? We have experience of ourselves, when we *see*, when we *hear*, when we *taste*, when we *imagine*, when we *fear*, when we *love*, when we *desire*; and so on. And we give names, as above, to distinguish what we experience of ourselves, on one of those occasions, from what we experience on another. We have experience of other men exhibiting *signs* of having similar experiences of themselves, that is, of *seeing, hearing*, and so on. It is necessary to explain, shortly, what is here meant by a sign. When we ourselves *see, hear, imagine*, &c. certain actions of ours commonly follow. We know, accordingly, that if any one, observing those actions, were to infer that we had been *seeing, hearing*, &c. the inference would be just. As often then as we observe similar actions in other men, we infer that they, too, have been seeing or hearing; and we thus regard the action as the sign.

Having got names to distinguish the state of experience of ourselves, when we say, *I see, I hear, I wish*, and so on; we find occasion for a name which will distinguish the having any (be it what it may) of those experiences, from the being altogether without them; and, for this purpose, we say, *I feel*, which will apply, generally, to any of the cases in which we say, *I see*, or *hear*, or *remember*, or *fear*, and comprehends the meaning of them all. The term *I think*, is commonly used for a purpose nearly the same. But it is not quite so comprehensive: there are several things which we should include under the term *our experience of our mind*, to which we should not extend the term *I think*. But there is nothing included under it to which we should not extend the term *I feel*. This is truly, therefore, the generic term.

All our experience, then, of the human mind, is confined to the several occasions on which the term *I feel* can be applied. And, now, What does all this experience amount to? What is the knowledge which it affords? It is, first, a knowledge of the *feelings* themselves; we can remember what, one by one, they were. It is, next, a knowledge of the order in which they follow one another; and this is all. But this description, though a just one, is so very general as to be little instructive. It is not easy, however, to speak about those feelings minutely and correctly; because the language which we must apply to them is ill adapted to the purpose.

Let us advert to the first branch of this knowledge, that of the feelings themselves. The knowledge of the simple cases, may be regarded as easy; the feeling is distinct at the moment of experience, and is distinctly remembered afterwards. But the difficulty is great with the complex cases. It is found, that a great number of simple feelings are apt to become so closely united, as often to assume the appearance of only one feeling, and to render it extremely difficult to distinguish from one another the simple feelings of which it is composed. And one of the grand questions which divide the philosophers of the present day, is, which feelings are simple, and which are complex. There are two sorts which all have regarded as simple: those which we have when we say, I hear, I see, I feel, I taste, I smell, corresponding to the five senses, and the copies of these sensations, called ideas of sense. Of these, the second take place only in consequence of the first, they are, as it were, a revival of them; not the same feelings with the sensations or impressions on the senses, but feelings which bear a certain resemblance to them. Thus, when a man sees the light of noon, the feeling he has is called an *impression*, – the impression of light; when he shuts his eyes and has a feeling, – the type of relict of the impression, – he is not said to *see* the light, or to have the *impression* of light, but to *conceive* the light, or have an idea of it.

These two, – *impressions*, and their corresponding *ideas*, – are simple feelings, in the opinion of all philosophers. But there is one set of philosophers who think that these are the only simple feelings, and that all the rest are merely combinations of them. There is another class of philosophers who think that there are original feelings beside impressions and ideas; as those which correspond to the words *remember, believe, judge, space, time*, &c. Of the first are Hartley and his followers in England, Condillac and his followers in France; of the second description are Dr Reid and his followers in this country, Kant and the German school of metaphysicians in general on the Continent.

It is evident, that the determination of this question with regard to the first branch of inquiry, namely, what the feelings are, is of very great importance with regard to the second branch, namely, what is the order in which those feelings succeed one another. For how can it be known how they succeed one another, if we are ignorant which of them enter into those several groups which form the component parts of the train? It is of vast importance, then, for the business of education, that the analysis of mind should be accurately performed; in other words, that all our complex feelings should be accurately resolved into the simple ones of which they are composed. This, too, is of absolute necessity for the accurate use of language; as the greater number of words are employed to denote those groups of simple feelings which we call complex ideas.

In regard to all events, relating to mind or body, our knowledge extends not beyond two points: The first is, a knowledge of the events themselves; the second is, a knowledge of the order of their succession. The expression in words of the first kind of knowledge is history; the expression of the second is philosophy; and to render that expression short and clear is the ultimate aim of philosophy.

The first steps in ascertaining the order to succession among events are familiar and easy. One occurs, and then another, and after that a third, and so on; but at first it is uncertain whether this order is not merely accidental, and such as may never recur. After a time it is observed, that events, similar to those which have already occurred, are occurring again and again. It is next observed, that they are always followed, too, by the same sort of events by which those events were followed to which they are similar; that these second events are followed, in the third place, by events exactly similar to those which followed the events which they resemble; and that there is, thus, an endless round of the same sequences.

If the order in which one event follows another were always different, we should know events only one by one, and they would be infinitely too numerous to receive names. If we could observe none but very short sequences, if, for example, we could ascertain that one event was, indeed, always followed by one other of the same description, but could not trace any constancy farther, we should thus know events by sequences of twos and twos. But those sequences would also be a great deal too numerous to receive names.

The history of the human mind informs us, that the sequences which are first observed are short ones. They are still, therefore, too numerous to receive names. But men compound the matter. They give names to sequences which they are most interested in observing, and leave the rest unnamed. When they have occasion to speak of the unnamed successions, they apply to them, the best way they can, the names which they have got; endeavouring to make a partial naming answer an universal purpose. And hence almost all the confusion of language and of thought arises.

The great object, then, is, to ascertain sequences more and more extensive, till, at last, the succession of all events may be reduced to a number of sequences sufficiently small for each of them to receive a name; then, and then only, shall we be able to speak wholly free from confusion.

Language affords an instructive example of this mode of ascertaining sequences. In language, the words are the events. When an ignorant man first hears another speak an unknown language, he hears the sounds one by one, but observes no sequence. At last he gathers a knowledge of the use of a few words, and then he has observed a few sequences; and so he goes on till he understands whatever he hears. The sequences, however, which he has observed, are of no greater extent than is necessary to understand the meaning of the speaker; they are, by consequence, very numerous and confusing.

Next comes the grammarian; and he, by dividing the words into different kinds, observes that these kinds follow one another in a certain order, and thus ascertains more enlarged sequences, which, by consequence reduces their number.

Nor is this all; it is afterwards observed, that words consist, some of one syllable, and some of more than one; that all language may thus be resolved into syllables, and that syllables are much less in number than words: that, therefore, the number of sequences in which they can be formed are less in number, and, by consequence, are more extensive. This is another step in tracing to the most comprehensive sequences the order of succession in that class of events wherein language consists.

It is afterwards observed, that these syllables themselves are compounded; and it is at last found, that they may all be resolved into a small number of elementary sounds corresponding to the simple letters. All language is then found to consist of a limited number of sequences, made up of the different combinations of few letters.

It is not pretended that the example of language is exactly parallel to the case which it is brought to illustrate. It is sufficient if it aids the reader in seizing the idea which we mean to convey. It shews the analogy between the analysing of a complex sound, namely, a word, into the simple sounds of which it is composed, to wit, letters; and the analysing of a complex feeling, such as the idea of a rose, into the simple feelings of sight, of touch, of taste, of smell, of which the complex idea or feeling is made up. It affords, also, a proof of the commanding knowledge which is attained of a train of events, by observing the sequences which are formed of the simplest elements into which they can be resolved; and it thus illustrates the two grand operations, by successful perseverance in which the knowledge of the human mind is to be perfected.

It is upon a knowledge of the sequences which take place in the human feelings or thoughts, that the structure of education must be reared. And, though much undoubtedly remains to be cleared up, enough is already known of those sequences to manifest the shameful defects of that education with which our supineness, and love of things as they are, rest perfectly satisfied.

As the happiness, which is the end of education, depends upon the actions of the individual, and as all the actions of man are produced by his feelings or thoughts, the business of education is, to make certain feelings or thoughts take place instead of others. The business of education, then, is to work upon the mental successions. As the sequences among the letters or simple elements of speech, may be made to assume all the differences between nonsense and the most sublime philosophy, so the sequences, in the feelings which constitute human thought, may assume all the differences between the extreme of madness and of wickedness, and the greatest attainable heights of wisdom and virtue: And almost the whole of this is the effect of education. That, at least, all the difference which exists between classes or bodies of men is the effect of education, will, we suppose, without entering into the dispute about individual distinctions, be readily granted; that it is education wholly which constitutes the remarkable difference between the Turk and the Englishman, and even that still more remarkable difference between the most cultivated European and the wildest savage. Whatever is made of any *class* of men, we may then be sure is possible to be made of the whole human race. What a field for exertion! What a prize to be won!

Mr. Hobbs, who saw so much further into the texture of human thought than all who had gone before him, was the first man, as far as we remember, who pointed out (which is peculiarly *knowledge* in this respect) the order in which our feelings succeed one another, as a distinct object of study. He marked, with sufficient clearness, the existence, and the cause of the sequences; but, after a very slight attempt to trace them, he diverged to other inquiries, which had this but indirectly for their object.

"The succession," he says (*Human Nature*, ch. 4) "of conceptions, in the mind, series or consequence" (by *consequence* he means *sequence*) "of one after another, may be casual and incoherent, as in dreams, for the most part; and it may be orderly, as when the former thought introduceth the latter. The cause of the coherence or consequence (*sequence*) of one conception to another, is their first coherence or consequence at that time when they are produced by sense; as, for example, from St. Andrew the mind runneth to St. Peter, because their names are read together; from St. Peter to a stone, for the same cause; from stone to foundation, because we see them together; and, according to this example, the mind may run almost from any thing to any thing. But, as in the sense, the conception of cause and effect may succeed one another, so may they, *after* sense, in the imagination." By the succession in the *imagination* it is evident he means the succession of *ideas*, as by the succession in *sense* he means the succession of sensations.

Having said that the conceptions of *cause* and *effect* may succeed one another in the sense, and after sense in the imagination, he adds, "And, for the most part, they do so; the cause whereof is the appetite of them who, having a conception of the *end*, have next unto it a conception of the next *means* to that end; as when a man from a thought of honour, to which he hath an appetite, cometh to the thought of wisdom, which is the next means thereunto; and from thence to the thought of study, which is the next means to wisdom." (Ib.) Here is a declaration with respect to three grand laws in the sequence of our thoughts. The first is, that the succession of ideas follows the same order which takes place in that of the impressions. The second is, that the order of cause and effect is the most common order in the successions in the imagination, that is in the succession of ideas. And the third is, that the appetites of individuals have a great power over the successions of ideas; as the thought of the object which the individual desires, leads him to the thought of that by which he may attain it.

Mr. Locke took notice of the sequence in the train of ideas, or the order in which they follow one another, only for a particular purpose; – to explain the intellectual singularities which distinguish particular men. "Some of our ideas," he says, "have a natural correspondence and connection one with another. It is the office and excellence of our reason to trace these, and hold them together in that union and correspondence which is founded in their peculiar beings. Besides this, there is another connexion of ideas, wholly owing to chance or custom; ideas that are not at all of kin come to be so united in some men's minds, that it is very hard to separate them; they always keep in company, and the one no sooner at any time comes into the understanding, but its associate appears with it; and if they are more than two which are thus united, the whole gang, always inseparable, show themselves together." There is no attempt here to trace the order of sequence, or to ascertain which antecedents are followed by which consequents; and the accidental, rather than the more general phenomena, are those which seem particularly to have struck his attention. He gave, however, a name to the matter of fact. When one idea is regularly followed by another, he called this constancy of conjunction *the association of the ideas*; and this is the name by which, since the time of Locke, it has been commonly distinguished.

Mr. Hume perceived much more distinctly than any of the philosophers who had gone before him, that to philosophize concerning the human mind, was to trace the order of succession among the elementary feelings of the man. He pointed out three great laws or comprehensive sequences, which he thought included the whole. Ideas followed one another, he said, according to *resemblance, contiguity* in time and place, and *cause and effect*. The last of these, the sequence according to cause and effect, was very distinctly conceived, and even the cause of it explained by Mr. Hobbs. That of contiguity in time and place is thus satisfactorily explained by Mr. Hume. "It is evident," he says, "that as the senses, in changing their objects, are necessitated to change them regularly, and take them as they lie contiguous to each other, the imagination must, by long custom, acquire the same method of thinking, and run along the parts of space and time in conceiving its objects." (*Treatise of Human Nature*, P. I. B. I. sect. 4.) This is a reference to one of the laws pointed out by Hobbs, namely, that the order of succession among the ideas, follows the order that took place among the impressions. Mr. Hume shows, that the order of sense is much governed by contiguity, and why; and assigns this as a sufficient reason of the order which takes place in the imagination. Of the next sequence, that according to resemblance, he gives no account, and only appeals to the consciousness of his reader for the existence of the fact. Mr. Hume farther remarked, that what are called our complex ideas, are only a particular class of cases belonging to the same law – the law of the succession of ideas; every complex idea being only a certain number of simple ideas, which succeed each other so rapidly, as not to be separately distinguished without an effort of thought. This was a great discovery; but it must at the same time be owned, that it was very imperfectly developed by Mr. Hume. That philosopher proceeded, by aid of these principles, to account for the various phenomena of the human mind. But though he made some brilliant developments, it is nevertheless true, that he did not advance very far in the general object. He was misled by the pursuit of a few surprising and paradoxical results, and when he had arrived at them he stopped.

After him, and at a short interval, appeared two philosophers, who were more sober-minded, and had better aims. These were Condillac and Hartley. The first work of Condillac appeared some years before the publication of that of Hartley; but the whole of Hartley's train of thought has so much the air of being his own, that there is abundant reason to believe the speculations of both philosophers equally original. They both began upon the ground that all simple ideas are copies of impressions; that all complex ideas are only simple ideas united by the principle of association. They proceeded to examine all the phenomena of the human mind, and were of opinion that the principle of association, or the succession of one simple idea after another, according to certain laws, accounts for the whole; that these laws might, by meditation, be ascertained and applied; and that then the human mind would be understood, as far as man has the means of knowing it.

The merit of Condillac is very great. It may yet, perhaps be truer to say, that he wrote admirably upon philosophy, than that he was a great philosopher. His power consists in expression; he conveys metaphysical ideas with a union of brevity and clearness which never has been surpassed. But though he professed rather to deliver the opinions of others, than to aim at invention, it cannot be denied that he left the science of the human mind in a much better state than he found it; and this is equivalent to discovery. As a teacher, in giving, in this field, a right turn to the speculations of his countrymen, his value is incalculable; and there is, perhaps, no one human being, with the exception of Locke, who was his master, to whom, in this respect, the progress of the human mind is more largely indebted. It is also true, that to form the conception of tracing the sequences among our simple ideas, as comprehending the whole of the philosophy of the human mind, even with the helps which Hume had afforded, and it is more than probable that neither Condillac nor Hartley had ever heard of a work which, according to its author, had fallen dead-born from the press, was philosophical and sagacious in the highest degree.

It must be allowed, however, that, in expounding the various mental phenomena, Condillac does not display the same penetration and force of mind, or the same comprehensiveness, as Dr. Hartley. He made great *progress* in showing how those phenomena might be resolved into the sequences of simple ideas, but Dr. Hartley made still greater. We do not mean to pronounce a positive opinion either for or against the grand undertaking of Dr. Hartley, to resolve the whole of the mental phenomena of man into sequences of impressions, and the simple ideas which are the copies of them. But we have no hesitation in saying, that he philosophizes with extraordinary power and saga-city; and it is astonishing how many of the mental phenomena he has clearly resolved; how little, in truth, he has left about which any doubt can remain.

We cannot afford to pursue this subject any farther. This much is ascertained, – that the character of the human mind consists in the sequences of its ideas; that the object of education, therefore, is, to provide for the constant production of certain sequences, rather than others; that we cannot be sure of adopting the best means to that end, unless we have the greatest knowledge of the sequences themselves.

In what has been already ascertained on this subject, we have seen that there are two things which have a wonderful power over those sequences. They are, Custom; and Pain and Pleasure. These are the grand instruments or powers, by the use of which, the purposes of education are to be attained.

Where one idea has followed another a certain number of times, the appearance of the first in the mind is sure to be followed by that of the second, and so on. One of the grand points, then, in the study of education, is to find the means of making, in the most perfect manner, those repetitions on which the beneficial sequences depend.

When we speak of making one idea follow another, and always that which makes part of a good train, instead of one that makes part of a bad train, there is one difficulty; that each idea, taken singly by itself, is as fit to be a part of a bad train as of a good one; for good trains and bad trains are both made out of the same simple elements. Trains, however, take place by sequences of twos, or threes, or any greater number; and the nature of these sequences, as complex parts of a still greater whole, is that which renders the train either salutary or hurt-ful. Custom is, therefore, to be directed to two points; first to form those sequences, which make the component parts of a good train; and secondly, to join those sequences together, so as to constitute the trains.

When we speak of making one idea follow another, there must always be a starting point; there must be some one idea from which the train begins to flow; and it is pretty evident that much will depend upon this idea. One grand question, then, is, "What are the ideas which most frequently operate as the commencement of trains?" Knowing what are the ideas which play this important part, we may attach to them by custom, such trains as are the most beneficent. It has been observed that most, if not all, of our trains, start from a sensation, or some impression upon the external or internal nerves. The question then is, which are those sensations, or aggregates of sensations, which are of the most frequent recurrence? it being obviously of importance, that those which give occasion to the greatest number of trains, should be made, if possible, to give occasion only to the best trains. Now the sensations, or aggregates of sensations, which occur in the ordinary business of life, are those of most frequent recurrence; and from which it is of the greatest importance that beneficial trains should commence. Rising up in the morning, and going to bed at night, are aggregates of this description, common to all mankind; so are the commencement and termination of meals. The practical sagacity of priests, even in the rudest ages of the world, perceived the importance, for giving religious trains an ascendancy in the mind, of uniting them, by early and steady custom, with those perpetually recurring sensations. The morning and evening prayers, the grace before and after meals, have something correspondent to them in the religion of, perhaps, all nations.

It may appear, even from these few reflections and illustrations, that, if the sensations, which are most apt to give commencement to trains of ideas, are skilfully selected, and the trains which lead most surely to the happiness, first of the individual himself, and next of his fellow-creatures, are by custom effectually united with them, a pro-vision of unspeakable importance is made for the happiness of the race.

Beside custom, it was remarked by Hobbs, that appetite had a great power over the mental trains. But appetite is the feeling toward pleasure or pain in prospect; that is, future pleasure or pain. To say that appetite, therefore, has power over the mental trains, is to say, that the prospect of pleasure or pain has. That this is true, every man knows by his own experience. The best means, then, of applying the prospect of pleasure and pain to render beneficent trains perpetual in the mind, is the discovery to be made, and to be recommended to mankind.

The way in which pleasure and pain affect the trains of the mind is, as ends. As a train commences in some present sensation, so it may be conceived as terminating in the idea of some future pleasure or pain. The intermediate ideas, between the commencement and the end, may be either of the beneficent description or the hurtful. Suppose the sight of a fine equipage to be the commencement, and the riches which afford it, the appetite, or the end of a train, in the mind of two individuals at the same time. The intermediate ideas in the mind of the one may be beneficent, in the other hurtful. The mind of the one immediately runs over all the honourable and useful modes of acquiring riches, the acquisition of the most rare and useful qualities, the eager watch of all the best opportunities of bringing them into action, and the steady industry with which they may be applied. That of the other recurs to none but the vicious modes of acquiring riches – by lucky accidents, the arts of the adventurer and impostor, by rapine and plunder, perhaps on the largest scale, by all the honours and glories of war. Suppose the one of these trains to be habitual among individuals, the other not: What a difference for mankind!

It is unnecessary to adduce farther instances for the elucidation of this part of our mental constitution. What, in this portion of the field, requires to be done for the science of education, appears to be, First, to ascertain, what are the ends, the really ultimate objects of human desire; Next, what are the most beneficent means of attaining those objects; and Lastly, to accustom the mind to fill up the intermediate space between the present sensation and the ultimate object, with nothing but the ideas of those beneficent means. We are perfectly aware that these instructions are far too general. But we hope it will be carried in mind, that little beyond the most general ideas can be embraced in so confined a sketch; and we are not without an expectation that, such as they are, these expositions will not be wholly without their use.

SECTION II
Qualities of Mind, to the Production of which the Business of Education should be directed

We come now to the second branch of the science of education, or the inquiry what are the qualities with which it is of most importance that the mind of the individual should be endowed. This inquiry we are in hopes the preceding exposition will enable us very materially to abridge. In one sense, it might undoubtedly be affirmed, that all the desirable qualities of the human mind are included in those benefi-cent sequences of which we have spoken above. But, as it would require, to make this sufficiently intelligible, a more extensive exposi-tion than we are able to afford, we must content ourselves with the ordinary language, and with a more familiar mode of considering the subject.

That intelligence is one of the qualities in question will not be denied, and may speedily be made to appear. To attain happiness is the object: and, to attain it in the greatest possible degree, all the means to that end, which the compass of nature affords, must be employed in the most perfect possible manner. But all the means which the compass of nature, or the system in which we are placed, affords, can only be known by the most perfect knowledge of that system. The highest measure of knowledge is therefore required. But mere knowledge is not enough; a mere magazine of remembered facts is an useless treasure. Amid the vast variety of known things, there is needed a power of choosing, a power of discerning which of them are conducive, which not, to the ends we have in view. The ingredients of intelligence are two, knowledge and sagacity; the one affording the materials upon which the other is to be exerted; the one, showing what exists; the other, converting it to the greatest use; the one, bringing within our ken what is capable, and what is not capable of being used as means; the other, seizing and combining, at the proper moment, whatever is fittest as means to each particular end. This union, then, of copiousness and energy; this possession of numerous ideas, with the masterly command of them, is one of the more immediate ends to which the business of education is to be directed.

With a view of happiness as the end, another quality will easily present itself as indispensable. Conceive that a man knows the materials which can be employed as means, and is prompt and unerring in the mode of combining them; all this power is lost, if there is anything in his nature which prevents him from using it. If he has any appetite in his nature which leads him to pursue certain things with which the most effectual pursuit of happiness is inconsistent, so far this evil is incurred. A perfect command, then, over a man's appetites and desires; the power of restraining them whenever they lead in a hurtful direction; that possession of himself which insures his judgement against the illusions of the passions, and enables him to pursue constantly what he deliberately approves, is indispensably requisite to enable him to produce the greatest possible quantity of happiness. This is what the ancient philosophers called temperance; not exactly the same with what is called the virtue or grace of temperance, in theological morality, which includes a certain portion (in the doctrines of some theological instructors, a very large portion) of abstinence, and not only of abstinence, or the gratuitous renunciation of pleasure, but of the infliction of voluntary pain. This is done with a view to please the God, or object of worship, and to provide, through his favour, for the happiness of a second, or future life. The temperance of the ancient philosophers had a view only to the happiness of the present life, and consisted in the power of resisting the immediate propensity, if yielding to it would lead to an overbalance of evil or prevent the enjoyment of a superior good, in whatever the good or evil of the present life consists. This resisting power consists of two parts; the power of resisting pleasure, and that of resisting pain, the last of which has an appropriate name, and is called Fortitude.

These two qualities, the intelligence which can always choose the best possible means, and the strength which overcomes the misguiding propensities, appear to be sufficient for the happiness of the individual himself; to the pursuit of which it cannot be doubted that he always has sufficient motives. But education, we have said, should be an instrument to render the individual the best possible artificer of happiness, not to himself alone, but also to others. What, then, are the qualities with which he ought to be endowed, to make him produce the greatest possible quantity of happiness to others?

It is evident enough to see what is the first grand division. A man can affect the happiness of others, either by abstaining from doing them harm, or by doing them positive good. To abstain from doing them harm, receives the name of Justice; to do positive good receives that of Generosity. Justice and generosity, then, are the two qualities by which man is fitted to promote the happiness of his fellow-creatures. And it thus appears, that the four cardinal virtues of the ancients do pretty completely include all the qualities, to the possession of which it is desirable that the human mind should be trained. The defect, however, of this description is, that it is far too general. It is evident that the train of mental events which conduce to the proposed results must be far more particularized to insure, in any considerable degree, the effects of instruction; and it must be confessed that the ethical instructions of the ancients failed by remaining too much in generals. What is wanting is, that the incidents of human life should be skilfully classified; both those on the occasion of which they who are the objects of the good acts are pointed out for the receipt of them, and those on the occasion of which they who are to be the instruments are called upon for the performance. It thus appears that the science of Ethics, as well as the science of Intellectuals, must be carried to perfection, before the best foundation is obtained for the science of Education.

SECTION III
Happiness, the End to which Education is devoted. – Wherein it consists, not yet determined

We have spoken of the qualities which are subservient to human happiness, as means to an end. But, before means can be skilfully adapted to an end, the end must be accurately known. To know how the human mind is to be trained to the promotion of happiness, another inquiry then, is necessary; Wherein does human happiness consist? This is a controverted question; and we have introduced it rather with a view to show the place which it occupies in the theory of education, than that we have it in our power to elucidate a subject about which there is so much diversity of opinion, and which some of the disputants lead into very subtle and intricate inquiries. The importance of the question is sufficiently evident from this, that it is the grand central point, to which all other questions and inquiries converge; that point, by their bearing upon which, the value of all other things is determined. That it should remain itself undetermined, implies, that this branch of philosophy is yet far from its highest point of perfection.

The speculation on this subject, too, may be divided into two great classes; that of those who trace up all the elements of happiness, as they do all those of intellect, to the simple sensations which, by their transformation into ideas, and afterwards into various combinations, compose, they think, all the intellectual and moral phenomena of our nature; another, that of those who are not satisfied with this humble origin, who affirm that there is something in human happiness, and in the human intellect, which soars high above this corporeal level; that there are intellectual as well as moral forms, the resplendent objects of human desire, which can by no means be resolved into the grosser elements of sense. These philosophers speak of eternal and immutable truths; truths which are altogether independent of our limited experience; which are truly universal; which the mind recognizes without the aid of the senses; and which are the objects of pure intellect. They affirm, also, that there is a notion of right and of wrong wholly underived from human experience, and independent of the laws which regulate, in this world, the happiness and misery of human life; a right and wrong, the distinction between which is perceived, according to some, by a peculiar sense; according to others, by the faculty which discerns pure truth; according to others, by common sense; it is the same, according to some, with the notion of the fitness and unfitness of things; according to others, with the law of nature; according to others with truth; and there is one eminent philosopher* who makes it depend upon sympathy, without determining very clearly whether sympathy depends upon the senses or not.

We cannot too earnestly exhort philosophers to perfect this inquiry; that we may understand at last, not by vague abstract terms, but clearly and precisely, what are the simple ideas included under the term happiness; and what is the real object to which education is pointed; since it is utterly impossible, while there is any vagueness and

---

*[Mill refers here to David Hume. – Ed.]

uncertainty with respect to the end, that there should be the greatest precision and certainty in combining the means.

SECTION IV
Instruments, and practical Expedients, of Education

We come at last to the consideration of the means which are at the disposal of man for endowing the human mind with the qualities on which the generation of happiness depends. Under this head the discussion of the practical expedients chiefly occurs; but it also embraces some points of theory. The degree in which the useful qualities of human nature are, or are not, under the powers of education, is one of the most important.

This is the subject of a famous controversy, with names of the highest authority on both sides of the question. Helvétius, it is true, stands almost alone, on one side. But Helvétius, alone, is a host. No one man, perhaps, has done so much towards perfecting the *theory* of education as Mons. Helvétius; and his books are pregnant with information of the highest importance. Whoever wishes to understand the groundwork of education, can do nothing more conducive to his end, than to study profoundly the expositions of this philosophical inquirer, whether he adopts his conclusions, in all their latitude, or not. That Helvétius was not more admired in his own country, is owing really to the value of his work. It was too solid, for the frivolous taste of gay circles of Paris, assemblies of pampered noblesse, who wished for nothing but amusement. That he has been so little valued, in this country, is, it must be confessed, owing a little to the same cause; but another has concurred. An opinion has prevailed, a false one, that Helvétius is a peculiarly dangerous enemy to religion; and this has deterred people from reading him; or rather the old people who do not read, have deterred the young who do. There is no book, the author of which does not disguise his unbelief, that can be read with more safety to religion. The author attacks nothing but priestcraft, and in one of the worst of its forms; the popish priestcraft of the dark and middle ages; the idea of which we are well accustomed, in this country, to separate from that of religion. When his phraseology at any time extends, and that is not often, to Christianity itself, or to religion in the abstract, there is nothing calculated to seduce. There is nothing epigrammatic, and sparkling in the expression; nothing sophistical and artfully veiled in the reasoning; a plain proposition is stated, with a plain indication of its evidence; and if your judgement is not convinced, you are not deluded through the fancy.

M. Helvétius says, that if you take men who bring into the world with them the original constituents of their nature, their mental and bodily frame, in that ordinary state of goodness which is common to the great body of mankind, – leaving out of the account the comparatively small number of individuals who come into the world imperfect, and manifestly below the ordinary standard, – you may regard the whole of this great mass of mankind, as equally susceptible of mental excellence; and may trace the causes which made them to differ. If this be so, the power of education embraces every thing between the lowest stage of intellectual and moral rudeness, and the highest state, not only of actual, but of possible perfection. And if the power of education be so immense, the motive for perfecting it is great beyond expression.

The conclusions of Helvétius were controverted directly by Rousseau; and defended, against the strictures of that writer, by the author himself. We recollect few writers in this country who have embraced them.* But our authors have contented themselves, rather with rejecting, than disproving; and, at the best, have supported their rejection only by some incidental reflection, or the indication of a discrepancy between his conclusions and theirs.

One of the causes, why people have been so much startled, by the extent to which Helvétius has carried the dominion of education, seems to us to be their not including in it nearly so much as he does. They include in it little more than what is expressed by the term schooling; commencing about six or seven years of age, and ending at latest with the arrival of manhood. If this alone is meant by education, it is no doubt true, that education is far indeed from being all-powerful. But if in education is included every thing, which acts upon the being as it comes from the hand of nature, in such a manner as to

---

*There is one brilliant authority on the side of Helvetius: "It was a favourite opinion of Sir Wm. Jones, that all men are born with an equal capacity of improvement." – Lord Teignmouth's *Life of Sir William Jones*, vol. ii, p. 211.

modify the mind, to render the train of feelings different from what it would otherwise have been; the question is worthy of the most profound consideration. It is probable, that people in general form a very inadequate conception of all the circumstances which act during the first months, perhaps the first moments, of existence, and of the power of those circumstances in giving permanent qualities to the mind. The works of Helvétius would have been invaluable, if they had done nothing more than prove the vast importance of these circumstances, and direct towards them the attention of mankind. Rousseau began this important branch of the study of education. He remarked a variety of important facts, which, till his time, had been almost universally neglected, in the minds of infants, and how much might be done, by those who surround them, to give good or bad qualities to their minds, long before the time at which it had been supposed that education could commence. But Helvétius treated the subject much more profoundly and systematically. He traced the circumstances to the very moment of birth; he showed at how early an age indelible characters may be impressed; nay, that some of the circumstances over which man has a control (for he speaks not of others), circumstances on which effects of the greatest importance depend, may be traced beyond the birth.

It is evident how much it imports the science of education, that these circumstances should, by careful and continued observation, be all ascertained, and placed in the order best adapted for drawing from them the most efficient practical rules. This is of more importance than determining the question, whether the prodigious difference, which exists among men ordinarily well organized, is owing wholly to the circumstances which have operated upon them since the first moment of their sensitive existence, or is in part produced by original peculiarities. Enough is ascertained to prove, beyond a doubt, that if education does not perform every thing, there is hardly anything which it does not perform: that nothing can be more fatal than the error of those who relax in the vigilance of education, because nature is powerful, and either renders it impossible for them to accomplish much, or accomplishes a great deal without them: that the feeling is much more conformable to experience, and much more conformable to utility, which ascribes every thing to education, and thus carries the motive for vigilance and industry, in that great concern, to its highest pitch. This much, at any rate, is ascertained, that all the difference which exists, or can ever be made to exist, between one class of men, and another, is wholly owing to education. Those peculiarities, if any such there be, which sink a man below, or elevate him above the ordinary state of aptitude to profit by education, have no operation in the case of large numbers, or bodies. But large numbers or bodies of men are raised to a high degree of mental excellence; and might, without doubt, be raised to still higher. Other large bodies, or whole nations, have been found in so very low a mental state, as to be little above the brutes. All this vast distance is undeniably the effect of education. This much, therefore, may be affirmed on the side of Helvétius, that a prodigious difference is produced by education; while, on the other hand, it is rather assumed than proved, that any difference exists, but that which difference of education creates.

Circumstances of the Physical Kind which operate upon the Mind in the way of Education

The circumstances which are included under the term Education, in the comprehensive sense in which we have defined it, may be divided, we have said, into Physical, and Moral. We shall now consider the two classes in the order in which we have named them; and have here again to remind the reader, that we are limited to the task of pointing out what we should wish to be done, rather than permitted to attempt the performance.

Three things are desirable with regard to the physical circumstances which operate in the way of education favourably or unfavourably; to collect them fully; to appreciate them duly; and to place them in the order which is most favourable for drawing from them practical rules.

This is a service (common to the sciences of education and mind) which has been very imperfectly rendered. It has been chiefly reserved to medical men to observe the physical circumstances which affect the body and mind of man; but of medical men few have been much skilled in the observation of mental phenomena, or have thought themselves called upon to mark the share which physical circumstances had in producing them. There are indeed some, and those remarkable, exceptions. There is Dr. Darwin in our own country, and M. Cabanis in France. They have both of them taken the mind as a part at least of their study; and we are highly indebted to them for the number and value of their observations. They are both philosophers, in the most important sense of the word; they both observed nature for themselves, observed her attentively, and with their view steadily directed to the proper end. But still it is not safe to rely upon them as guides. They were in too great a haste to establish conclusions; and were apt to let their belief run before their evidence. They were not sufficiently careful to distinguish between the different degrees of evidence, and to mark what is required to constitute proof. To do this steadily seems, indeed, to be one of the rarest of all endowments; and was much less the characteristic of the two philosophers we have named, than a wide range of knowledge, from which they collected the facts, and great ingenuity in combining and applying them. Dr. Darwin was the most remarkable, both for the strength and the weakness of which we speak. The work of Darwin, to which we chiefly allude, is the *Zoönomia*; though important remarks to the same effect are scattered in his other publications. Cabanis entitled his great work, *Rapports du Physique et du Moral de l'Homme*. And there are some works recently announced by German physiologists, the titles of which promise aids in the same endeavour. But though we expect from them new facts, and ingenious hints, we have less hope of any great number of sound conclusions.

There are certain general names already in use, including the greater number of the physical circumstances which operate in the way of education upon the mind. It will be convenient, because of their commonness, to make use of them on the present occasion, though neither the enumeration which they make is complete, nor the distribution logical.

All the physical circumstances which operate upon the mind are either, 1. inherent in the body; or, 2. external to the body. Those which are external to the body, operate upon the mind, by first operating upon the body.

Of the first kind, the more remarkable seem to be healthiness or sickliness, strength or weakness, beauty or deformity, the temperament, the age, the sex.

Of the second sort, the more remarkable seem to be the aliment, the labour, the air, temperature, action, rest.

Previous to the inquiry concerning the power which physical circumstances exert in the formation of the mind, it may seem that we ought to determine the speculative question respecting the nature of the mind: that is, whether the phenomena of mind may possibly result from a certain organization of matter; or whether something of a different kind, and which we call spiritual, must not be conceived, as the source and organ of thought. We do not mean to enter into this controversy, which would detain us too long. It is not, in the least degree, necessary, for the end which we have in view. Whether the one hypothesis, with respect to the mind, be adopted, or the other, the distribution of the circumstances, which operate in the formation of human character, into those commonly called Physical, and those commonly called Moral, will be as convenient as any distribution which the present state of our knowledge enables us to make; and all that inquiry can do, in regard to those circumstances, is, to trace them accurately, and to observe their effects; that is, to ascertain what they are, and what the order of the mental events by which they are followed. This is simply matter of experience, and what we experience is the same, whether we adopt one opinion, or another, with regard to the nature of that which thinks. It is in what we experience, all ascertained, and put into the best possible shape for ease of comprehension, and ready application to practice, that all useful knowledge on this, as on all other subjects, consists.

I. First, we are to consider the circumstances of the body which have an effect upon the mental sequences. The object is, to ascertain which have a tendency to introduce those sequences which are favourable, which to introduce those that are unfavourable, to human happiness, and how to turn this knowledge to account.

Health and sickness, or the states of body which those names most peculiarly express, are the first of the circumstances which we have enumerated under this head. That these states have a tendency to introduce very different trains of thought, is matter of vulgar experience; but very little has been done to examine such trains, and to ascertain what in each is favourable, and what is unfavourable to human happiness.

We have already seen, that the trains which are favourable to Intelligence, Temperance, Justice, and Generosity, are the trains favourable to human happiness. Now, with respect to Intelligence, it will be seen, that Health is partly favourable, and partly unfavourable; and the same is the case with Sickness. Health is favourable, by allowing that time to be given to study, which many kinds of sickness withdraw, and by admitting a more vigorous attention, which the pain and langour of sickness often impair. It is unfavourable, by introducing that flow of pleasurable ideas which is called high spirits, adverse at a certain pitch to the application of attention; and by leading to that passionate pursuit of pleasure, which diminishes, if it does not destroy, the time for study. The mode in which disease operates upon the mental sequences is a subject of great complexity, and in which little has yet been done to mark distinctly the events, and ascertain the order of their succession. Cabanis, in his seventh memoir, entitled, *De l'Influence des Maladies sur la Formation des Idées et des Affections Morales*, has made a useful beginning toward the elucidation of this subject; but here, as elsewhere, he is too often general and vague. Instruction may also be gleaned from Darwin; but the facts which bear upon this point rather drop from him incidentally, than are anywhere put together systematically for its elucidation. As they were both physicians, however, of great experience, and of unusual skill in the observation of mental phenomena, their opinions are entitled to the greatest respect. The result of the matter is, that an improved medicine is no trifling branch of the art and science of education. Cabanis, accordingly concludes his memoir with the two following propositions:

"1mo. L'état de maladie influe d'une manière directe sur la formation des idées et des affections morales: nous avons même pu montrer dans quelques observations particulières, comment cette influence s'exerce."

"2do. L'observation et l'expérience nous ayant fait decouvrir les moyens de combattre assez souvent avec succés l'état de maladie, l'art qui met en usage ces moyens, peut donc modifier et perfectionner les opérations de l'intelligence et les habitudes de la volonté."

As it is chiefly through the nervous system, and the centre of that system, the brain, that the mental sequences are affected, and as all the sensitive parts have not an action equally strong, nor equally direct, upon the nerves and brain, diseases affect the mental sequences differently, according to the parts which they invade. The system of the nerves and brain is itself subject to different states of disease. Classified with regard to the functions which that system performs, as the organ of sensibility and of action, these states are thus described by M. Cabanis: "1. Excess of sensibility to all impressions on the one part; excessive action on the organs of motion on the other. 2. Unfitness to receive impressions, in sufficient number, or with the due degree of energy; and a diminution of the activity necessary for the production of the motions. 3. A general disturbance of the functions of the system, without any remarkable appearance of either excess or defect. 4. A bad distribution of the cerebral virtue, either when it exerts itself unequally in regard to time, having fits of extraordinary activity, followed by others of considerable remission; or when it is supplied in wrong proportion to the different organs, of which some are to a great degree abandoned, while there appears in others a concentration of sensibility, and of the excitations or powers by which the movements are affected."

The effects upon the mental sequences are represented in the following general sketch, which has the advantage of being tolerably comprehensive, though it is unhappily both vague and confused: "We may lay it down as a general fact, that, in all the marked affections of the nerves, irregularities, less or greater, take place, relative both to the mode in which impressions are received, and to the mode in which the determinations, automatic or voluntary, are formed. On one part, the sensations vary incessantly and rapidly with respect to their vivacity, their energy, and even their number; on another, the strength, the readiness, the facility of action exhibit the greatest inequalities. Hence perpetual fluctuation, from great excitement to languor, from elevation to dejection; a temper and passions variable in the highest degree. In this condition, the mind is always easily pushed to extremes. Either the man has many ideas, with great mental activity and acuteness; or, he is, on the contrary, almost incapable of thinking. It has been well observed, that hypochondriacal persons are by turns both courageous and cowardly; and as the impressions are habitually faulty either by excess or defect, in regard to almost all objects, it is seldom that the images correspond to the reality of things; that the desires and the will obtain the proper force and direction. If, along with these irregularities, which arise from the nervous system, should be found a weakness of the muscular organs, or of some important viscus, as, for example, of the stomach, – the phenomena, though still analogous in the main, will be distinguished by remarkable peculiarities. During the interval of languor, the debility of the muscles renders the sense of weakness, the fainting and drooping, still more complete and oppressive; life appears ready to escape at every instant. The passions are gloomy, excited by trifles, selfish; the ideas are petty, narrow, and bear only upon the objects of the slightest sensations. At the times of excitation, which arrive the more suddenly the greater the weakness; the muscular determinations do not obey the impulses of the brain, unless by starts, which have neither energy nor duration. These impulses serve only to convince the patient more profoundly of his real imbecility; they give him only a feeling of impatience, of discontent, and anxiety. Desires, often sufficiently keen, but commonly repressed by the habitual feeling of weakness, still more increase the discouraging impression. As the peculiar organ of thought cannot act without the concurrence of several others, and as, at that moment, it partakes in some degree of the weakness which affects the organs of movement, the ideas present themselves in crowds; they spring up, but do not arrange themselves in order; the necessary attention is not enjoyed; the consequence is, that this activity of the imagination, which we might expect to afford some compensation for the absence of other faculties, becomes a new source of dejection and despair."

In this passage, the mental sequences which particular states of disease introduce are clearly shown to have a prodigious influence upon human happiness; but the effects which are produced in respect to intelligence, temperance, generosity and justice, are mixed up together; and the author rather shows how much this subject deserves to be studied, than gives us information from which any considerable degree of practical utility can be derived. The connexion between particular states of body, and particular mental trains, ought to be carefully watched and recorded. When the events, one by one, are accurately distinguished, and made easy to be recognized, and when the order in which they follow one another is known, our power over the trains of those events, power to prevent such as are unfavourable, to produce such as are favourable, to human happiness, will then be at its height; and how to take care of his health will be one of the leading parts of the moral and intellectual education of man.

The state of the body, with regard to health and disease, is the inherent circumstance of the greatest importance, and we must pass over the rest with a cursory notice. The next we mentioned, are, Strength and Weakness, meaning chiefly muscular strength and weakness; and the natural, habitual, not the accidental, or diseased, state. It is a common observation, that muscular strength is apt to withdraw the owner from mental pursuits, and engage him in such as are more of the animal kind; the acquisition and display of physical

powers. Few men of great bodily powers have been much distinguished for mental excellence; some of the greatest ornaments of
human nature have been remarkable for bodily weakness. Muscular
strength is liable to operate unfavourably upon the moral as well as
the intellectual trains of thought. It diminishes that respect for other
men, which is so necessary to resist the impulses of passion; it
presents innumerable occasions for playing the tyrant with impunity;
and fosters, therefore, all that train of ideas, in which the tyrannical
vices are engendered. Cabanis remarks, and the fact is worthy of the
greatest attention, – "Presque tous les grands scélérats sont des hommes d'une structure organique vigoureuse, remarquables par la
fermeté et la tenacité de leurs fibres musculaires." It is evident,
therefore, how deeply it concerns the happiness of mankind, that the
mental trains, which this circumstance has a tendency to raise, should
be accurately known, as thus alone the means can be known, how that
which is hurtful may be avoided, that which is useful be introduced.

Of beauty and deformity, as circumstances affecting the mental
trains, much will not be necessary to be said. Illustrations will occur to
every body, to prove, that their power is not inconsiderable; so little,
however, has been done to ascertain the facts, and record them in the
best possible order, that any thing which deserves the name of knowledge on the subject hardly exists; and the principal service we can
render is to point it out for study; to exhort future inquirers to observe
diligently the trains which flow from beauty and deformity as their
source, and to trace to the largest possible sequences, as above described, the connexions which take place between them. Beauty and
deformity, it may be observed, operate upon the mental trains in
somewhat a different way from health and disease; rather mediately
than immediately. It is the idea of their effect upon other people that
is the more immediate cause of the trains to which they give occasion.
The idea that beauty commands their favourable regards, is apt to
introduce the well known trains, denoted by the terms, vanity, pride,
contemptuousness, trains not very favourable to the virtues. The idea
that deformity is apt to excite their unfavourable regards, is often
observed to lead to acuteness and vigour of intellect, employed as
instruments of protection, but to moroseness, and even malignity of
temper. The mode, however, in which beauty and deformity operate
upon the mental trains, namely, through the idea of their effect upon
other people, is common to them with a great many other advantages

or disadvantages, which derive their value chiefly from their influence upon other people; and materials for the illustration of this subject have been supplied by various writers upon the human mind.

To the word Temperament, no very precise idea has hitherto been annexed. It may be conceived in the following manner: The bodily structure, the composition of elements in the body of every individual, is different from that in the body of any other. It is observed, however, that the composition is more nearly resembling in some, than in others; that those who thus resemble may be arranged in groups; and that they may all be comprehended in four of five great classes. The circumstances, in which their bodily composition agrees, so as to constitute one of those large classes, have been called the Temperament; and each of those more remarkable characters of the body has been observed to be attended with a peculiar character in the train of ideas. But the illustration of the trains of ideas, and hence of the qualities of mind, which are apt to be introduced by temperament, and by the diversities of age and of sex, we are obliged, by the rapid absorption of the space allotted us wholly to omit. The subject in itself is not very mysterious. Accurate observation, and masterly recordation alone are required. To be sure, the same may be said of every object of human inquiry. But in some cases, it is not so easy to conceive perfectly what observation and recordation mean. On these topics, also, we are happy to say, that Cabanis really affords very considerable helps.

2. We come now to the second sort of physical circumstances, which have the power of introducing habitually certain trains of ideas, and hence of impressing permanent tendencies on the mind, – the circumstances which are external to the body. Some of these are of very great importance. The first is Aliment.

Aliment is good or evil, by quality and quantity. Hartley has remarked long ago, that though all the impressions from which ideas are copied, are made on the extremities of the nerves which are ramified on the surface of the body, and supply the several organs of sense, other impressions are nevertheless made on the extremities of the nerves which are ramified on the internal parts of our bodies, and that many of those impressions are associated with trains of ideas; that the impressions made upon the extremities of the nerves which are ramified on the alimentary canal, are associated with the greatest number of those trains; and of such trains, that some are favourable to happiness, some altogether the reverse. If the quantity and quality of the aliment be the principal cause of those impressions, here is a physiological reason, of the greatest importance, for an accurate observation and recordation of the events occurring in this part of the field; what antecedents are attended by what consequents, and what the largest sequences that can be traced. Cabanis confirmed the doctrine of Hartley with regard to the internal impressions, and added another class. He said that not only the extremities of the nerves which terminate internally, but the centre of the nervous influence, the brain itself, received impressions, and that thus there were no fewer than three sources of mental and corporeal movements of man; one external, from which almost all our distinct ideas are copied; and two internal, which exert a very great influence upon the trains of ideas, and hence upon the actions of which these trains are the antecedents or cause.

On this too, as on most of the other topics, belonging to the physical branch of education, we must note, as still uncollected, the knowledge which is required. It is understood in a general way, that deep impressions are by this means made upon the mind; but how they are made, is a knowledge which, in any such detail and accuracy as to afford useful practical rules, is nearly wanting. There is a passage in Hartley, which we esteem it important to quote: "The sense of feeling may be distinguished into that of the external surface of the body, and that of the cavities of the nose, mouth, fauces, alimentary duct, pelvis, of the kidneys, uterus, bladder or urine, gall bladder, follicles, and ducts of the glands, &c. The sensibility is much greater in the last than in the first, because the impressions can more easily penetrate through the soft epithelium with which the internal cavities are invested. In the mouth and nose this sensibility is so great, and attended with such distinguishing circumstances, as to have the names of taste and smell assigned respectively to the sensations impressed upon the papillae of these two organs." . . . "The taste may also be distinguished into two kinds; viz. the general one which extends itself to the insides of the lips and cheeks, to the palate, fauces, oesophagus, stomach, and whole alimentary duct, quite down to the anus . . . The pleasures of the taste, considered as extending itself from the mouth through the whole alimentary duct, are very considerable, and frequently repeated; they must, therefore, be one chief means by which pleasurable states are introduced into the brain and nervous system. These pleasurable states must, after some time, leave miniatures of themselves, sufficiently strong to be called up upon slight occasions, viz. from a variety of associations with the common visible and audible objects, and to illuminate these and their ideas. When groups of these miniatures have been long and closely connected with particular objects, they coalesce into one complex idea, appearing, however, to be a simple one; and so begin to be transferred upon other objects, and even upon tastes back again, and so on without limits. And from this way of reasoning it may now appear, that a great part of our intellectual pleasures are ultimately deducible from those of taste; and that one principal final cause of the greatness and constant recurrency of these pleasures, from our first infancy to the extremity of old age, is to introduce and keep up pleasurable states in the brain, and to connect them with foreign objects. The social pleasures seem, in a particular manner, to be derived from this source, since it has been customary in all ages and nations, and is in a manner necessary, that we should enjoy the pleasures of taste in conjunction with our relations, friends, and neighbours. In like manner, nauseous tastes and painful impressions upon the alimentary duct give rise and strength to mental pains. The most common of these painful impressions is that from excess, and the consequent indigestion. This excites and supports those uneasy states, which attend upon melancholy, fear, and sorrow. It appears also to me, that these states are introduced in a great degree during sleep, during the frightful dreams, agitations, and oppressions, that excess in diet occasions in the night. These dreams and disorders are often forgotten; but the uneasy states of body which then happen, leave vestiges of themselves, which increase in number and strength every day from the continuance of the cause, till at last they are ready to be called up in crowds upon slight occasions, and the unhappy person is unexpectedly, and at once, as it were, seized with a great degree of the hypochondriac distemper, the obvious cause appearing no ways proportionable to the effect. And thus it may appear that there ought to be a great reciprocal influence between the mind and alimentary duct, agreeably to common observation." Cabanis, in like manner, says, "Quoique les médecins aient dit plusieurs choses hazardées, touchant l'effet des substances alimentaries sur les organs de la pensée, ou sur les principes physiques de nos penchans, il n'en est pas moins certain que les differentes causes que nous appliquons journellement à nos corps, pour en renouveller les mouvements, agissent avec une grande efficacité sur nos dispositions morales. On se rend plus propre aux travaux de l'esprit par certaines precautions de régime, par l'usage, ou la suppression de certains alimens. Quelques personnes ont été guéries de violens accés de colère, auxquels elles étoient sujêtes, par la seule diète pythagorique, et dans le cas même où des délires furieux troublent toutes les facultés de l'âme, l'emploi journalier de certaines nourritures ou de certaines boissons, l'impression d'une certaine température de l'air, l'aspect de certaines objets; en un mot, un système diététique particulier suffit souvent pour y remener le calme, pour faire tout rentrer dans l'ordre primitif."

As it is impossible for us here to attempt a full account of the mode in which aliments operate to produce good or bad effects upon the train of ideas, we shall single out that case, which, as operating upon the greatest number of people, is of the greatest importance; we mean that, in which effects are produced by the *poverty* of the diet; proposing, under the term poverty, to include both badness of quality, and defect of quantity. On badness of quality, we shall not spend many words. Aliments are bad in a variety of ways, and to such a degree as to impair the bodily health. Of such, the injurious effect will not be disputed. Others, which have in them no hurtful ingredient, may contain so insignificant a portion of nourishment, that to afford it in the requisite degree, they must produce a hurtful distention of the organs. The saw-dust, which some northern nations use for bread, if depended upon for the whole of their nourishment, would doubtless have this effect. The potato, where solely depended upon, is not, perhaps, altogether free from it. Bad quality, however, is but seldom resorted to, except in consequence of deficient quantity. That is, therefore, the principal point of inquiry.

It is easy to see a great number of ways in which deficient quantity of food operates unfavourably upon the *moral* temper of the mind. As people are ready to sacrifice every thing to the obtaining of a sufficient quantity of food, the want of it implies the most dreadful poverty; that state, in which there is scarcely any source of pleasure, and in which almost every moment is subject to pain. It is found by a very general experience, that a human being, almost constantly in pain, hardly visited by a single pleasure, and almost shut out from hope, loses by degrees all sympathy with his fellow creatures; contracts even a jealousy of their pleasures, and at last a hatred; and would like to see all the rest of mankind as wretched as himself. If he is habitually wretched, and rarely permitted to taste a pleasure, he snatches it with an avidity, and indulges himself with an intemperance, almost unknown to any other man. The evil of insufficient food acts with an influence not less malignant upon the intellectual, than upon the moral part of the human mind. The physiologists account for its influence in this manner. They say, that the signs, by which the living energy is manifested, may be included generally under the term *irritability*, or the power of being put in action by stimulants. It is not necessary for us to be very particular in explaining these terms; a general conception will for the present suffice. A certain degree of this irritability seems necessary to the proper state, or rather the very existence of the animal functions. A succession of stimulants, of a certain degree of frequency and strength, is necessary to preserve that irritability. The most important by far of all the useful stimulants applied to the living organs is food. If this stimulant is applied, in less than a sufficient degree, the irritability is diminished in proportion, and all those manifestations of the living energy which depend upon it, mental as well as corporeal, are impaired; the mind loses a corresponding part of its force. We must refer to the philosophical writers on medicine for illustrations and facts, which we have not room to adduce, but which will not be difficult to collect. Dr. Crichton places *poor diet* at the head of a list of causes which "weaken attention, and consequently debilitate the whole faculties of the mind."* From this fact, about which there is no dispute, the most important consequences arise. It follows, that when we deliberate about the means of introducing intellectual and moral excellence, into the minds of the principal portion of the people, one of the first things which we are bound to provide for, is, a generous and animating diet. The physical causes must go along with the moral; and nature herself forbids, that you shall make a wise and virtuous people, out of a starving one. Men must be happy themselves, before they can rejoice in the happiness of others; they must have a certain vigour of mind, before they can, in the midst of habitual suffering, resist a presented pleasure; their own lives, and means of well-being, must be worth something, before they can value, so as to respect, the life, or well-being, of any other person. This or that individual may be an extra-

*An Inquiry into the Nature and Origin of Mental Derangement, &c. By A. Crichton, M.D.T. 274.

ordinary individual, and exhibit mental excellence in the midst of wretchedness; but a wretched and excellent people never yet has been seen on the face of the earth. Though far from fond of paradoxical expressions, we are tempted to say, that a good diet is a necessary part of a good education; for in one very important sense it is emphatically true. In the great body of the people all education is impotent without it.

Labour is the next of the circumstances in our enumeration. We have distinguished labour from action, though action is the genus of which labour is one of the species; because of those species, labour is so much the most important. The muscular operations of the body, by which men generally earn their bread, are the chief part of the particulars which we include under that term. The same distinction is useful here as in the former case; labour is apt to be injurious by its *quality*, and by its *quantity*. That the quality of the labour, in which a man is employed, produces effects, favourable or unfavourable upon his mind, has long been confessed; Dr. Smith made the important remark, that the labour in which the great body of the people are employed, has a tendency to grow less and less favourable, as civilization and the arts proceed. The division and subdivision of labour is the principal cause. This confines the attention of the labourer to so small a number of objects, and so narrow a circle of ideas, that the mind receives not that varied exercise, and that portion of aliment, on which almost every degree of mental excellence depends. When the greater part of a man's life is employed in the performance of a few simple operations, in one fixed invariable course, all exercise of ingenuity, all adaptation of means to ends, is wholly excluded, and the faculty lost, as far as disuse can destroy the faculties of the mind. The minds, therefore, of the great body of the people are in danger of really degenerating, while the other elements of civilization are advancing, unless care is taken, by means of the other instruments of education, to counteract those effects which the simplification of the manual processes has a tendency to produce.

The *quantity* of labour is another circumstance which deserves attention in estimating the agents which concur in forming the mind. Labour may be to such a degree severe, as to confine the attention almost wholly to the painful ideas which it brings; and to operate upon the mind with nearly the same effects as an habitual deficiency of food. It operates perhaps still more rapidly; obliterating sympathy, inspiring cruelty and intemperance, rendering impossible the reception of ideas, and paralysing the organs of the mind. The attentive examination, therefore, of the facts of this case, is a matter of first-rate importance. Two things are absolutely certain; that without the bodily labour of the great bulk of mankind the well-being of the species cannot be obtained; and that if the bodily labour of the great bulk of mankind is carried beyond a certain extent, neither intellect, virtue, nor happiness can flourish upon the earth. What, then, is that previous middle point, at which the greatest quantity of good is obtained with the smallest quantity of evil, is, in this part of the subject, the problem to be solved.

The state of defective food and excessive labour, is the state in which we find the great bulk of mankind; the state in which they are either constantly existing, or into which they are every moment threatening to fall. These are two, therefore, in settling the rank among the circumstances which concur in determining the degree of intellect and morality capable of being exhibited in the societies of men, which ought to stand in a very eminent place: the mode of increasing to the utmost, the quantity of intellect, morality, and happiness, in human society, will be very imperfectly understood, till they obtain a new degree of consideration.

We named, besides these, among the physical circumstances which contribute to give permanent characters to the mind, air, temperature, action, and rest. But of these we must leave the illustration wholly to other inquirers. It is mortifying to be obliged to relinquish a subject, on which so much depends, and for which so little has been done, with so very imperfect an attempt for its improvement. We shall, however, have performed a service of some utility to education, if what we have said has any tendency to lead men to a juster estimate of the physical circumstances which concur in fashioning the human mind, and hence to greater industry and care in studying and applying them.

Circumstances of the Moral Kind which operate upon the Mind in the way of Education

The Moral circumstances which determine the mental trains of the human being, and hence the character of his actions, are of so much importance, that to them the term education has been generally confined: or rather, the term education has been generally used in so narrow a sense, that it embraces only one of the four classes into which we have thought it convenient to distribute the moral circumstances which operate to the formation of the human mind.

1. The first of these classes we have comprehended under the term DOMESTIC EDUCATION. To this the groundwork of the character of most individuals is almost wholly to be traced. The original features are fabricated here; not, indeed, in such a manner as to be unsusceptible of alteration, but in such a manner, decidedly, as to present a good or bad subject for all future means of cultivation. The importance, therefore, of domestic education, needs no additional words to explain it; though it is difficult to restrain a sigh, when we reflect, that it has but now begun to be regarded as within the pale of education; and a few scattered remarks, rather than a full exposition of the subject, is all the information upon it, with which the world has been favoured.

By Domestic Education, we denote all that the child hears and sees, more especially all that it is made to suffer or enjoy at the hands of others, and all that it is allowed or constrained to do, in the house in which it is born and bred, which we shall consider, generally, as the parental.

If we consider, that the mental trains, as explained above, are that upon which every thing depends, and that the mental trains depend essentially upon those sequences among our sensations which have been so frequently experienced as to create a habit of passing from the idea of the one to that of the other, we shall perceive immediately the reasons of what we have advanced.

It seems to be a law of human nature, that the first sensations experienced produced the greatest effects; more especially, that the earliest repetitions of one sensation after another produce the deepest habit; the strongest propensity to pass immediately from the idea of the one to the idea of the other. Common language confirms this law, when it speaks of the susceptibility of the tender mind. On this depends the power of those associations which form some of the most interesting phenomena of human life. From what other cause does it arise, that the hearing of a musical air, which, after a life of absence, recalls the parental mansion, produces as it were a revolution in the whole being? That the sympathies between brothers and sisters are what they are? On what other cause originally is the love of country founded? – that passionate attachment to the soil, the people, the manners, the woods, the rivers, the hills, with which our infant eyes were familiar, which fed our youthful imaginations, and with the presence of which the pleasures of our early years were habitually conjoined!

It is, then, a fact, that the early sequences to which we are accustomed form the primary habits; and that the primary habits are the fundamental character of the man. The consequence is most important; for it follows, that, as soon as the infant, or rather the embryo, begins to feel, the character begins to be formed; and that the habits, which are then contracted, are the most pervading and operative of all. Education, then, or the care of forming the habits, ought to commence, as much as possible, with the period of sensation itself; and, at no period, is its utmost vigilance of greater importance, than the first.

Very unconnected, or very general instructions, are all that can be given upon this subject, till the proper decompositions and recompositions are performed; in other words, till the subject is first analysed, and then systemized; or, in one word, *philosophized*, if we may use that verb in a passive signification. We can, therefore, do little more than exhort to the prosecution of the inquiry.

The steady conception of the End must guide us to the Means. Happiness is the end; and we have circumscribed the inquiry, by naming Intelligence, Temperance, and Benevolence, of which last the two parts are Generosity and Justice, as the grand qualities of mind, through which this end is to be attained. The question, then, is, how can those early sequences be made to take place on which the habits, conducive to intelligence, temperance, and benevolence, are founded; and how can those sequences, on which are founded the vices opposite to those virtues, be prevented?

Clearness is attained, by disentangling complexity; we ought, therefore, to trace the sequences conducive to each of those qualities in their turn. A part, however, must suffice when we cannot accomplish the whole. Intelligent trains of ideas constitute intelligence. Trains of ideas are intelligent, when the sequences in the ideas correspond to the sequences in nature. A man, for example, knows the order of certain words, when his idea of the one follows that of the other, in the same order in which the events themselves took place. A man is sagacious in devising means for the production of events when his ideas run easily in trains which are at once agreeable to knowledge, that is, to the trains of events, and at the same time new in the combination. They must be agreeable to knowledge; that is, one of the ideas must follow another in the order in which the objects of which they are the ideas follow one another in nature, otherwise the train would consist of mere chimeras, and, having no connexion with things, would be utterly useless. As the event, however, is not in the ordinary course; otherwise sagacity would not be required to give it existence; the ordinary train of antecedents will not suffice; it must be a peculiar train, at once correspondent with nature, and adapted to the end. The earliest trains, produced in the minds of children, should be made to partake as much as possible of those characters. The impressions made upon them should correspond to the great and commanding sequences established among the events on which human happiness principally depends. More explicitly, children ought to be made to see, and hear, and feel, and taste, in the order of the most invariable and comprehensive sequences, in order that the ideas which correspond to their impressions, and follow the same order to succession, may be an exact transcript of nature, and always lead to just anticipations of events. Especially, the pains and pleasures of the infant, the deepest impressions which he receives, ought, from the first moment of sensation, to be made as much as possible to correspond to the real order of nature. The moral procedure of parents is directly the reverse; they strive to defeat the order of nature, in accumulating pleasure for their children, and preventing the arrival of pains, when the children's own conduct would have had very different effects.

Not only are the impressions, from which ideas are copied, made, by the injudicious conduct of those to whom the destiny of infants is confided, to follow an order very different from the natural one, or that in which the grand sequences among events would naturally produce them; but wrong trains of ideas, trains which have no correspondence with the order of events, are often introduced immediately by words, or other signs of the ideas of other men. As we can only give very partial examples of a general error, we may content ourselves with one of the most common. When those who are about children express by their words, or indicate by other signs, that terrific trains of ideas are passing in their minds, when they go into the dark; terrific trains, which have nothing to do with the order of events, come up also in the minds of the children in the dark, and often exercise over them an uncontrollable sway during the whole of their lives. – This is the grand source of wrong education; to this may be traced the greater proportion of all the evil biases of the human mind. – If an order of ideas, corresponding with the order of events, were taught to come up in the minds of children when they go into the dark, they would think of nothing but the real dangers which are apt to attend it, and the precautions which are proper to be taken; they would have no wrong feelings, and their conduct would be nothing but that which prudence, or a right conception of the events, would prescribe. – If the expressions, and other signs of the ideas of those who are about children, indicate that trains, accompanied with desire and admiration, pass in their minds when the rich and powerful are named, trains accompanied with aversion and contempt when the weak and the poor, the foundation is laid of a character stained with servility to those above, and tyranny to those below them. If indication is given to children that ideas of disgust, of hatred, and detestation, are passing in the minds of those about them, when particular descriptions of men are thought of; as men of different religions, different countries, or different political parties in the same country; a similar train becomes habitual in the minds of the children; and those antipathies are generated which infuse so much of its bitterness into the cup of human life.

We can afford to say but very few words on the powers of domestic education with regard to Temperance. That virtue bears a reference to pain and pleasure. The grand object evidently is, to connect with each pain and pleasure those trains of ideas which, according to the order established among events, tend most effectually to increase the sum of pleasures upon the whole, and diminish that of pains. If the early trains create a habit of over-valuing any pleasure or pain, too much will be sacrificed, during life, to obtain the one, or avoid the other, and the sum of happiness, upon the whole, will be impaired. The order in which children receive their impressions, as well as the order of the trains which they copy from others, has a tendency to create impatience under privation; in other words, to make them in prodigious haste to realize a pleasure as soon as desired, to extinguish a pain as soon as felt. A pleasure, however, can be realized in the best possible manner, or a pain removed, only by certain steps, – frequently numerous ones; and if impatience hurries a man to overlook those steps, he may sacrifice more than he gains. The desirable thing would be, that his ideas should always run over those very steps, and none but them; and the skilful use of the powers we have over the impressions and trains of his infancy would lay the strongest foundation for the future happiness of himself, and of all those over whom his actions have any sway. It is by the use of this power that almost every thing is done to create what is called the temper of the individual; to render him irascible on the one hand, or forbearing on the other; severe and unforgiving, or indulgent and placable.

Intelligence and Temperance are sometimes spoken of, as virtues which have a reference to the happiness of the individual himself: Benevolence as a virtue which has a reference to the happiness of others. The truth is, that intelligence and temperance have a reference not less direct to the happiness of others than to that of the possessor; and Benevolence cannot be considered as less essential to his happiness than intelligence and temperance. In reality, as the happiness of the individual is bound up with that of his species, that which affects the happiness of the one, must also, in general, affect that of the other.

It is not difficult, from the expositions we have already given, to conceive in a general way how sequences may take place in the mind of the infant which are favourable to benevolence, and how sequences may take place which are unfavourable to it. The difficulty is, so to bring forward and exhibit the details, as to afford the best possible instruction for practice. We have several books now in our own language, in particular those of Miss Edgeworth, which afford many finely selected instances, and many detached observations of the greatest value, for the cultivation of benevolence in the infant mind. But the great task of the philosopher, that of *theorizing* the whole, is yet to be performed. What we mean by "theorizing the whole," after the explanations we have already afforded, is not, we should hope, obscure. It is to observe exactly the facts; to make a perfect collection of them, nothing omitted that is of any importance, nothing included of none; and to record them in that order and form, in which all that is best to be done in practice can be most immediately and certainly perceived.

The order of the impressions which are made upon the child, by the spontaneous order of events, is, to a certain degree, favourable to benevolence. The pleasures of those who are about him are most commonly the cause of pleasure to himself; their pains of pain. When highly pleased, they are commonly more disposed to exert themselves to gratify him. A period of pain or grief in those about him, is a period of gloom – a period in which little is done for pleasure – a period in which the pleasures of the child are apt to be overlooked. Trains of pleasurable ideas are thus apt to arise in his mind, at the thought of the pleasurable condition of those around him; trains of painful ideas at the thought of the reverse; and he is thus led to have an habitual desire for the one, aversion to the other. But if pleasures, whencesoever derived, of those about him, are apt to be the cause of good to himself, those pleasures which they derive from himself, are in a greater degree the cause of good to himself. If those about him are disposed to exert themselves to please him when they are pleased themselves, they are disposed to exert themselves in a much greater degree to please him, in particular, when it is he who is the cause of the pleasure they enjoy. A train of ideas, in the highest degree pleasurable, may thus habitually pass through his mind at the thought of happiness to others produced by himself; a train of ideas, in the highest degree painful, at the thought of misery to others produced by himself. In this manner the foundation of a life of beneficence is laid.

The business of a skilful education is, so to arrange the circumstances by which the child is surrounded, that the impressions made upon him shall be in the order most conducive to this happy result. The impressions, too, which are made originally upon the child, are but one of the causes of the trains which are rendered habitual to him, and which, therefore, obtain a leading influence in his mind. When he is often made to conceive the trains of other men, by the words, or other signs by which their feelings are betokened, those borrowed trains become also habitual, and exert a similar influence on the mind. This, then, is another of the instruments of education. When the trains, signified to the child, of the ideas in the minds of those about him are trains of pleasure at the thought of the happiness of other human beings, trains of the opposite kind at the conception of their misery; and when such trains are still more pleasurable or painful as the happiness or misery is produced by themselves, the association becomes in time sufficiently powerful to govern the life.

The grand object of human desire is a command over the wills of other men. This may be attained, either by qualities and acts which excite their love and admiration, or by those which excite their terror.

When the education is so wisely conducted as to make the train run habitually from the conception of the good end to the conception of the good means; and as often, too, as the good means are conceived, viz. the useful and beneficial qualities, to make the train run on to the conception of the great reward, the command over the wills of men; an association is formed which impels the man through life to pursue the great object of desire, fitting himself to be, and by actually becoming, the instrument of the greatest possible benefit to his fellow men.

But, unhappily, a command over the wills of men may be obtained by other means than by doing them good; and these, when a man can command them, are the shortest, the easiest, and the most effectual. These other means are all summed up in a command over the pains of other men. When a command over the wills of other men is pursued by the instrumentality of pain, it leads to all the several degrees of vexation, injustice, cruelty, oppression, and tyranny. It is, in truth, the grand source of all wickedness, of all the evil which man brings upon man. When the education is so deplorably bad as to allow an association to be formed in the mind of the child between the grand object of desire, the command over the wills of other men, and the fears and pains of other men, as the means; the foundation is laid of the bad character, – the bad son, the bad brother, the bad husband, the bad father, the bad neighbour, the bad magistrate, the bad citizen, – to sum up all in one word, the bad man. Yet, true, it is, a great part of education is still so conducted as to form that association. The child, while it yet hangs at the breast, is often allowed to find out by experience, that crying, and the annoyance which it gives, is that by which chiefly it can command the services of its nurse, and obtain the pleasures which it desires. There is not one child in fifty, who has not learned to make its cries and wailings an instrument of power; very often they are an instrument of absolute tyranny. When the evil grows to excess, the vulgar say the child is spoiled. Not only is the child allowed to exert an influence over the wills of others, by means of their pains; it finds, that frequently, sometimes most frequently, its own will is needlessly and unduly commanded by the same means, pain, and the fear of pain. All these sensations concur in establishing a firm association between the idea of the grand object of desire, command over the acts of other men, and the idea of pain and terror, as the means of acquiring it. That those who have been subject to tyranny, are almost always desirous of being tyrants in their turn; that is to say, that a strong association has been formed in their minds, between the ideas of pleasure and dignity, on the one hand, and those of the exercise of tyranny, on the other, is a matter of old and invariable observation. An anecdote has just been mentioned to us, so much in point, that we will repeat it, as resting on its own probability, though it is hearsay evidence (very good, however, of its kind) on which we have received it. At Eton, in consequence, it is probable, of the criticisms which the press has usefully made upon the system of *fagging* (as it is called), at the public schools, a proposition was lately made, among the boys themselves, for abolishing it. The idea originated with the elder boys, who were in possession of the power; a power of a very unlimited and formidable description; and by them was warmly supported. It was, however, opposed with still greater vehemence by the junior boys, the boys who were then the victims of it. The expected pleasure of tyrannizing in their turn, outweighed the pain of their present slavery. In this case, too, as in most others, the sources of those trains which govern us are two – the impressions made upon ourselves, and the trains which we copy from others. Besides the impressions just recounted, if the trains which pass in the minds of those by whom the child is surrounded, and which he is made to conceive by means of their words, and other signs, lead constantly from the idea of command over the wills of other men, as the grand object of desire, to the ideas of pain and terror as the means, the repetition of the copied trains increases the effect of the native impressions, and establishes and confirms the maleficent character. These are the few things we can afford to adduce upon the subject of Domestic Education.

2. In the next place comes that we have denominated TECHNICAL EDUCATION. To this the term Education has been commonly confined; or, rather, the word Education has been used in a sense so unhappily restricted, that it has extended only to a part of that which we call Technical Education. It has not extended to all the arts, but only to those which have been denominated liberal.

The question here occurs – What is the sort of education required for the different classes of society, and what should be the difference in the training provided for each? Before we can treat explicitly of technical education, we must endeavour to show, in what manner, at least, this question ought to be resolved.

There are certain qualities, the possession of which is desirable in all classes. There are certain qualities, the possession of which is desirable in some, not in others. As far as those qualities extend which ought to be common to all, there ought to be a correspondent training for all. It is only in respect to those qualities which are not desirable in all, that a difference in the mode of training is required.

What then are the qualities, the possession of which is desirable in all? They are the qualities which we have already named as chiefly subservient to the happiness of the individual himself, and of other men; Intelligence, Temperance, and Benevolence. It is very evident that these qualities are desirable in all men; and if it were possible to get them all in the highest possible degree in all men, so much the more would human nature be exalted.

The chief difficulty respects Intelligence; for it will be readily allowed, that almost equal care ought to be taken, in all classes, of the trains leading to the settled dispositions which the terms Temperance and Benevolence denote. Benevolence, as we have above described it, can hardly be said to be of more importance to the happiness of man in one class than in another. If we bear in mind, also, the radical meaning of Temperance, that it is the steady habit of resisting a present desire, for the sake of a greater good, we shall readily grant, that it is not less necessary to happiness in one rank of life than in another. It is only necessary to see, that temperance, though always the same disposition, is not always exerted on the same objects, in the different conditions of life. It is no demand of temperance, in the man who can afford it, to deny himself animal food; it may be an act of temperance in the man whose harder circumstances require that he should limit himself to coarser fare. It is also true, that the trains which lead to Temperance and Benevolence may be equally cultivated in all classes. The impressions which persons are made to receive, and the trains of others which they are made to copy, may, with equal certainty, be guided to the generating of those two qualities in all the different classes of society. We deem it unnecessary, (here indeed, it is impossible) to enter into the details of what may be done in the course of technical education, to generate, or to confirm, the dispositions of Temperance and Benevolence. It can be nothing more than the application of the principles which we developed, when we endeavoured to show in what manner the circumstances of domestic education might be employed for generating the trains on which these mental qualities depend.

Technical Education, we shall then consider, as having chiefly to do with *Intelligence*.

The first question, as we have said before, respects what is desirable for all, – the second, what is desirable for each of the several classes. Till recently, it was denied, that intelligence was a desirable quality in the great body of the people; and as intelligence is power, such is an unavoidable opinion in the breasts of those who think that the human race ought to consist of two classes, – one that of the oppressors, another that of the oppressed. The concern which is now felt for the education of the working classes, shows that we have made a great step in knowledge, and in that genuine morality which ever attends it.

The analysis of the ideas decides the whole matter at once. If education be to communicate the art of happiness; and if intelligence consists of two parts, a knowledge of the order of those events of nature on which our pleasures and pains depend, and the sagacity which discovers the best means for the attaining of ends; the question, whether the people should be educated, is the same with the question, whether they should be happy or miserable. The question, whether they should have more or less of intelligence, is merely the question, whether they should have more or less of misery, when happiness might be given in its stead. It has been urged that men are, by daily experience, evinced not to be happy, not to be moral, in proportion to their knowledge. It is a shallow objection. Long ago it was observed by Hume, that knowledge and its accompaniments, morality and happiness, may not be strictly conjoined in every individual, but that they are infallibly so in every age, and in every country. The reason is plain; a natural cause may be hindered of its operation in one particular instance, though in a great variety of instances it is sure to prevail. Besides, there may be a good deal of knowledge in an individual, but not knowledge of the best things; this cannot easily happen in a whole people; neither the whole nor the greater part will miss the right objects of knowledge, when knowledge is generally diffused.

As evidence of the vast progress which we have made in right thinking upon this subject, we cannot help remarking, that even Milton and Locke, though both men of great benevolence toward the larger family of mankind, and both men whose sentiments were democratical, yet seem, in their writings on education, to have had in view no education but that of the *gentleman*. It had not presented itself, even to their minds, that education was a blessing in which the indigent orders could be made to partake.

As we strive for an equal degree of justice, an equal degree of temperance, an equal degree of veracity, in the poor as in the rich, so ought we to strive for an equal degree of intelligence, if there were not a preventing cause. It is absolutely necessary for the existence of the human race, that labour should be performed, that food should be produced, and other things provided, which human welfare requires. A large proportion of mankind is required for this labour. Now, then, in regard to all this portion of mankind, that labours, only such a portion of time can by them be given to the acquisition of intelligence, as can be abstracted from labour. The difference between intelligence and the other qualities desirable in the mind of man, is this, That much of time, exclusively devoted to the fixing of the associations on which the other qualities depend is not necessary; such trains may go on while other things are attended to, and amid the whole of the business of life. The case is to a certain extent, the same with intelligence; but, to a great extent, it is not. Time must be exclusively devoted to the acquisition of it; and there are degrees of command over knowledge to which the whole period of human life is not more than sufficient. There are degrees, therefore, of intelligence, which must be reserved to those who are not obliged to labour.

The question is (and it is a question which none can exceed in importance), What is the degree attainable by the most numerous class? To this we have no doubt, it will, in time, very clearly appear, that a most consolatory answer may be given. We have no doubt it will appear that a very high degree is attainable by them. It is now almost universally acknowledged, that, on all conceivable accounts, it is desirable that the great body of the people should not be wretchedly poor; that when the people are wretchedly poor, all classes are vicious, all are hateful, and all are unhappy. If so far raised above wretched poverty, as to be capable of being virtuous; though it be still necessary for them to earn their bread by the sweat of their brow, they are not bound down to such incessant toil as to have no time for the acquisition of knowledge, and the exercise of intellect. Above all, a certain portion of the first years of life are admirably available to this great end. With a view to the productive powers of their very labour, it is desirable that the animal frame should not be devoted to it before a certain age, before it has approached the point of maturity. This holds in regard to the lower animals; a horse is less valuable, less, in regard to that very labour for which he is valuable at all, if he is forced upon it too soon. There is an actual loss, therefore, even in productive powers, even in good economy, and in the way of health and strength, if the young of the human species are bound close to labour before they are fifteen or sixteen years of age. But if those years are skilfully employed in the acquisition of knowledge, in rendering all those trains habitual on which intelligence depends, it may be easily shown that a very high degree of intellectual acquirements may be gained; that a firm foundation may be laid for a life of mental action, a life of wisdom, and reflection, and ingenuity, even in those by whom the most ordinary labour will fall to be performed. In proof of this, we may state, that certain individuals in London, a few years ago, some of them men of great consideration among their countrymen, devised a plan for filling up those years with useful instruction; a plan which left the elements of hardly any branch of knowledge unprovided for; and at an expense which would exceed the means of no class of a population, raised as much above wretched poverty as all men profess to regard as desirable. Mr. Bentham called this plan of instruction by the Greek name *Chrestomathia*; and developed his own ideas of the objects and mode of instruction, with that depth and comprehension which belong to him, in a work which he published under that name.* Of the practicability of the scheme no competent judge has ever doubted; and the difficulty of collecting funds is the only reason why it has not been demonstrated by experiment, how much of that intelligence which is desirable for all may be communicated to all.†

---

* *Chrestomathia* [= 'useful learning' – Ed.], being a collection of papers, explanatory of the design of an institution proposed to be set on foot, under the name of Chrestomathic day school, &c. By Jeremy Bentham, Esq.

† We mention with extraordinary satisfaction, that an idea of education, hardly less extensive than what is here alluded to, has been adopted by that enlightened and indefatigable class of men, the Baptist Missionaries in India, for the population, poor as well as ignorant, of those extensive and populous regions. A small volume, entitled "*Hints relative to Native Schools, together with the Outline of an Institution for their extension and Management*," was printed at the mission press at Serampore in 1816; and, as it cannot come into the hands of many of our readers, we gladly copy from it the following passage, in hopes that the example may be persuasive with many of our countrymen at home.

"It is true, that when these helps are provided, namely, a correct system of orthography, a sketch of grammar, a simplified system of arithmetic, and an extended vocabulary, little is done beyond laying the foundation. Still, however, this foundation must be laid, if any superstructure of knowledge and virtue be attempted relative to the inhabitants of

Beside the knowledge or faculties, which all classes should possess in common, there are branches of knowledge and art, which they cannot all acquire, and, in respect to which, education must undergo a corresponding variety. The apprenticeships, for example, which youths are accustomed to serve to the useful arts, we regard as a branch of their education. Whether these apprenticeships, as they have hitherto been managed, have been good instruments of education, is a question of importance, about which there is now, among enlightened men, hardly any diversity of opinion. When the legislature undertakes to do for every man, what every man has abundant motives to do for himself, and better means than the

India. Yet, were the plan to stop here, something would have been done. A peasant or an artificer, thus rendered capable of writing as well as reading his own language with propriety, and made acquainted with the principles of arithmetic, would be less liable to become a prey to fraud among his own countrymen; and far better able to claim for himself that protection from oppression which it is the desire of every enlightened government to grant. But the chief advantage derivable from this plan is, its facilitating the reception of ideas which may enlarge and bless the mind in a high degree, – ideas for which India must be indebted to the West, at present the seat of science, and for the communication of which, generations yet unborn, will pour benedictions on the British name.

"1. To this, then, might be added a concise, but perspicuous account of the solar system, preceded by so much of the laws of motion, of attraction, and gravity, as might be necessary to render the solar system plain and intelligible. These ideas, however, should not be communicated in the form of a treatise, but in that of simple axioms, delivered in short and perspicuous sentences. This method comes recommended by several considerations; – it agrees with the mode in which doctrines are communicated in the *Hindoo Shastras,* and is therefore congenial with the ideas of even the learned among them; it would admit of these sentences being written from dictation, and even committed to memory with advantage, as well as of their being easily retained; and, finally, the conciseness of this method would allow of a multitude of truths and facts relative to astronomy, geography, and the principal phenomena of nature, being brought before youth within a very small compass.

"2. This abstract of the solar system might be followed by a compendious view of geography on the same plan – that of comprising every particular in concise but luminous sentences. In this part it would be proper to describe Europe particularly, because of its importance in the present state of the world; and Britain might, with propriety, be allowed to occupy in the compendium, that pre-eminence among the nations which God of Providence has given her.

"3. To these might be added a number of popular truths and facts relative to natural philosophy. In the present improved state of knowledge, a thousand things have been ascertained relative to light, heat, air, water to meteorology, mineralogy, chemistry, and natural history, of which the ancients had but a partial knowledge, and of which the natives of the East have as yet scarcely the faintest idea. These facts, now so clearly ascertained, could be conveyed in a very short compass of language, although the process of reasoning, which enables the mind to account for them, occupies many volumes. A knowledge of the facts themselves, however, would be almost invaluable to legislature; the legislature takes a very unnecessary, commonly a not very innocent trouble. Into the details, however, of the best mode of teaching, to the working people, the arts by which the different commodities useful or agreeable to man are provided, we cannot possibly enter. We must content ourselves with marking it out as a distinct branch of the subject, and an important object of study.

With respect to the education of that class of society who have wealth and time for the acquisition of the highest measure of intelligence, there is one question to which every body must be prepared

the Hindoos, as these facts would rectify and enlarge their ideas of the various objects of nature around them; and while they, in general, delighted as well as informed those who read them, they might inflame a few minds of a superior order with an unquenchable desire to know *why* these things are so, as thus urge them to those studies, which in Europe have led to the discovery of these important facts.

"4. To this view of the solar system of the earth, and the various objects it contains, might, with great advantage, be added such a compendium of history and chronology united, as should bring them acquainted with the state of the world in past ages, and with the principal events which have occurred since the creation of the world. With the creation it should commence, describe the primitive state of man, the entrance of evil, the corruption of the antediluvian age, the flood, and the peopling of the earth anew from one family, in which the compiler should avail himself of all the light thrown on this subject by modern research and investigation; he should particularly notice the nations of the east, incorporating, in their proper place, the best accounts we now have both of India and China. He should go on to notice the call of Abraham, the giving of the decalogue, the gradual revelations of the Scriptures of Truth, the settlement of Greece, its mythology, the Trojan war, the four great monarchies, the advent of the Saviour of men, the persecutions of the Christian church, the rise of Mahometanism, the origin of the papacy, the invention of printing, of gunpowder, and the mariner's compass, the reformation, the discovery of the passage to India by sea, and the various discoveries of modern science. Such a synopsis of history and chronology, composed on the same plan, that of comprising each event in a concise but perspicuous sentence, would exceedingly enlarge their ideas relative to the state of the world, certainly not to the disadvantage of Britain, whom God has now so exalted as to render her almost the arbitress of nations.

"5. Lastly, It would be highly proper to impart to them just ideas of themselves, relative both to body and mind, and to a future state of existence, by what may be termed a Compendium of Ethics and Morality. The complete absence of all just ideas of this kind, is the chief cause of that degradation of public morals so evident in this country.

"These various compendiums, after being written from dictation, in the manner described in the next section, might also furnish matter for reading; and when it is considered that, in addition to the sketch of grammar, the vocabulary, and the system of arithmetic, they include a view of the solar system, a synopsis of geography, a collection of facts relative to natural objects, an abstract of general history, and a compendium of ethics and morality, they will be found to furnish sufficient matter for reading while youth are at school."

Why should not the same idea be pursued in England, and as much knowledge conveyed to the youth of all classes at school, as the knowledge of the age, and the allotted period of schooling will admit?

with an answer. If it be asked, whether, in the constitution of any establishment for the education of this class; call it university, call it college, school, or any thing else; there ought to be a provision for perpetual improvement; a provision to make the institution keep pace with the human mind; or whether, on the other hand, it ought to be so constituted as that there should not only be no provision for, but a strong spirit of resistance to, all improvement, a passion of adherence to whatever was established in a dark age, and a principle of hatred to those by whom improvement should be proposed; all indifferent men will pronounce, that such institution would be a curse rather than a blessing. That he is a *progressive* being is the grand distinction of Man. He is the only progressive being upon this globe. When he is the most rapidly progressive, then he most completely fulfils his destiny. An institution for *education* which is hostile to progression, is, therefore, the most preposterous, and vicious thing, which the mind of man can conceive.

There are several causes which tend to impair the utility of old and opulent establishments for education. Their love of ease makes them love easy things, if they can derive from them as much credit, as they would from others which are more difficult. They endeavour, therefore, to give an artificial value to trifles. Old practices, which have become a hackneyed routine, are commonly easier than improvements; accordingly, they oppose improvements, even when it happens that they have no other interest in the preservation of abuses. Hardly is there a part of Europe in which the universities are not recorded in the annals of education, as the enemies of all innovation. "A peine la compagnie de Jesus," says d'Alembert, "commençait elle à se montrer en France, qu'elle essuya des difficultés surtout firent les plus grands efforts, pour écarter ces nouveaux venus. Les Jesuites s'annonçaient pour enseigner gratuitement, ils comptoient déjà parmi eux des hommes savans et célèbres, supérieures peut être à ceux dont les universités pouvaient se glorifier; l'interêt et la vanité pouvaient donc suffire à leurs adversaires pour chercher à les exclure. On se rappelle les contradictions semblables que les ordres mendians essuyerent de ces mêmes universités quand ils voulurent s'y introduire; contradictions fondées à peu près sur les mêmes motifs." (*Destruction des Jesuites en France.*) The celebrated German philosopher, Wolf, remarks the aversion of the universities to all improvement, as a notorious fact, derived from adequate motives: "Non adeo impune turbare licet scholarium quietem, et docentibus lucrosam, et discentibus jucundam." – (Wolfii *Logica*, Dedic. p. 2.)

But though such and so great are the evil tendencies which are to be guarded against in associated seminaries of education; evil tendencies which are apt to be indefinitely increased, when they are united with an ecclesiastical establishment, because, whatever the vices of the ecclesiastical system, the universities have in that case an interest to bend the whole of their force to the support of those vices, and to that end to vitiate the human mind, which can only be rendered the friend of abuses in proportion as it is vitiated intellectually, or morally, or both; it must, notwithstanding, be confessed, that there are great advantages in putting it in the power of the youth to obtain all the branches of their education in one place; even in assembling a certain number of them together, when the principle of emulation acts with powerful effect; and in carrying on the complicated process according to a regular plan, under a certain degree of discipline, and with the powerful spur of publicity. All this ought not to be rashly sacrificed; nor does there appear to be any insuperable difficulty, in devising a plan for the attainment of all those advantages, without the evils which have more or less adhered to all the collegiate establishments which Europe has yet enjoyed.

After the consideration of these questions, we ought next to describe, and prove by analysis, the exercises which would be most conducive in forming those virtues which we include under the name of intelligence. But it is very evident, that this is a matter of detail far too extensive for so limited a design as ours. And though, in common language, Education means hardly any thing more than making the youth perform those exercises; and a treatise on Education means little more than an account of them; we must content ourselves with marking the place which the inquiry would occupy in a complete system, and proceed to offer a few remarks on the two remaining branches of the subject, *Social Education*, and *Political Education*.

The branches of moral education, heretofore spoken of, operate upon the individual in the first period of life, and when he is not as yet his own master. The two just now mentioned operate upon the whole period of life, but more directly and powerfully after the technical education is at an end, and the youth is launched into the world under his own control.

3. SOCIAL EDUCATION is that in which Society is the Institutor.

That the Society in which an individual moves produces great effects upon his mode of thinking and acting, every body knows by indubitable experience. The object is, to ascertain the extent of this influence, the mode in which it is brought about, and hence the means of making it operate in a good, rather than an evil direction.

The force of this influence springs from two sources: the principle of imitation; and the power of the society over our happiness and misery.

We have already shown, that when, by means of words and other signs of what is passing in the minds of other men, we are made to conceive, step by step, the trains which are governing them, those trains, by repetition, become habitual to our own minds, and exert the same influence over us as those which arise from our own impressions. It is very evident, that those trains which are most habitually passing in the minds of all those individuals by whom we are surrounded, must be made to pass with extraordinary frequency through our own minds, and must, unless where extraordinary means are used to prevent them from producing their natural effect, engross to a proportional degree the dominion of our minds. With this slight indication of this source of the power which society usurps over our minds, that is, of the share which it has in our education, we must content ourselves, and pass to the next.

Nothing is more remarkable in human nature, than the intense desire which we feel of the favourable regards of mankind. Few men could bear to live under an exclusion from the breast of every human being. It is astonishing how great a portion of all the actions of men are directed to these favourable regards, and to no other object. The greatest princes, the most despotical masters of human destiny, when asked what they aim at by their wars and conquests, would answer, if sincere, as Frederic of Prussia answered, *pour faire parler de soi*; to occupy a large space in the admiration of mankind. What are the ordinary pursuits of wealth and of power, which kindle to such a height the ardour of mankind? Not the mere love of eating and of drinking, or all the physical objects together, which wealth can purchase or power command. With these every man is in the long run speedily satisfied. It is the easy command, which those advantages procure over the favourable regards of society, – it is this which renders the desire of wealth unbounded, and gives it that irresistible influence which it possesses in directing the human mind.

Whatever, then, are the trains of thought, whatever is the course of action which most strongly recommends us to the favourable regards of those among whom we live, these we feel the strongest motive to cultivate and display; whatever trains of thought and course of action expose us to their unfavourable regards, these we feel the strongest motives to avoid. These inducements, operating upon us continually, have an irresistible influence in creating habits, and in moulding, that is, educating us, into a character conformable to the society in which we move. This is the general principle; it might be illustrated in detail by many of the most interesting and instructive phenomena of human life; it is an illustration, however, which we cannot pursue.

To what extent the habits and character, which those influences tend to produce, may engross the man, will no doubt depend, to a certain degree, upon the powers of the domestic and technical education which he has undergone. We may conceive that certain trains might, by the skilful employment of the early years, be rendered so habitual as to be uncontrollable by any habits which the subsequent period of life could induce, and that those trains might be the decisive ones, on which intelligent and moral conduct depends. The influence of a vicious and ignorant society would in this case be greatly reduced; but still, the actual rewards and punishments which society has to bestow, upon those who please, and those who displease it; the good and evil, which it gives, or withholds, are so great, that to adopt the opinions which it approves, to perform the acts which it admires, to acquire the character, in short, which it "delighteth to honour," can seldom fail to be the leading object of those of whom it is composed. And as this potent influence operates upon those who conduct both the domestic education and the technical, it is next to impossible that the trains which are generated, even during the time of their operation, should not fall in with, instead of counteracting, the trains which the social education produces; it is next to impossible, therefore, that the whole man should not take the shape which that influence is calculated to impress upon him.

4. The POLITICAL EDUCATION is the last, which we have undertaken to notice, of the agents employed in forming the character of man. The importance of this subject has not escaped observation. Some writers have treated of it in a comprehensive and systematical manner. And a still greater number have illustrated it by occasional

and striking remarks. It is, nevertheless, true, that the full and perfect exposition of it yet remains to be made.

The Political Education is like the key-stone of the arch; the strength of the whole depends upon it. We have seen that the strength of the Domestic and the Technical Education depends almost entirely upon the Social. Now it is certain, that the nature of the Social depends almost entirely upon the Political; and the most important part of the Physical (that which operates with greatest force upon the greatest number, the state of aliment and labour of the lower classes), is, in the long-run, determined by the action of the political machine. The play, therefore, of the political machine acts immediately upon the mind, and with extraordinary power; but this is not all; it also acts upon almost every thing else by which the character of the mind is apt to be formed.

It is a common observation, that such as is the direction given to the desires and passions of men, such is the character of the men. The direction is given to the desires and passions of men by one thing, and one alone; the means by which the grand objects of desire may be attained. Now this is certain, that the means by which the grand objects of desire may be attained, depend almost wholly upon the political machine. When the political machine is such, that the grand objects of desire are seen to be the natural prizes of great and virtuous conduct – of high services to mankind, and of the generous and amiable sentiments from which great endeavours in the service of mankind naturally proceed – it is natural to see diffused among mankind a generous ardour in the acquisition of all those admirable qualities which prepare a man for admirable actions; great intelligence, perfect self-command, and over-ruling benevolence. When the political machine is such that the grand objects of desire are seen to be the reward, not of virtue, not of talent, but of subservience to the will, and command over the affections of the ruling few; interest with the *man above* to be the only sure means to the next step in wealth, or power or consideration, and so on; the means of pleasing the man above become, in that case, the great object of pursuit. And as the favours of the man above are necessarily limited – as some, therefore, of the candidates for his favour can only obtain the objects of their desire by disappointing others – the arts of supplanting rise into importance; and the whole of that tribe of faculties denoted by the words intrigue, flattery, back-biting, treachery, &c., are the fruitful offspring of that political education which government, where the interests of the subject many are but a secondary object, cannot fail to produce.

PRISONS AND PRISON DISCIPLINE.

I.
Introduction – Ends of Imprisonment.

The arrangements, necessary to adapt prisons to the ends for which they are designed, seem to require little more than the exercise of good sense; and yet the manner in which the practice of the world blunders on from one absurdity, and very often from one atrocity, to another, shows pretty distinctly, how little public affairs have hitherto had the benefit of that practical faculty, or of any thing that resembles it.

Ends of Imprisonment.

Prisons have been applied to three purposes; 1*st*, That of safe-custody; 2*dly*, That of punishment; 3*dly*, That of reformation.

It is very evident, that each of these purposes requires an arrangement of means peculiar to itself.

Though each requires a combination of means peculiar to itself, it does not follow that of the means required for each a portion may not be the same in all. Every body will acknowledge that this is the case.

The means of safe-custody, for instance, are required for those who are imprisoned in order to be punished and those who are imprisoned in order that they may be reformed, as well as for those who are imprisoned to the sole end of their being made present at a particular time and place.

The arrangements, then, for safe-custody, form a basis, on which every combination of means for attaining any of the other ends of imprisonment must always be erected. Other means for the attainment of those ends are to be considered as accessions to those required for the first.

It is a corollary from this position, that the same house may, at one and the same time, be employed for all three purposes. Those properties in the building which make it fittest, at the least expence, for safe-custody, make it fittest also for purposes, either of punishment, or of reformation. This will be rendered abundantly apparent in the sequel; and is nearly proved by the single circumstance, that the means of punishment and reformation are only additions to those of safe-custody. If the arrangements needed, for those who are to be punished and for those who are to be reformed, interfere not with one another, or with those needed on account of the persons in safe custody merely, the truth of the corollary is indisputable, for nobody will deny that, in point of economy, there must be very great advantage.

II.
Means of Safe-custody.

I. We shall consider, first of all, what is the best combination of means for safe-custody. Dungeons and fetters are the expedient of a barbarous age. In respect of prisons, as of every thing which comes within the precincts of law, the expedients of a barbarous age are, with great industry, retained in those which are civilized. They are, indeed, preserved with a success which, if it were not experienced, would be altogether incredible. As the expedients of a barbarous age still exist in many other arrangements for the purpose of law, so it is but of yesterday that the prisons of our forefathers have been regarded as fit for reform; or that the means which those sages in their ancestorial wisdom devised for attaining the ends of imprisonment were supposed capable of being altered for the better, by their less instructed sons.

It is at least, however, allowed, that inspection is a means for safe custody, which renders unnecessary all but very ordinary means of any other description. Thus, so long as a man is, and knows that he is, under the eyes of persons able and willing to prevent him, there is very little danger of his making an attempt, which he sees would be vain, to effect a breach in the wall, or force open the door, of his cell. Any great strength, therefore, in such wall or door, or fetters upon any part of his body, are wholly unnecessary, since the attempts are sure of not being made, or of being instantly frustrated.

The plan of a prison, in which the power of inspection is rendered so complete, that the prisoner may be, and cannot know but that he is, under the eyes of his keepers, every moment of his time, a plan which we owe to General Bentham,* so universally known for his mechanical genius, is described by his brother, in his work entitled *Panopticon*, or *Inspection House*; where also a system of management is delineated, and its principles are expounded, so perfectly, that they who proceed in this road, with the principle of utility before them, can do little else than travel in his steps.

An idea of the contrivance may be conveyed in a few words. It is a circular building, of the width of a cell, and of any height; carried round a space, which remains vacant in the middle. The cells are all open inwards, having an iron grating instead of a wall, and, of course, are visible in every part to an eye properly placed in the vacant space. A narrow tower rises in the middle of that space, called the inspection tower, which serves for the residence of the keepers, and in which, by means of windows and blinds, they can see without being seen; the cells, by lights properly disposed, being capable of being rendered as visible by night as by day.

Thus, we have provision for safe custody; and along with it, five other important purposes are gained. First of all, there is great economy; the vast expense of thick, impenetrable walls, being rendered unnecessary. Secondly, All pretence for subjecting prisoners to the torture and degradation of irons is taken away. Thirdly, No misbehaviour of the prisoners can elude observation, and instant correction. Fourthly, No negligence, or corruption, or cruelty, on the part of the subordinate agents in the prison, can escape the view of their principals. And, Fifthly, No misconduct towards the prisoners, on the part of their principals, can remain unknown to the public, who may obtain a regulated admittance into the inspection tower, and regulated communication with the prisoners.

* [Samuel Bentham, Jeremy Bentham's brother. – Ed.]

The persons who are liable to be in prison, for safe-custody merely, are of three classes. First, Persons apprehended, and about to be put on their trial, for the commission of a crime: Secondly, Persons convicted of a crime, and about to receive their punishment: and, Thirdly, Debtors.

Under a good system of law, very little provision would need to be made for these cases. It is one of the essential properties of a good system of law to permit as little time as possible to intervene between the apprehension and trial, and between the conviction and punishment, of a person for a crime. There would never, therefore, be many such persons in any prison at a time. And under a good system of law, there never would be any body in a prison on account of debt.* This is mentioned merely to show how little, under a good system of law, the apparatus and expense of a separate prison, for this set of cases, would be wanted.

These persons being inmates of a prison, for insuring their presence merely, the question is, What treatment they ought to receive?

Persons in prison before trial, and debtors, are persons of whom nothing is certainly known, but that they are unfortunate. They are, therefore, entitled to all the benevolence which is due to the unfortunate.

What is done for them in a prison must, however, be done at the expense of the community, that is, by sacrifices demanded of those who are not in prison; and those sacrifices ought, undoubtedly, to be the smallest possible. The question is, therefore, to be settled by a compromise between the principle of benevolence, and the principle of economy.

The principle of benevolence undoubtedly requires that the health of the prisoners should not be impaired; for this, importing the premature loss of life, is in reality the punishment of death, inflicted upon those to whom no punishment is due.

That health may not be impaired, three things are indispensable: – 1. A wholesome apartment; 2. A sufficiency of wholesome food; 3. Sufficient clothing.

---

* If fraud were committed in contracting the debt, or if the property of others obtained by loan, had been dishonestly spent, or dishonestly risked, such fraud, or dishonesty, being crimes, not a debt, might justly subject a man to imprisonment, or any other sort of due punishment.

The principle of economy, with equal certainty, exacts, that all those should be of the cheapest kind.

All this is abundantly clear. It is equally clear, that, with respect to those who are in prison for safe custody merely, the principle of benevolence requires, and the principle of economy does not forbid, that they should be free to use any indulgence, which costs nothing, or which they provide for themselves; and that no farther restraint should be placed upon their liberty than what the custody of their persons, and the rule of economy, which prescribes the limits and accommodations of the place, may demand.

Few words will be necessary to show what is appropriate to the case of the man, who is in prison during the interval between his sentence and his punishment.

By the supposition, in this case, his punishment is something distinct from his imprisonment; because, if not, it is a case which comes under another head, namely, that of persons who are in prison for the sake of punishment; and will be fully considered in another part of this discourse.

If he is in prison for detention merely, his punishment, as meted out and fixed by the judge, being something wholly separate, every particle of hardship imposed upon him, not necessary for this detention, is without law, and contrary to law; is as much injustice and a crime, when inflicted upon him, as if inflicted upon any other member of the community. The same considerations, which, as we found above, ought to regulate the imprisonment of debtors, and persons in custody before trial, namely, the compromise between the principle of benevolence and the principle of economy; apply, without the smallest difference, to the case of persons who, during the interval between their sentence and its execution, are in prison for the mere purpose of preventing their escape.

We foresee a difficulty, or rather an objection, for there is really no difficulty in the case.

Persons come into prisons, who have been accustomed, in the preceding part of their lives, to all degrees of delicate and indulgent living, to whom, therefore, the hard fare prescribed by the principle of economy will occasion very different degrees of uneasiness.

Such persons, when in prison for safe-custody merely (what is required when persons are in prison for punishment, or for reformation, will be seen hereafter), may be allowed to make use of any funds, which they may possess, for procuring to themselves all unexceptionable indulgences. They may be also allowed the exercise of any lucrative art, consistent with the nature of the prison, for procuring to themselves the means of such indulgence. This the principle of benevolence dictates, and there is nothing in the principle of economy which forbids it.

We shall be told, however, that there are persons, who have been accustomed to a delicate mode of living, and who come into prison without the command of any funds, or the knowledge of any art, by which they may soften the hardship of their lot: and we shall be asked what is the course which our philosophy recommends for the treatment of them? The course which it recommends is very clear. Such persons are paupers, and whatsoever treatment is fit for paupers, of the description to which they belong, is fit also for them. If there are any funds, to which as paupers they can apply, the application should be open to them. If there is not any, nor any person to whose benevolence they can resort, the effects of such a destitute situation must be sustained, the same way in a prison, as they must be, when any person falls into it, out of a prison.

III.
Means of Punishment.

II. Having stated what appears to us necessary for illustrating the principles which ought to regulate the imprisonment of those, in respect to whom safe-custody is the end in view, we come, in the next place, to the case of those, in respect to whom, in addition to safe-custody, punishment is to be effected through the same medium.

This subject we shall unfortunately be under the necessity of treating superficially; because, in order to explain it fully, we ought to have before us the whole doctrine of punishment; and, for this purpose, a development, too extensive for the present occasion, would be required.

This we may assume as an indisputable principle; That whatever punishment is to be inflicted, should be determined by the judge, and by him alone, that it should be determined by its adaptation to the crime; and that it should not be competent to those to whom the execution of the sentence of the judge is entrusted, either to go beyond the line which he has drawn, or to fall short of it.

We have already established, on what seemed sufficient reasons, that for persons, confined, on account of safe-custody merely, the cheapest accommodation, not importing injury to health, in respect to apartment, food, and clothing, should alone be provided at the public expense.

Unless in the case of those whom the judge might condemn to lose a portion of their health, by the sufferings of an unwholesome prison, unwholesome food, or improper clothing, this accommodation ought to be afforded, even to those who are placed in prisons for the sake of punishment. And if it should be thought that the loss of health never can be a proper punishment, if it has never been regarded as such even by savages, and is repudiated by every principle of reason, then it follows, that the accommodations which we have described in the former part of this discourse, as required in the case of prisoners detained for safe-custody, are required in the case of prisoners of every description.

This is a basis, therefore, upon which every thing is to rest. In every rational system of prison management, this is an essential condition. We are now to see in what manner, upon this footing, punishment, by means of imprisonment, is to be effected.

One mode is sufficiently obvious and sufficiently known. The punishment may be rendered more or less severe by its duration. Want of liberty is, in almost all cases, a source of uneasiness; want of liberty, added to the denial of all pleasures of sense, can hardly ever fail to be a source of great uneasiness. A long imprisonment, there-fore, with the cheapest accommodation not importing injury to health, must be a severe punishment. This, it is evident, may be graduated to more or less of severity, not only by degrees of time, but of the use of such means as the prisoner might command for procuring accom-modations and indulgences.

To this imprisonment may be added solitude. But though we men-tion this, as a practicable addition to simple imprisonment, it is well known how little, unless for short periods, and on very particular occasions, it is to be recommended.

The modes, which lately have been most in repute, of adding to the severity of simple imprisonment, for the purpose of punishment, have

been two; 1st, Hard labour; and 2dly, Bad prisons, with bad management in those prisons.

1. The species of labour which appears to have obtained the preference is that of treading in a wheel.

If a criminal in a prison is ever to be let out again, and to mix in
society, it is desirable that nothing should be done, and least of all
done on purpose, to make him a worse member of society than when
he went in. There cannot be a worse quality of a punishment, than
that it has a tendency to corrupt and deteriorate the individual on
whom it is inflicted; unless, indeed, he is a prisoner for life; in that
case, people of a certain temper might say, that making worse his
disposition is a matter of little importance; and to them we have no
time to make any reply.

Most of those persons who come into prison as criminals, are bad,
because they have hated labour, and have had recourse to other
means than their industry of attaining the supply of their wants and
the gratification of their desires. People of industry, people who love
labour, seldom become the criminal inmates of a prison.

One thing, however, is pretty certain, that men seldom become in
love with their punishments. If the grand cause of the crimes which
have brought a man to punishment is his not having a love but hatred
of labour; to make labour his punishment, is only to make him hate it
the more. If the more a man hates labour, the more he is likely to act
as a bad member of society; to punish a man with labour, and then to
turn him out upon society, is a course of legislation which savours not
of the highest wisdom.

Besides, in treating labour as an instrument of punishment, call it
hard labour, if you will, what sort of a lesson do you teach to the
industrious and laborious class, who form the great body of your
people? to those whose lot is labour, whose lot is hard labour, harder
than any which it is in your power to impose? What compulsory labour
is so hard as many species of voluntary labour?

As an instrument of reformation, labour, as we shall presently see,
is invaluable. As an instrument of punishment, hardly any thing can
be conceived more exceptionable. That which is the source of all that
mankind enjoy, that which is the foundation of every virtue in the
most numerous class of the community, would you stamp with
ignominy and dishonour, by inflicting it as a punishment upon the
worst and basest of your people? Is this your expedient for rendering

it, what every wise legislator would wish to render it, honourable, and thence desirable?

There are other objections, perfectly decisive, against labour as a punishment. It operates with more inequality than almost any other instrument of punishment that ever has been invented. The same degree of labour would kill one man, that to another would be only a pastime. From this source we may apprehend the most horrid abuses, in the continuance of those tread-mills. We may be very sure, that the most atrocious cruelty will often be inflicted upon those who, with strength below the average standard, are placed in those penal engines; while, in the case of those whose strength is much above that standard, they will hardly operate as a punishment at all.

It is impossible that the judge can measure out this punishment; because the judge has not the means of ascertaining the relative strength of the parties who come before him. It must, therefore, be left to the jailor. The jailor, not the judge, will mete out and determine the degree of suffering which each individual is to undergo. The jailor, not the judge, is the man who adapts the punishment to the crime. Hence one of the stains which mark a careless and stupid legislation.

It is a far inferior, though still no inconsiderable proof of a blundering legislation, that the labour, if labour it must be, is not of such a sort as to be useful. The turning of a wheel, by human labour, when so many better means of turning it are possessed in abundance is destitute of even this recommendation. It stands upon a similar footing with the contrivance of the jailor, whom Mr. Bentham celebrates: "We are told somewhere," he says, "towards the close of Sully's *Memoirs*, that for some time after the decease of that great and honest minister, certain high mounts were to be seen at no great distance from his house. These mounts were so many monuments of his charity. The poor in his neighbourhood happened to have industry to spare, and the best employment he could find for it was, to remove dirt from the place where it lay to another where it was of no use. By the mere force of innate genius, and without having ever put himself to school to learn economy of a French minister, a plain English jailor, whom Howard met with, was seen practising this revived species of pyramid architecture in miniature. He had got a parcel of stones together, shot them down at one end of his yard, and set the prisoners to bring them to the other; the task achieved, Now, says he, you may fetch them back again. Being asked what was the object of this industry, his answer was, 'To plague the prisoners.'" In a note on this passage, Mr. Bentham says, "I beg the jailor's pardon; what is above was from memory; his contrivance was the setting them to saw wood with a blunt saw, made blunt on purpose. The removers of mounts were a committee of justices."

2. Bad prisons, and bad management in those prisons, is a mode of punishment, the recommendation of which has lately been revived, after we might have hoped that, in this country at least, it was exploded for ever. The language of such recommendation has, on several recent occasions, been heard in Parliament; and an article on Prison Discipline, which lately appeared in the *Edinburgh Review*, cannot, if the writer is to be considered as speaking in earnest (which, perhaps, may be doubted), be interpreted in any other sense. Even the Committee of the Society for the Improvement of Prison Discipline have not been able to withstand the force of what they may have supposed to be fashionable doctrine. In their *Fourth Report*, lately published, which we are sorry to say evinces more of good intention than of enlightened views for its guidance, they say, "No charge can be more mistaken and unfounded, than that the plans recommended by this institution are calculated to introduce comfort into gaols. The committee are of opinion, and have always contended, that severe punishment must form the basis of an effective system of prison discipline," thereby confounding two things, punishment, and prison discipline; things totally distinct; and between which, it is of so much importance to preserve the distinction, that without preserving it not a rational idea can be entertained about either.

No doubt crimes must be punished. Who needs instruction upon that head? But when the judge has prescribed, that, in a particular way, which he points out, a particular measure of pain shall be inflicted upon an individual; and when the individual is taken, and made to sustain the operations through which the pain is generated; what has this to do with the discipline of the prison? It is an act or series of acts, *sui generis*; acts not forming any part of the ordinary course of prison management; acts which would not have taken place, which ought not to have taken place, if the judge had not commanded them, and which were performed solely and exclusively in obedience to his commandment. This is the nature of punishment – other punishment than this there ought to be none.

The committee would make severe punishment the basis of prison discipline! What business have the committee with punishment? The assigning of punishment the legislature have given to other and fitter hands; to those who take cognizance of the offence, and alone ought to measure the punishment. Saying they would make punishment the basis of prison discipline, what do they intend by this ill-contrived expression? Do they mean, that their jailor shall hold the scales, and weigh out the proper quantity? If not, how are they to be understood? for if not the jailor but the judge is to weigh, and the jailor is to do nothing but punctually carry the prescription of the judge into execution, then is punishment in no proper sense of the word, any part of prison discipline. It is a separate operation, performed on a particular occasion, because prescribed by the judge, and in the exact manner in which the judge has prescribed it. If it is, on the other hand, a part of prison discipline, then all the horrid consequences, inseparable from making the jailor the judge and meter of punishment, present themselves to the imagination; and he who can endure to look at them may dwell upon the picture of a prison, wherein the poor will not be more comfortable than at home, nor by the charms of imprisonment enticed to the commission of crimes.

Nothing can more clearly indicate that vulgar state of mind, which consists in confusion of ideas, than the vague language which we hear about the necessity of making prisons the seats of wretchedness, that crimes, they say, may not receive encouragement.

We have already seen, that, unless it is part of a man's punishment, expressly ordained, that he shall lose a portion of his health; that is, that his life shall be cut short; that is, that along with a portion of torture, he shall receive a capital punishment; a wholesome apartment, a sufficiency of wholesome food, proper clothing, all of the cheapest kind, must be provided for every body. When people talk about making prisons seats of wretchedness, do they mean something worse than this?

Many of them will no doubt answer; Yes, we mean hard labour in addition. We ask again, Do you mean hard labour, according to the prescription of the judge, or without the prescription of the judge? If according to the prescription of the judge, the case is the same with that which we have previously examined. This instrument of punishment is exceptionable, only because it is a bad instrument.

The whole matter evidently comes to this. If more wretchedness is desired than what is implied in confinement under the worst accommodation which the preservation of health admits, it must be meted out, either at the pleasure of the jailor, or the pleasure of the judge. The writers in the *Edinburgh Review*, and the Committee of the Society for the Improvement of Prison Discipline, speak as if they had never reflected upon the difference.

We do not mean to bestow a word upon that theory, which, for the prevention of offences, would make prisons scenes of wretchedness at the pleasure of the jailor.

The only question which can deserve a solution is, what mode of inflicting evil in a gaol can the judge make use for best attaining the ends of punishment? The answer is not difficult. Unless, where that course of reformatory discipline, which we shall delineate under the next head, suffices; and we allow, that, though it may be made to involve no small degree of punishment, there are cases in which it would not suffice; it will certainly appear, that prisons are not the best instruments of punishment.

A single consideration suffices for the proof of this proposition. Punishment in a prison loses the grand requisite of a punishment, that of engendering the greatest quantity of terror in others, by the smallest quantity of suffering in the victim. The principal, perhaps the sole end of punishment, is, to restrain by the example; because, with respect to the individual whom you have got, if you think society in any danger from him, you can keep him in sight, and no more is required. Yet, the language we hear about the tread-mill, and hear from mouths of high persons, implies, that hardly any thing more is in their minds, than the effect upon the individual sufferers. "Nothing finer than the tread-mill; a fellow who has been in the tread-mill never comes back again." Be it so, but by your leave, this is a very insignificant part of the question.

The choice of expedients, for obtaining the punishment best adapted to the several cases for which a course of reformatory discipline does not suffice, belongs to another head of inquiry, and must, for the present purpose, be regarded as determined. All that it is necessary for us to show here is, that a prison is not the proper scene for it, nor the instruments of a prison the proper instruments. To render a punishment the most efficacious in accomplishing the great end of punishment, it must be a punishment calculated to make the strongest impression upon the senses, and, through the senses, upon the imagination, of the public at large; more especially of that part of the public who lie under the strongest temptations to the commission of similar crimes. But the punishments inflicted in a prison are with-drawn from the senses of the public, and seem as if they were intended to make the smallest possible, not the greatest possible, impression upon the imaginations of those who are to be deterred from crime. They are defective, therefore, in the most essential quality of a punishment, and can always be supplied by better means of attaining the same end.

The proper idea of a prison is that of a place of custody, and that alone. This idea ought to be clearly, and distinctly, and steadily preserved in the mind, in all disquisitions respecting prison discipline. Punishment and reformatory discipline may be annexed to safe custody; and in as far as they consist of a series of operations, requir-ing time for their performance, it is essential to them. As reformatory discipline consists wholly in such a series, imprisonment is a necess-ary condition of it. Since many, also, of the best kinds of punishment are not such as can be executed all at once, but require a period of time, imprisonment is equally necessary for these punishments. But though you must have safe-custody to enable you to execute certain punishments, and also to enable you to carry into effect a course of reformatory discipline, safe-custody is not the same thing with punishment, nor the same thing with reformatory discipline; and no conclusions can be depended upon, in which ideas so distinct are confounded.

IV.
Reformatory Discipline.

III. Having thus considered prisons, as instruments of safe-custody, and as instruments of punishment; two of the purposes to which they have been applied as means; it remains, that we consider them, as instruments of reformatory discipline, the third of the purposes to which they have been applied.

It is necessary, first of all, to state a clear idea of reformatory discipline.

When offences, against which it is necessary that society should have protection, are committed, it is desirable that the punishment of the offender should have three properties; 1*st*, That it should deter all other persons from committing a similar offence, which is its most important property. 2*dly*, That it should have the effect of deterring the man himself from a repetition of the offence. 3*dly*, That it should have the effect of removing his former bad habits, and planting useful habits in their stead. It is this last property which is sought to be communicated to his punishment by reformatory discipline.

As the creating and destroying of habits is the work of time, and as safe-custody, and restraints from all indulgences, except under certain conditions, is necessary to reformatory discipline, whatever punishment is involved in such protracted coercion, is a necessary part of reformatory discipline.

What is desired is, to create a habit of doing useful acts, break the habit of doing hurtful acts. To accomplish this, means must be obtained of making the individual in question perform certain acts, abstain from the performance of certain other acts.

The means to be employed for producing performance cannot be of more than two sorts; the pleasurable, and the painful. A man may be induced to perform certain acts, either by punishment, or reward. He may be made to abstain from performing certain acts by an additional means, by withholding the power of performing them.

The latter is the means chiefly applicable for preventing the performance of hurtful acts in prisons; not only crimes, but acts of intemperance, gaming, or any others, the tendency of which is towards crimes. As this is nearly the universal practice, the reasons of it must be so generally known, as not to need repetition.

The inquiry which chiefly calls for our attention is, What are the best means of producing the performance of those acts, the habit of performing which we desire to render so perfect, that it may be relied upon for the effect, even in a state of freedom?

The persons on whom reformatory discipline is intended to operate, belong to the class of those who depend upon their industry for their support. So nearly, at least, do they belong to this class exclusively, that the immaterial exceptions may, in this general inquiry, be omitted.

The necessary foundation, in the case of such persons, not only for all virtues, but for abstinence from crime, is the habit of performing some one of those series of acts, which are denominated lawful industry, and for which the performers obtain payment or reward.

Labour, therefore, in some of its useful branches, is to be regarded as the foundation of all reformatory discipline. But as the object of this discipline is to train the man to love, not to hate labour, we must not render the labour in such a case any part of his punishment. The labour must, for this important purpose, be a source of pleasure, not of pain.

The way in which labour becomes agreeable to men out of prison, is the way in which it can be made agreeable to them in a prison; and there is no other. Advantages must accrue from the performing of it.

The way of attaching to it advantages the most intensely persuasive, in a reformatory prison or penitentiary, is exceedingly obvious.

There, it is easy to prevent the attaining of any pleasure, except through the medium of labour.

What is provided in the prison, according to the principles already explained, is lodging, food, and clothing, all of the very cheapest kind not producing injury to health. In the monotony of a prison, there is no one who will not intensely desire pleasure in addition to this.

In the sentence of a criminal, who is subjected to reformatory discipline, it may, and as often as the case requires, it ought, to be rendered a part, that he shall not be permitted to make any additions to this hard fare from any source belonging either to himself or others, except his labour; but that what he earns by his labour he may, in a certain way, lay out to procure to himself better food, or any other indulgence (certain hurtful ones excepted) which he may desire. Few cases, indeed, will be found in which this simple contrivance will not produce steadiness of application.

We have now then attained what is of principal importance. For if we have got the inmates of a prison to labour steadily in some useful branch of industry, to look to labour as the great or only source of their enjoyments, and to form habits of so doing, sufficiently confirmed to be depended upon for governing their conduct in a state of freedom, we have prepared them for being useful members of society, and our purpose is accomplished.

Here, then, comes the question. By what arrangements, in detail, can the business of confining, maintaining, and setting offenders to work, be most advantageously performed?

In other words, In what hands should the government of penitentiaries be placed, and under what rules should it be ordained for them to act?

It is an universal axiom in morals, that no security is equally to be depended upon for any desirable result, as the interest of those upon whom its accomplishment depends. If, in devolving upon man the task of bringing about a particular end, we make it his interest to bring it about in the best possible manner, especially if we make it his interest in any high degree, we can hardly be disappointed in counting upon his most strenuous exertions. On the other hand, if he has no interest, or a very inconsiderable interest, in the end which he is intrusted to bring about; if little cognizance will be taken of his proceedings, whether good or bad; if to attend to the business would be exceedingly troublesome, to neglect it will produce little inconvenience; we may be very sure that, by a great majority of men, the business of the task devolved upon them will be very imperfectly performed. If they can make a profit out of oppression, or if, as is the case to so great a degree in prisons, they can consult their ease by imposing additional and mischievous restraints upon the prisoners, their interests are strongly set against their duties, and ill conduct is still more perfectly secured.

This last, how deplorable soever the confession, is the state of management of all British prisons, with hardly any exception. There is a jailor, who receives a salary and power; and is told to manage the prison well; and there is a number of justices, that is, gentlemen of the neighbourhood, who obtain not a little power, and a great deal of praise, for undertaking to do certain public duties of a local nature, with little interest in doing them well, and no little interest in doing them in many respects exceedingly ill, who have the charge of looking after him. Varieties we cannot afford to particularize. This is the general description.

The management, then, of the prison, is the joint concern of the jailor and the justices, or magistrates, including sheriffs, who, jointly or severally, have no such interest, as can be expected generally to produce any considerable effect, in any thing more than such a kind of management as will not excite attention and indignation by its badness. All the degrees of bad management, which are within those limits, they, having little or no interest to prevent, have abundant interest to permit.

It is surely not necessary, that we should go far into the detail of this case, to show the causes which it places in operation, and their natural effects.

First of all, it is sufficiently evident, that the jailor has an interest in obtaining his salary, and other emoluments, with as little trouble to himself as possible.

It is not less evident, that the magistrates have an interest in getting the power and credit, attached to their office, with as little trouble to themselves as possible.

This is enough. The book of human nature is clear upon the subject. This principle, at uncontrolled work in a prison, is perfectly sufficient to generate all the evils which those abodes of misery can be made to contain.

It is undeniable, that so far as those, who thus have the super-intendence of jailors, are disposed to consult their ease, and to per-form negligently a troublesome duty, which they may perform well or ill just as they please, so far they will be indisposed to listen to any complaints against the jailor. It saves them a good deal of trouble to confide in the jailor. They speedily come, therefore, to look upon confidence in the jailor, and to speak of it, as a good thing, a duty. "Has not the jailor been most carefully and judiciously selected for his office, by wise and good men? (viz. ourselves). Would it not be an injury to a man of his character to distrust him? And to distrust him – for what? For the complaints of prisoners. But prisoners are always complaining, always giving trouble. Jailors are a good set of men. Prisoners are a bad set of men; especially complaining prisoners. They are the very worst kind of men – they are, therefore, to be silenced; and it is often very difficult to silence them; nothing but harsh measures will do it; when harsh measures, however, are absolutely necessary, it is the duty of jailors to use them, and the duty of magistrates to protect such men in the discharge of so important a duty."

Such are the feelings and conclusions which are undeniably prompt-ed, by the mere love of ease, in the bosoms of such men as English magistrates.

So far as the magistrates consult their ease (men generally do consult their ease when they have not a preponderating motive to the contrary), the jailor is at liberty to consult his ease.

In the jailor's consulting his ease, every thing that is horrid in a prison finds its producing cause.

What the jailor has chiefly to guard against is, the escape of his prisoners, because that is a result which cannot be hidden, and will not escape animadversion. But the love of ease prompts him to take the easiest means for this purpose, locking up in dungeons, loading with irons, and prohibiting communication from without: in other words, all the measures which are the most tormenting to the prisoner. If the prisoner, confiding in his ingenuity, or his strength, makes any attempts to free himself from this misery, by escaping, the disturbance which is thus given to the ease of the jailor is a cause of pain, proportional to the love with which he cherishes his ease; this pain, excites resentment, resentment calls for vengeance, and the prisoner is cruelly punished. The demon despotism reigns in his most terrific form.

This is only one half of the evil. The servants of the jailor, the turn-keys, as they are called, and others who wait upon the prisoners, are as fond of their ease as the jailor is of his. If the jailor has not adequate motives to make him take care that the business of the prison is well done, he will repose the same confidence in his servants, which the magistrates so liberally exercise towards him. He will leave them to indulge their ease, as he could not do otherwise without disturbing his own.

From the servants of the prison indulging their ease, neglect of the prisoners is the immediate and unavoidable consequence. From neglect of prisoners, that is, of men placed in a situation destitute of all the means of helping themselves, all those evils, which, in another situation, could be produced only by the most direful oppression, immediately ensue.

By the servants of a gaol, cherishing their ease, and left by their superintendents, to do so, every call of a prisoner for help, for relief from any annoyance, is felt as an injury, and resented as such. Cruelty speedily comes, as a co-operator with neglect, to fill up the measure of the prisoner's calamity.

The prisoner, finding himself destitute of all remedy, except he can prevail upon the people who approach him to remove some of the causes of the misery which he endures, has recourse to bribery, when he can possibly command the means; and then pillage, without limit and without mercy, is added to all the evils of this den of horrors.

If such are the consequences of entrusting the management of prisons to persons who have no interest, or not a sufficiency of interest, in good management, we have next to consider the important question, By what means a sufficiency of interest in good management can be created? We need not have any doubt, that if a sufficiency of good accrues to the managers from every particle of good management, and a sufficiency of evil from every particle of bad, we shall have as much as possible of the good, and as little as possible of the evil.

1. The grand object, as we have stated, of reformatory discipline is, to create habits of useful industry.
2. A second object is, to preserve the health of the prisoners, and impose upon them no suffering, not implied in the conditions of their confinement, or prescribed by the judge.
3. A third is, by moral and religious tuition, to generate and strengthen good dispositions.
4. A fourth is, to attain those ends at the smallest possible expense.

It is not difficult to give the manager or keeper of a reformatory prison or penitentiary, a very strong interest in all these important results.

We have already seen, that the mode of giving to the prisoner a motive to labour, is, by giving him a share in the produce of his labour.

It is evident that an equally certain mode of giving to the jailor a motive for obtaining as much of that labour as possible, that is, for doing all that depends upon him to make the prisoners labour as much as possible, and as productively as possible, is by giving him also a share in the produce of their labour.

It may be said, however, that if the jailor receives a share of the labour of the prisoners, he will have a motive for making them labour too much: labour may be so excessive as to equal the severest torture.

Effectual expedients, however, for the prevention of this evil, are easy and obvious. In the first place, it does not seem necessary that the labour should be in any degree compulsory. If a prisoner is, according to the rule above laid down with respect to the cheapest fare, confined to the coarsest kind of bread, and to water, if he does not labour, but has it in his power to add to his enjoyments by labouring, more especially if he may labour in company, but if he will not labour, must remain in solitude, the cases will be exceedingly few in which compulsion will be needful; and these might, if it were deemed of sufficient importance, be specially provided for by the legislature.

If a man may work, or not work, as he pleases, and much or little as he pleases, there is no need of any farther security against excessive labour. If there were, it would be afforded by the interest which it is easy to give to the jailor in the health of the prisoner.

Giving to the jailor a share in the produce of the labour of a prisoner has two happy effects; not only that of giving him an interest in rendering the value of that produce as great as possible, but that, also, of giving him an interest in the health of the prisoner, because the produce of a man's labour is greater when he is in health than when he is not.

This may be encreased by giving to the jailor, through a very obvious channel, an interest, and an interest to any amount, in the life of each prisoner. It being ascertained what is the proportion of persons of a similar age that die annually, when not confined in a prison, all that is necessary is, to entitle the jailor to a sum of money for each of the individuals above that proportion whom he preserves alive, and to make him forfeit a sum for each individual above that proportion who dies. This sum, it is evident, may be sufficiently high, to ensure, on the part of the jailor, a strong desire for the life, and thence a proper attention to the health of the prisoners.

Another particular in this case requires attention. It is obvious that the motive of the prisoner to render the quantity or value of his labour the greatest, is, when the share which he enjoys of it is the greatest. It is equally obvious, that the motive of the jailor to promote the augmentation of this quantity or value is the greatest when his share is the greatest.

If the whole of the produce of the labour of each of the prisoners were left to be divided between himself and the jailor, the motives of the two parties, taken jointly, would be at the highest. And the question then would be, according to what proportion should the division be made?

The peculiar circumstances of this case permit the most decisive answer to be returned. No evil can accrue, and every good purpose is best gained, by allowing the jailor to take as much as he pleases. It being first established that he can employ no compulsory methods, that the prisoner must have as much of the coarsest fare and accommodation as he needs, whether he works or not, and that work can thus be obtained from him only by the operation of reward, it will be the interest of the jailor to make his reward sufficiently high to obtain from him all the work which he can perform, and, in his situation as a criminal, he ought, generally speaking, to receive no more. The propriety of this regulation, therefore, rests on conclusive evidence.

Here, however, an objection, worthy of attention, occurs. If the jailor receives so great a proportion of the produce of the labour of the prisoners, he may receive a much higher remuneration than the nature of his duties requires; and so far the public is deprived of a fund which ought to be available for the public service.

This observation is true; and the question is, in what manner can the separation of what is necessary in remuneration of the jailor, and what should be detached for the benefit of the public, be most advantageously made?

If the situation of the jailor affords more than an adequate reward, he will be willing to give something annually in order to retain that situation. And for measuring exactly what he ought to give, there is a sure and a well tried expedient: it is, to lay the thing open to competition.

By this expedient, a double advantage is gained: for both the public receives as great a share of the produce of the labour of the prison, as is compatible with the due remuneration of the jailor; and the jailor, he being entitled, in the first instance, to share the whole of the produce with the labourers, having both to pay what he owes to the government, and obtain his own remuneration out of his share, has a motive as strong as if the whole were his own, to render the produce as great as possible.

It will be easily seen that this contract between the public and the jailor, if sufficient securities can be taken for its being cancelled, as soon as misconduct on his part should render it desirable that it should be so, ought, for important reasons, to be concluded for a considerable number of years, or for his life. It is of importance that those individuals, who are to undergo the reformatory discipline, and who are unacquainted with any trade, should, especially if they are young, be taught the trade in which their labours can be turned to the greatest account: and, to make it the interest of the jailor to have them taught, it is evident that he must have the prospect of enjoying the benefit of their skilled labour for a sufficient length of time. This short illustration we hope will suggest to the reader sufficient reflection, for evidence of this point; and we must hasten to the remainder.

We have now shown, to how great an extent, upon the plan which we have thus briefly sketched, the interest of the jailor is rendered co-incident with the ends which are in view, and the most effectual of all securities is obtained for the goodness of his management. We proceed to show what additional securities this plan enables us to provide.

Let us, first of all, attend to the power of inspection, which may be afforded in a degree altogether unparalleled. By the admirable properties of the building which we have recommended, not only is the conduct of the prisoners rendered wholly transparent to the jailor, but the conduct of the jailor may be rendered equally transparent to his inspectors. And as the central lodge, or tower of inspection, may be entered by any number, without giving the least disturbance to the prisoners, without their even knowing that any body is there, the public may be admitted on such terms, as to afford the full benefit of public inspection, – the most efficient of all inspections, – over the whole economy of the prison. By means of whispering tubes, oral communication might be permitted with the prisoners, at such times, and under such regulations, as would prevent it from interfering with the working hours, or other parts of the discipline, to all persons who might have a wish to hear if they had any complaints.

Another very simple expedient would make an important addition to the list of securities. It ought to be an obligation on the jailor to keep a book, in which all complaints of the prisoners should be entered, and, as often as they could write, signed with their names. Along with the complaint should be entered a statement of what had been done for removing the ground of the complaint, or of the reasons for doing nothing. And this book should be open to the perusal of the public, and should lie in a place convenient for the inspection of all the visitors of the prison.

A still more important and indispensable security would be, the obligation of the jailor to present, annually, to the principal court of justice, such as the Court of King's Bench in England, a report on the management and state of the prison during the preceding year, containing, with all other points of useful information, exact accounts of the receipts and disbursements; to verify those statements by his oath; to print and publish them at his own expense; and to answer, upon oath, all interrogatories, made to him, in open court, by the judge, or by any other person, how much soever the answer might tend to his own crimination; and this as often as the judge might call upon him for such a purpose. By this means, with the obvious security afforded for other still more important ends, so perfect a knowledge would be communicated of the gains of the jailor, and the mode of obtaining them, as would ensure an accurate bargain, rigidly proportioned to the amount of them, as often as the contract came to be renewed.

The last thing which we think it necessary to recommend in the shape of a security, would operate as a test of the efficacy of the management in its character of a reformatory discipline. The jailor should be held bound to pay a certain sum, varying in proportion to the length of time during which the prisoner had been subject to his discipline, for each of the prisoners who, after liberation, should be convicted of a crime.

Connected with the important part of the subject relating to the labour of the prisoners, it is proper to bring to view the advantage of a subsidiary establishment for receiving and employing those who might be liberated from the prison. It is a well known ground of lamentation, that persons liberated from a prison, find often great difficulty in obtaining employment, and are constrained, by a kind of necessity, to betake themselves to their former evil courses, though with the inclination to have devoted themselves to honest industry, had the means not been denied them. The best mode of obviating this great evil would be, to have a subsidiary establishment, the architectural form the same as that of the prison, in which the jailor should be obliged to receive all persons who have been liberated from the prison, and who make application for admittance, and to employ them on the same terms as the prisoners, with the single exception of its being in their power to remove when they please, and to make, in respect to terms, all such stipulations with the jailor as may be for their mutual advantage.

The next part of the subject to which we proceed, is the plan according to which the prison shall be supplied with the articles which the prisoners are enabled by their labour to purchase.

As there are certain articles, such as intoxicating liquors, which ought to be altogether withheld, unless for special reason permitted, and as the jailor could not have a sufficient command over the articles conveyed into the prison, unless he had, in his own hands, the power of supply; as the intercourse, also, which would be created with strangers, if the prisoners were at liberty to purchase of whom they pleased, would be incompatible with the discipline of the prison, the power of supplying articles of purchase to the prisoners ought to be confined to the jailor.

If it be objected that the jailor would thus have the power of oppressing the prisoners, by selling bad articles, or good articles too dear, the answer is, That he could not. We have already seen, that in order to derive from the prisoners the greatest quantity of profit to himself, he must give to them a reward for their labour sufficient to make them labour to the most profitable account. But if he sells articles to them at more than the usual price, this is merely a reduction of the reward left to them for their labour: this he cannot reduce beyond a certain point, without reducing the amount of his profit; and any greater reward than up to this point, the nature of the case renders undesirable.

We have now then stated all that seems necessary to be said on the three great subjects; 1*st*, Of the structure and form of the prison. 2*dly*, The securities which may be applied for obtaining good conduct on the part of the jailor; and 3*dly*, The first and principal part of reformatory discipline, namely, voluntary labour.

The remaining conditions of reformatory discipline will not require much explanation.

1. Separation, as far as concerns the sexes, and as far as concerns the good from the bad, is now so generally attended to as an object of importance, that the danger sometimes is of other things being too much overlooked in the comparison.

In a prison, such as we have described, in which, by means of moveable partitions, the cells may be enlarged or contracted at pleasure, and in which the prisoners are all under continual inspection, the power of separation, to any desired extent, is complete.

The two sexes, though inmates of the same prison, and simultaneously subject to the same inspection, may be as completely disjoined as if they were inhabitants of a different region. By a piece of canvas, and nothing more costly, extended in the form of a curtain, from the boundary on each side of the female cells, in the direction of a radius across the central area to the inspection lodge, the females would be as completely cut off from seeing, or being seen by the male prisoners, as if they were separated by seas and mountains; the same effect would be obtained as to hearing, by merely leaving a cell vacant between those of the males and females; and thus the space appropriated to each of the two sexes might, in the easiest manner, be diminished or enlarged, as their relative numbers might require.

A much more complete and desirable separation, than that which is aimed at as the utmost in other prisons, is easily attainable in this. The ordinary separation of young offenders from old, of the greatly corrupted from those who are presumed to be less deeply infected, is still apt to leave associations too promiscuous, and too numerous, not to be unfavourable to the progress of reformation.

The prisoners should be put together in companies of twos, and threes, and fours, seldom more; each company occupying a separate cell. It would be the interest of the jailor to put them together in such assortments as would be most conducive to the quantity and value of work they could perform, and to the goodness of their behaviour; that is, to the most perfect operation of the reformatory discipline: and his experience of their dispositions and faculties would of course fit him beyond anyone else for making the selection.

It will have been all along understood, that, to attain the ends of inspection and economy, the same rooms or cells which form the day and working rooms on our plan, form also the sleeping rooms. Not the smallest inconvenience from confusion of things in the apartment can thence be derived; because the hammocks, which would be more convenient than beds, could be stowed away in little compass during the day.

It is also to be particularly observed, that whatever degree of seclusion might either be indulged to the feelings of an individual, or might be deemed conducive to his mental improvement, might still, upon this plan, be easily secured; because, by means of screens, a portion of the cell might be formed into as many private apartments as might be desired; and where experience of good conduct had laid a foundation for confidence, periods of seclusion, even from the eye of the inspector, might be allowed.

2. Nothing of great importance to be mentioned in this summary sketch seems now to remain, except schooling, and religious instruction.

The Sunday is the appropriate period for both. Sunday-schools are found by experience to be sufficient for communicating to children the important arts of reading, writing, and accounts. It would be obligatory on the jailor to afford the means of instruction in these respects to every prisoner who might not have attained them; together with all other means, not incompatible with the case, of promoting their moral and intellectual improvement.

3. The religious services proper to the day, and such other devotional exercises as might be thought requisite on other days, would be conducted by the chaplain, the prison affording remarkable facilities for bringing all the prisoners into a situation conveniently to hear; and also, which would be a circumstance of great importance, bringing the public from without, to participate in the religious services of the prison, for whom temporary accommodation in the vacant central area might be provided, and to whom, by the charms of eloquence and music, and the power of curiosity, it would be the interest of the jailor, by letting the seats, to provide sufficient attraction.

It seems to be necessary, before concluding, to obviate an objection, which, though it has seldom been urged as a reason against reformatory discipline, is yet considered as requiring a great deduction to be made in the estimate formed of its advantages. The objection is, that, by affording the means of employment to prisoners, we take away those means from a corresponding number of persons who are not prisoners, and thus sacrifice the deserving to the worthless.

This objection is drawn from some of the conclusions of Political Economy. That which affords the means of employment to labour is capital; in other words, the means of subsistence to the labourer, the tools he works with, and the raw material on which he is employed. When labourers are too numerous for the means of employment, it is evident that, if any new ones are added to the number, you can give employment to them only by taking it away from the old ones. It is, therefore, said, that by giving employment to prisoners, we make an equal number of honest workmen paupers.

In this objection, however, as is generally the case with false reasoning, a part only of the essential circumstances, not the whole, is taken into the account. In the first place, with regard to the prisoners, one principal part of the capital which puts labour in motion, namely, subsistence, is afforded to them of course, whether they labour or not.

In the next place, the objection proves too much: for, if it would be better, for the sake of affording employment to others, that the man should do nothing in prison, it would equally be better that he should have done nothing out of prison; better that we should have a portion of our population useless than productive. According to this doctrine, the proper rule, whenever population exceeds the demand for labour, and wages are low, would be to give subsistence to a portion of the people, on the condition of their abstaining from labour.

Thus much of the allegation is true, namely, that when to the subsistence, which you would have given at any rate, you add tools and raw materials, you so far diminish the quantity of tools and raw materials which can be furnished to others. But, counting only this circumstance, another most important circumstance is left out of the computation. This deduction of tools and raw materials is made once for all. The productive labourer replaces the capital, which employs him, with a profit. Advance to him, for one year, the food and other articles which he needs, you never need to advance any thing more. What he produces in the course of the year, replaces the food and all other articles which he has used, with a profit. But if he has not laboured, he has produced nothing; you have to supply him, therefore, with the means of subsistence, not one year, but every year, from the produce of other men's labour. If he labours, you have to give him once, out of the general stock of means for the employment of labour, subsistence for a year, with tools and raw material, and you have no occasion to give him any more. If he is to be idle, you give him, it is true, only subsistence, without tools and raw material, the first year; but you have to give him subsistence, that is, so far to diminish the means of employing other men's labour, every year; whereas, if he is a productive labourer, for the advance which you make to him the first year, he not only exempts you from all farther deductions from the means of employing other men, but he every year adds to those means, by the whole amount of the profit made upon his labour. To make those persons, therefore, productive labourers, whom you must at any rate subsist, is to increase, not to diminish the means of employing others.

As to another objection which is sometimes offered, that the commodities produced in a prison glut the market, and injure other manufacturers, this is still more evidently founded upon the consideration of part of the determining circumstances without consideration of the remainder. If it is meant to apply not to one class, or two classes of commodities, but to the mass of commodities in general, it may instantly be seen to be untrue. The men who become sellers of the articles produced in a prison, become buyers to the same amount. Whenever a man sells a greater amount of articles than before, he gets the means of buying an equally greater amount. He always brings as much of a new demand into the market as he brings of a new supply. If he introduces more of some one commodity than the market requires, and reduces the profits on producing it, capital leaves that employment till the inequality is redressed. If the number of people is the same, and the quantity of commodities is encreased, it is a contradiction in terms, to say that the circumstances of such a people are not improved.

Having answered these objections, it does not occur to us that there is any thing more which in this outline it is necessary for us to add. The plan, both of construction and management, appears to us simple, and easy to be understood; and to offer securities for the attainment of the end, such as the imperfection of the human powers, seldom permit to be realized. In the delineation presented, the only merit we have to claim is that (if our endeavour has been successful) of adding perspicuity to compactness. There is not, we believe, an idea which did not originate with Mr. Bentham, whose work ought to be the manual of all those who are concerned in this material department of public administration.

THE BALLOT
(1830)

This article is destined to the consideration of the Ballot; leaving out of account, for the present, all the other ingredients, which go to the formation of a true Representative System, and are indispensable to the establishment of good government.

In proceeding to prove the utility of the ballot, this uncomfortable feeling intrudes itself, – that the task is useless. The evidence is so clear and incontestible, that it seems a loss of time to put it in words. The same considerations, one imagines, must occur to every other mind, and strike it with similar conviction.

Another feeling is produced, by the arguments of those who assume the part of enemies of the ballot. What they say has not the countenance, the colour, not one of the marks, of *bona-fide* reasons; such grounds as a man rests upon for the truth of an opinion really held. All their allegations bear upon them the broad appearance of mere pretexts; the sham pleas, which are invented and set up, as often as men are summoned to defend opinions, which they have adopted and are determined to maintain, from other considerations than those of their truth, or falsehood.

As matters stand, at present, in England, we should never forget, that in determining our preference of the secret or open mode of voting for a Member of Parliament, the real question is this; Whether the people who vote, should really have the choice of the Member of Parliament; Or should only go through the formalities, the mummery of voting, including in it the prostitution of an oath, little regarded by a religious people; – while the whole power of choosing, should be really possessed by other parties.

It may indeed be affirmed, – it is not often so done in plain words, though it is of course habitually assumed, – that the last is the proper result; that the House of Commons ought to be chosen, – that is, a majority of the House, – by a few of the most powerful and wealthy men of the kingdom.

Allowing this assumption for the moment, overlooking all that is monstrous in the averment, – that a few men, who may, by their choice of Members of Parliament, employ, and abuse, the property and the persons of the rest of the community, for their own purposes, – will make a better choice for the community, than the community will make for themselves; we are then met by the inevitable question; Why, if this be so, – if it is indubitably true, that the small number will choose better than the great, and that the choice is actually and fortunately secured to them, – do we not abolish the fraudulent pretence which we now uphold? Why give to the people the appearance of a choice, which is nothing but a delusion? Is there not such a thing as lying by acts, as well as by speech? Is the turpitude of the mendacity less, when it is effected through the medium of the deed, than the word? Is there a more perfect instance, in the whole compass of imposture, of mendacity by deed, than that which is exhibited in the process of open voting for Members of Parliament in England?

If it be affirmed that the fraud and mendacity are, in this instance, good, in consideration of the end; because, though it be very undesirable that the people should have, in their rude and shapeless hands, any security for good government, it is very desirable that they should have the belief of it, – to this an unanswerable objection occurs, – that all hope of upholding such delusion has become vain. There is a new element among the working principles of human society, on the effects of which the retainers of this hope would do well to ponder. The art of printing exists. And the irresistible progress of the information which it diffuses necessitates, not a change merely, but a perfect revolution, in the art of governing mankind. In the times that are gone, the art of government has consisted in a mixture of fraud and force; in which, commonly, the fraud predominated. In the times that are to come, as fraud will be impracticable, and a knowledge of what is good and what evil in the mode of managing the national affairs cannot be withheld from the nation, government will be left either to rational conviction, or to naked force. This is the grand revolution of modern times. This is the new era. And another thing in this altered condition of human affairs may deserve the serious consideration of those who have to do with the powers of government. All history proves, that force alone is inadequate to the government of mankind: even the approaches to the use of it have uniformly failed. The resort to fraud is alone complete evidence of the impotence of force by itself; for, doubtless, the fraud – always imposing shackles, more or less – would never had been submitted to, had the naked force been adequate to the end. – What is the conclusion? – As fraud has, heretofore, been combined with force; fraud must be supplanted by knowledge, in the future history of the world; and force left by itself is not competent to insure the obedience of mankind. It follows, that rational conviction alone is left for the auxiliary of force. But rational conviction will not afford its aid upon any terms except its own. It then becomes the governing power: and becoming the governing power, it becomes the sole power; for rational conviction needs not the aid of force.

But, to pass from these clear revelations of reason, which hold forth, as in a mirror, the future history of mankind; one remark is yet necessary to be made, upon the conduct of those abettors of delusion to whom this part of our discourse is more particularly addressed. This their plea for mendacity and imposture, – to which religion ministers as a handmaid, in the instrumentality of the oath – stands directly opposed to the argument, which we shall have occasion to handle more particularly farther on, – that the ballot is unfavourable to that grand principle of morality, Truth. What are we to think of the morality and faith of those men, who display all the vehemence of outraged moral feeling, when they contemplate the chance that, under the safeguard of secrecy, the voter for a member of Parliament may break the promise – extorted from him by a villain – to violate his conscience and betray the trust confided to him by his country; while at the same time they uphold the virtue and excellence of the grand practical train of mendacity by which the people are to be cheated into a belief, that they have a power, of which they are wholly deprived? Was there ever a more glaring exposure of a hollow pretence? What is different, in the two cases, upon the shewing of these persons themselves, is not the mendacity but – the end. In the one case, the end is, to place the powers of government, without limit or control, in the hands of the few. For that end, according to them, active mendacity is laudable. In the other case, the end is, to limit the exercise of the powers of government to the attainment of the public good, by rendering the men, to whom the powers are confided, responsible to the nation at large. For this end mendacity, or the very chance of it, is to be treated as the most detestable of all conceivable things. We understand this morality; and we understand the men who seek credit upon the strength of it.

Besides the class, of whom we have hitherto spoken, who think that only the farce of voting should exist, – there is another class of our public men, who say, that they to whom the suffrage is given ostensibly, in England, exercise it substantially.

These men, of course, hold, that such a portion of the people as, in England, have the shew, should have the reality, of voting; otherwise they would belong to the class of whom we have already treated, and of whom it is not at present necessary to say any thing more.

It is implied in the supposed existence of such a class, that they believe the true, not the pretended, exercise of the power of choosing by the people who vote, to be necessary to good government.

The good arising from the freedom of suffrage being upon this supposition the greatest possible, the evil from corrupted suffrage, corrupted either by hope of reward or dread of punishment, the greatest possible – what would men do, who were in earnest about the attainment of this good, escape from this evil?

1. They would shew a great anxiety about the securities as they are, to know whether they are as complete as they can be made.
2. They would shew a great anxiety about the securities as they ought to be – that is, the means of making them as perfect as possible.

It will be very instructive to take a view, in these two respects, of the conduct of the class, who, assuming that the suffrage is now free, treat the proposition of ballot as contemptible or odious; in which class are comprehended the major part of the public men of England.

First, let us contemplate the pains which they take to make sure that the suffrage is now free; that there is no mistake in a matter of such vast importance; that the men who vote are really secure from any undue influence, and never lend themselves to the election of any but the men whom their innermost thoughts prefer. Did any of us ever observe any such anxiety? Men in earnest about an affair of so much importance would shew great jealousy of every suspicious appearance.

Elections are of two kinds; those for counties and those for boroughs. Take the first, the county elections. What do we observe in regard to them? Are they perfectly free from suspicion? Does every honourable or right honourable person know with certainty, that no application is ever made to a county voter, which can hang a bias on his mind, and stain his vote with the character of corruption? If this were the case, the absence of all solicitude on this subject, so conspicuous in their conduct, would be perfectly accounted for, without impeachment of their sincerity and truth.

Let us advert to the real matter of fact. A large majority of all those who vote for county members, vote, under such circumstances of dependance, that they cannot vote contrary to what they know to be the inclination of such and such men, without the prospect of serious, often ruinous, consequences to themselves. This is a matter of fact, so notorious, that no man who desires to be treated as a gentleman would venture to deny it, in any other place than an assembly of representatives, chosen according to this impure principle. That, indeed, is a place, where men, under the guidance of a common interest, do make assertions, pleasing to one another, which the rest of the world hear with astonishment; and, when they hear, turn round to one another and say, "If these men were to use words to us for such purposes in private life, after what fashion should we treat them?"

Is there among those honourable and right honourable persons one, who has either been candidate for a county, or supported a candidate; and who has not, himself, to the utmost of his power, exerted both engines of corruption; both the dread of evil, where that engine was at his command; and the prospect of good, where it was not?

Is this the fact? And do we still witness, in an assembly so chosen, the language and countenance of men, who maintain, that the members of a representative assembly ought to be chosen without corruption – and that the representative system of Great Britain ought to be preserved as it is?

There is a pretext which is employed, and often successfully, to create and to spread delusion upon this subject. It may be necessary to expose this piece of sophistry before we proceed any farther. It is contained in the language which is held about the legitimate influence of property. We are asked if we would destroy the legitimate influence of property? They accuse us of a desire to preclude the legitimate influence of property; and under the shield of an equivocal expression, they vent a quantity of moral indignation. Those are exceedingly wicked people, who desire to destroy the legitimate influence of property. They who desire secrecy of voting, desire to destroy the legitimate influence of property. Can there be a more complete demonstration against them? Can any men be more completely made to appear the proper objects of insult? richly meriting at once the scorn and the hatred of all those to whom property is dear; that is, of all but the most worthless and detestable of mankind, for how can society exist, or the innumerable benefits of it be preserved, if property is not secure? Thus the friends of the ballot are represented, obliquely at least, as the enemies of property; and then come all the images of spoliation, confiscation, anarchy, bloodshed, to annex odium to the individuals, and discredit to the cause.

The extreme folly of all this is easy to be made appear. It is only necessary to compel those fair and honourable opponents, to show what they mean by the legitimate influence of property. We, the friends of the ballot, the plebeian, the democratical, the base, are fully persuaded, that there are two influences of property; one good, moral, beneficent; another bad, immoral, pregnant with the most baneful consequences. The first of these we are so far from desiring to see extinguished, that all our endeavour is to increase it. We can prove to demonstration, – at least before such men as care for evidence upon these subjects, and know how to value it, – that the course we propose to follow is not only calculated to raise the moral influence of property, to its greatest height, but that it is the only course by which it can be so raised. With respect to the immoral, the baneful, influence of property, we confess that we are democratical enough to wish to see it wholly destroyed. The men whose mouths are full of the talk about legitimate influence, did not like to be so explicit. We will explain the reason. Their terms, "the legitimate influence of property," includes both meanings; the moral, and the immoral, influence of property both together. This is exceedingly convenient. In this we see an example of the main artifice by which discourse is rendered the instrument of fraud. – Let two things, one good, and one evil, be confounded under one name; it is not difficult to transfer the approbation, the attachment, or, on the other hand, the detestation and abhorrence, which they severally deserve, from the one to the other. And this delusion is always most easy, in things which are remote from the familiar knowledge of the senses, things which can be apprehended distinctly only by a certain clearness and force of the intellect. It is worth while to attend to the working of this sophistical machinery. The moral influence of property deserves all the approbation which its eulogizers bestow upon it. That we may have clear ideas upon the subject, let us think for a little what it is. Riches, to the purpose we are now contemplating, mean, a certain quantity of power: power of bestowing – good more or less extensively – and also of inflicting evil on our fellow creatures. It is possible, we all know, for a man who is possessed of this power, to exercise it in such a manner as to become the object of the affection and reverence, not only of all those who come within the sphere of his virtues, but, by sympathy with them, of all those to whom the knowledge of his character is diffused. The opinions, the wishes, of such a man, become a motive to his fellow creatures. We desire to be able to concur with him in his opinions, we desire to be able to forward the objects of his wishes. If such a man expresses a decided preference of one of two candidates; the opinion of his virtue, that he would not recommend the man whom he did not inwardly prefer; and of his wisdom, that he would not be deceived, together with the unavoidable pleasure of giving him pleasure, would always go far to determine the choice of those who live under the influence of his virtues. This is the legitimate influence of property, in the sense in which it is moral. This is an influence which is as safe under the ballot, as without the ballot. The man who proceeds to the scene of election with that reverence in his heart, which the moral influence of property implies, will not be deserted of that moral impulse, when he places his vote in secrecy. The effect of it is as sure as if it were delivered before an assembled world; because it is the mind of the man that acts. The will, the choice, are his own.

Let us next contemplate the other, the immoral influence of property; to which also, by a vile profanation, the term "legitimate influence" is applied. We all know that, commonly, riches are so employed as to create no affection towards the possessor of them; to produce no reverence of his wisdom, and no sympathy with his desires, in the mass of the people by whom he is surrounded. This is not to be imputed, with any degree of harshness, as blame to the individuals. The effect cannot be otherwise, in a country, where the social relations are so ill constituted, as to afford no adequate motive to a more virtuous course. On the contrary, praise is to be awarded to those, as often as we find them, who think that one good of riches is to earn the love and esteem of those among whom they live. We are not without examples of persons who so employ their property – of not a few, who so employ it in the lower degrees, – of some, even in the higher. It is notorious, however, that these are not the great body of opulent persons. The rest seek their influence in a different way. That way is so familiar to us all, that nothing more is wanted for the account of it, than the few words which are necessary to suggest it. We see, by daily example, how easy it is, for those who employ little or no part of their fortune to obtain the favourable sentiments of their countrymen, – nevertheless to make such a use of it as places a considerable number of persons in their dependence, – so to arrange their own permanent position with regard to such and such individuals, as to possess a great power over their happiness; the power of taking from them, or leaving with them, important means of well-being. This power over their happiness is unavoidably attended with a great power over their wills. Men do not choose to act in opposition to the desires of a man who can injure them greatly, when they have great reason to apprehend, that, by so acting, they will ensure whatever evil he can bring upon them.

This we call the immoral influence of property. This is an influence which can be used by the worst of men, as easily as by the best; supposing it for the moment an influence which any good man would consent to use; – an influence, which can be as easily used for the worst, as for the best of ends. The very opposite is the case with the moral influence of property; the native, inborn tendency in the human breast to promote the wishes of the man who has so employed the means of happiness at his disposal, as to fill our hearts with affection and esteem. This can be exercised only by virtuous men – can be employed only for virtuous purposes.

Let us now ask ourselves, under which of these influences, if we had our choice, should we desire our country to be governed. Suppose we had it in our power to give full scope to the exercise of the moral influence, and suppress entirely the immoral, will any man say that it should not be done? – What we affirm of the ballot is, – that it

234

has this precious quality. It does bestow upon us this invaluable power. This is what we doubt not to be able presently to prove.

To return however for a little to the working of the immoral influence. Let us put before us a case. Let us suppose a country in which the representative system has been long established; and on such a footing that the powers of government are substantially placed in the hands of the representative body. Let us also suppose that portion of the community by whom the representatives are chosen to be so circumstanced that a large majority of them can be placed, and are at last effectually placed, mediately, or immediately, under the immoral influence of the property of a small number of men; in other words, that they vote such men to be representatives, as that small number bid them, under compulsion of the evil which disobedience would bring upon them. Let us rest our thoughts, for a moment, upon the qualities of this social order, – upon such a relation of human beings to one another in the political union.

Let us first observe the obligations of those, to whom the function of voting is consigned. They are elected, and set apart from the rest of their fellow citizens, for the performance of a service to their country, upon which its vital interests depend. They are Trustees for the Community to which they belong; and in a Trust, importing the greatest good or evil, to the vast majority of their countrymen. Can there be a more sacred obligation? Is there any thing binding upon the conscience of man, if this is not to be considered binding in the highest degree? Is it not an act of virtue to be faithful to this Trust? Not an act of vice, to be unfaithful to it? Is there any thing in any conceivable act of treachery to render it odious, which is not in this act? Is not the habitual consciousness of treacherous acts, the perpetual feeling that a man is a villain? Is not the habitual consciousness of having been, and being now a villain, with the intention of continuing to be so, a complete perversion of the moral faculty? Is not such a man completely degraded from the rank of a moral being?

Let us now apply our serious thoughts to the condition of the men who are vested with this trust in our own country. It is matter of fact, notorious, and undisputed, that a certain number of opulent men hold the great majority of them in such a state of dependence, that they command their votes. Whatever may be the opinion of any individual of this large majority respecting the superior fitness of one of two candidates, he will vote for the other, if the man on whom his fears or hopes depend commands him, to what degree soever he may deem him unfit for the exercise of the power, with which he so contributes to invest him. The nature and quality of the proceeding are obvious to all men's perception. The opulent man applies to the voting man the means which are in his power to make him commit an act in the highest degree criminal, – to betray a trust of unspeakable importance, committed to him by his country.

We are told that the voters ought not to be guilty of such criminal compliance. True. So say we. They ought to perish rather. And so they would, under a social order morally constituted. But what is to be expected, in a state of things which has no tendency to generate the high feelings of public virtue; a state of things in which the hollow pretence of public virtue is indeed in sufficient repute, but any effective display of the reality excites only feelings of hatred; a state of things in which the interests of the men who have the lead in the country, and who set the fashion, in morals, as in clothes, are habitually pursued in opposition to the interests of the country; a state of things in which not only the morals of the people (at least any morals except those which are cultivated for the benefit of Priests and Masters) are neglected from their infancy, but the means are withheld by which even the seeds of morality could be sown in their breasts? Does their country in this manner abandon the care of the people's morals; and does it reproach them with the want of them? Inconsistency here is not all; – the inconsistency has dishonesty for the cause of it. The people are placed in circumstances in which they cannot have morals – the grand morals we now speak of – the ennobling sentiment in the breast of every man to regard the public interest as his own. We upbraid them with this; and what next? What is the inference we draw? Only this – that the care of the public ought to be abandoned; and a few men ought to have the power placed in their hands of sacrificing, according to their discretion, the interests of their country to their own. Is the inference fairly drawn? Is it supported by the premises? The virtue of the people, you say, is weak. Unhappily it is so, deplorably weak; What then? Would it not be good to take all possible means to prevent it from being exposed to strong temptation? So say the men, who recommend the ballot. This is denied by the men, who resist the ballot, and who of course desire that the bad morals of the people, and all their pernicious consequences, should remain; as he who rejects the remedy, clings to the disease. Who are the men who profit by these bad morals? The men in whose hands, through that odious instrumentality, the powers of government are placed. Have they any interest in improving the morals, by the badness of which they derive advantage of such importance? – Is it not a dreadful state into which a nation is brought, when its leading men have an interest in the badness of the morals of the people? Is it in the nature of things that, so situated, the morals of the people should be good?

Acknowledging, as we do most fully, the criminality of the voters; deeply sensible of the degree to which they are demoralized and degraded, by the part they act in returning members to parliament, let us now turn to the men who influence their votes, and endeavour to make an honest estimate of their virtues.

Let us first look at their conduct in its essence, and afterwards consider it in its circumstances. What is the nature of the act, when a man attains the end he has in view, by being the cause of the criminal act of another person? Suppose the object, is to avoid the payment of a just debt; and that the man in question hires a person to make a false oath, which secures him that advantage; he is of course regarded as guilty of the perjury, in a higher degree, if possible, than the man by whose lips it is performed. Suppose the object is, to obtain possession of a fortune by the death of the person who holds it; and that the man we are supposing hires an assassin who executes his purpose: is not he who hires the assassin the real author of the murder?

Who is there that has not already made the application to the case which it is our present business to illustrate? The voter for a member of parliament has a trust placed in his hands, on the discharge of which the highest interests of his country depend. Moral obligation is without a meaning, if the faithful discharge of this is not among the highest of all moral acts; the faithless discharge one of the basest of all immoral ones. To render this high obligation more binding still, the sanction of an oath is added. The voter solemnly swears, that he will not betray, but will faithfully execute, his trust. What happens? The unfortunate voter is in the power of some opulent man; the opulent man informs him how he must vote. Conscience, virtue, moral obligation, religion, all cry to him, that he ought to consult his own judgment, and faithfully follow its dictates. The consequences of pleasing, or offending, the opulent man, stare him in the face; the oath is violated, the moral obligation is disregarded, a faithless, a prostitute, a pernicious vote is given. Who is the author of this perjury, this prostitution, this treachery? There are two odious criminals; but assuredly the voter is the least criminal, and the least odious of the two.

Observe the horrid spectacle; two sets of men, the one comparatively rich, the other poor, so placed with respect to one another, that they act upon one another, for mutual corruption; that they gain their ends upon one another, only by a renunciation of the most sacred obligations, and the commission of the greatest crimes; that, in order to have inward peace, in such a course of acting, they must succeed in obliterating every trace of the higher morals from their minds. The sense of obligation to the community to which they belong, the regard due to a trust, are not compatible with their situation. The men who have occasion for the prostitution, the perjury, the faithlessness of voters, and the most perfect indifference on their part to the interests of their country, must beware how they appear to have any regard for morality before such persons, or any regard for country. The appearance they put on is a curious one: it is that of a feigned scorn for all the public virtues, and a real hatred. This mixture of feeling gives a curious character even to the countenances of persons of the higher ranks in this country, distinguishable in most, and very marked in some.

When men have renounced the real virtues, they look out for substitutes, to conceal the state of their character, and, if possible, make its outside fair. It would be inconvenient, in almost any state of the world, for a set of men to proclaim their indifference to the good of the community in which they live; even where they are exerting themselves with the utmost energy to place the interests of the community permanently in a state of sacrifice to their own. What do they do? They find out whereon to display their zeal something which may be made to appear the interest of the community, but is in reality their own. Thus, under the old monarchy of France, the privileged classes possessed Loyalty in a high degree – an ardent love of the *grand monarque*; in other words, an ardent love of seeing placed as much as possible of other men's property at the disposal of the king, which he with royal bounty distributed among them. Our own gentry have a still better cry. It is the constitution – the British constitution! When trampling on every moral obligation in their way to their object, they still claim to be patriots, on the strength of a love to the constitution. Their actions interpret their words. Their love of the constitution is a love of suborned and prostituted votes; a love of the power, thus placed in their hands, of raising taxes without limit upon the community, and dividing the proceeds among themselves. Loyalty, constitution, are pretty sounds. But what they mean is, Plunder.

The prostituted voter, we said, is less criminal, than his corrupter. Not only is he less criminal in the principal act; he being to a great degree the passive tool, the other the active agent; his crime being single, that of the suborner multiplied in every individual whose villainy he has secured; he is also less criminal in the circumstances of his act, they almost all in his case being extenuating, almost all in his suborner's case aggravating circumstances, of the guilt.

For what is the object of the suborner? – To seat himself in parliament. This may be for a public purpose, or a selfish one. The public purpose is not that of the majority of candidates. No man, even a member of parliament, out of the House of Commons, will pretend that it is. No man, who knows his countrymen, and who means not to counterfeit or deceive, will deny, that those who go into the House constitute two classes; those who go in for the vanity of the thing; and those who go in for plunder: and that the rest, at the highest estimate, constitute a miserable exception. Take the most favourable case, that of the man who gets into the House with a virtuous intention; this is not one of those motives, which urging a man with vehemence in a particular direction, takes off from the odiousness of a bad action. But pass this case, and go to those which so nearly include the whole body. Take one of the men whose object is mere vanity – the distinction of being a member of parliament. Is there any thing, in this petty, vulgar, motive, to extenuate the guilt of an enormous crime? The motive of that proportion of candidates who seek admission for the sake of plunder, is itself wicked, and of course adds to the wickedness of the conduct by which the admission is procured.

Contrast with these motives that of the voter on whom the immoral influence of property takes its effect. His situation, most commonly, is that of an occupant of the land, or of a house, of the man by whom his vote is suborned. His prospect is that of being turned out of such occupation, if he does not lend himself to the designs of his suborner. In general this is a calamity of the severest kind. Often it is ruin, or something little short of it. In most cases, it is a great revolution in the circumstances of the man, and his family; full of anxiety, full of labour, full of risk. Not to incur such a catastrophe must always be among the strongest desires, the most overpowering motives, of a human being. It is a crime in any one, even for such a motive as this, to betray his trust, to violate his faith pledged to his country, and, as far as he is concerned, to deliver it up to misgovernment and plunder. But assuredly, if temptation makes any difference in the degree of crime, and every system of law in the world assumes that it makes the greatest, there is no comparison between the turpitude of the man who gives a dishonest vote in such circumstances, and the turpitude of him who suborns it.

Another tremendous accusation lies upon the class of suborners. They are the class by whom chiefly the moral character of the voting classes is formed. The opinions which they spread of what is honourable, and what dishonourable, become the governing opinions. But the habits of thinking, about what is right and wrong, what is shameful, what the contrary, diffused among any people, constitute the moral character of that people. If pains are successfully taken with them to prevent their thinking a certain course of action shameful, though it really be so, they lose by degrees all moral feeling on the subject; in other words, are reduced to the most frightful state of moral corruption; they obey every temptation to any vicious act of the kind supposed, without the smallest self-condemnation or moral repugnance; the most feeble, the most contemptible of motives, therefore, is always adequate to the production of the crime.

Those who desire to get possession in their own country of the powers of government, exempt from all real responsibility, that is, for the purposes of plunder – for in such circumstances the motives to public plunder are irresistible – have no stronger interest, than in preventing, as far as they can, the existence of any such opinion as that public plunder is disgraceful; that is to say, public plunder in the essence of the thing; for as to certain forms of it – if such as they have no occasion to practise – they care not to what degree public opinion may be turned against them; nay, are ready with their aid to heap disgrace upon them, as a convenient method of diverting attention from the forms in which they indulge and preventing them from being duly considered and understood. If they have such an interest in preventing public plunder from being reputed disgraceful, they have no less an interest in saving from such moral condemnation all the crimes which minister to that result, and are necessary to its attainment. Among these the most important by far is the prostitution of votes. And, accordingly, no more remarkable instance can be produced of the power of the leading classes over the moral sentiments of mankind; the efficacy with which the successful prosecution of their sinister interests generates moral corruption in the body of the people; than the utter extinction of moral feeling in England with regard to voting for members of parliament. Shallow, thoughtless men, even if they are not corrupt, can hardly be made to conceive the extent of this calamity; for, along with the extinction of the moral feeling in regard to voting, must go the moral feeling in regard to acts in general, by which the common good and evil rarely are affected; the very notion of virtue and vice therefore becomes divorced from the thought of public acts as such; and men may be wicked to the highest degree in public transactions, without becoming disgraceful. This is nearly the last stage of public calamity: for there remains but one alternative; – the eternal existence of the misrule; – or a convulsion to obtain deliverance from it.

We conceive that little more remains, to demonstrate the utility and the necessity of the ballot: for we affirm, and think we shall be able in a few words to prove, that the ballot is a remedy for a great portion of all this evil; easy of application, and of all remedies, possible to be applied, the most unexceptionable, on account of any evil conse-quences arising out of itself. We reason thus: – If it be proved that any where an enormous amount of evil exists, that an agency may be applied which will remove, if not the whole, a great part, of all this evil, and that to this agency no hurtful consequences are attached, which can be reputed an equivalent for one of the millions of evils which it will remove, the argument for its application seems to be as complete as demonstration can in moral subjects be. We know but one objection which can be made to it – that it is too complete. This is an objection not unlikely to be made. There are people who, precisely because it is complete, and, being complete, is not conducive to their ends, may call it an *a priori* argument, or by some such unpopular name; and will, on that ground, with much briskness, infer, that it is good for nothing. People who have their reasons for not liking a conclusion to which demonstration leads, have nothing for it but to decry demonstration. They indeed obtain credit only among the blockheads. But then the blockheads are the greatest both in number and power. It is not every man's ambition that goes higher than this. We suppose ourselves to be arguing with persons, who really hold that there is a difference between one government and another: that it is of great importance to the community, whether the persons, to whom the management of their affairs is confided, do or do not act under an efficient responsibility to them. We suppose that we are arguing with persons who hold the British constitution to be something more than a name. All the eulogies we hear pronounced upon it proceed upon the assumption, that there is an immeasurable distance between a good government and a bad; that in the good government there are securities for the good conduct of those to whom the management of the public affairs is confided; and that in the bad government there is a want of those securities.

Representative government is a contrivance for affording those securities, by giving to the public the choice of the persons who have the management or at least a perfect control over the management of the public affairs. But where are those securities, if the people have not this choice – if they have nothing but the name of choosing, with some vain and fraudulent formalities; while the real power of choosing is exercised uniformly and steadily by the same small number of men. This small number of men are really, then, the governors, under no responsibility at all. Is it possible that in these circumstances the public affairs should not be mismanaged; – that they should not be managed under a perfect subserviency to the interests of that small number; in other words, that the interests of the governed should not, under a government so constituted, be habitually sacrificed to the interest of the governors? Does badness of government consist in any thing else than this?

Now is not the time to enter upon the display of all that is contained under the dreadful term, badness of government; or of the items in the shocking catalogue which are most remarkable in the government of our own country; though nothing is more important than the frequent recounting of those evils, which they who suffer them always know, but of which they lose the accurate and pungent sense, if the thought of them is not frequently and vividly renewed.

The question we have to resolve will now be seen to be easy, because it turns upon a single point. All the evils of misgovernment, which we suffer, and to which we are liable, cumulated with all the evils of that horrid immorality which results from the giving and suborning prostitute votes, arise from this; – that the people of England do not choose the members of parliament, that the majority of them are chosen by a small number of men.

It is so clear as not to admit of being rendered clearer by argument, that what gives this small number of men the power of choosing, is the openness of the voting. It is the openness, therefore, of the voting that corrupts the government of England, and corrupts the morals of the people of England. That which enables the men, who hold the voters in dependence, to suborn the votes, is their knowing how the vote is given. Render it impossible for them to know how any vote is given, and their power over it is gone. The power either of rewarding a prostitute vote, or punishing an honest one, is useless, whenever it has been made impossible to be known whether the prostitute or the honest vote has been given. Effect this impossibility; take away the power of knowing how the man who votes for a member of parliament has bestowed his vote, and see the consequences. You give effectual securities to the public, that the affairs of the public will be managed for their interest, not sacrificed to the interest of their rulers; and you take away at the same time one of the most terrible engines of moral depravation, which ever was wielded for the pollution and degradation of any portion of mankind. Are not these important effects to be derived from so simple a cause? And is not the cause which produces such effects the more to be cherished and esteemed because of its simplicity?

The men in parliament who allow themselves to speak without repugnance of parliamentary reform at all, generally confine their favour to moderate reform. If the actions of these men corresponded with their words, we should have them with us on the question of the ballot. For can there be any change more moderate, than that of converting an open vote into a secret one? Allow every thing else to remain as it is. Keep to the same voters exactly, and distribute them after the same manner. Do not even alter the duration of parliaments. Not that these things are as they should be. They might be altered, we think, for the better. But the ballot would operate so powerfully as an instrument of good, that the inconveniences which might still arise from these defects, if we had the ballot, would be far less severely felt.

This moderate, very moderate reform, could obviously have none of those effects, which are commonly painted in tragic colours, to frighten weak, fearful people, from every thought of reform. It cannot possibly have any farther effect, than that of bringing the practice of the English constitution into a conformity with its theory – that theory, which renders it "the envy of surrounding nations, and the admiration of the world." That theory, undoubtedly, is, that the people choose. The practice is, that they do not choose. The ballot, and that alone, can enable them to choose, and render the British constitution in reality what it now is only in pretence.

There is another important argument in favour of the ballot. Nothing else can render the constitution of England conformable to the conception and expectations of its kings. When they, upon some great emergency, have recourse to a new, as a fitter instrument than an old, parliament, they declare that they have recourse to the sense of their people; meaning, of course, that the sense of their people is expressed in the choice of members of parliament. They know not, it seems, that it is not the sense of their people which is so expressed, but the sense of a small number of suborners of votes.

There are two blemishes in our representative system, as it stands, which even those who admire it as it stands, allow to be blemishes; and on which they are often pleased to descant as great and horrible evils. These are – expense of elections, and bribery in corrupt boroughs. Often have they tried their hands at legislating for a remedy of those evils. Notwithstanding the greatness of their efforts, notwithstanding the magnitude of the expended power, – the difficulties have still overmatched them. The collective wisdom of the nation has been baffled in a contest with cost, and corruption; and these blemishes still remain. It ought, with such parties, to be a strong recommendation of the ballot, and would be, if they were honest and sincere in what they say, that it would radically cure these acknowledged diseases of the parliament. See how clearly and immediately the result appears. With regard to bribery, who would go to the expense of paying any man for a vote, when, for aught he knew, it was given against himself? As money for votes rendered in secret can have no effect whatever to secure the vote for which it is given, the man would be mad, who would throw it away in that manner.

Let us next attend to the cost incurred at elections, without regarding what it consists in, expense of conveying distant voters, entertainments; or favours of other description, money, or money's worth; the ballot would put an end to it all. Men will not incur expense for the attainment of an object, when it is clear that such expense can have no effect whatever in procuring the object. This is most indubitably the case with money spent on account of a vote given in such secrecy, that whether it is given for you or against you, you never can know. Under such a system the practical consequences would be, that only those men would vote who could do so free of expense, or were willing to defray their own charges.

We observed toward the beginning of this article, that the enemies of the ballot in parliament are divided into two classes: one, that of the men who admit the limited number of real choosers, and defend it as the perfect state of the British constitution; the other, that of the men who, though they partly admit, partly also deny, the limitation of the number of real choosers by the operation of open voting, but who loudly express their conviction that voting ought to be free, and ought not to be perverted from its honesty by either of the two instruments of corruption, dread of evil, or prospect of reward. The former class are a very small minority in parliament, and the ground they take so very untenable, that they deserve no more of our regard. The latter class may be considered as making up the body of parliament. To them we now address ourselves, with an assurance of accomplishing one or other of two objects; either gaining their co-operation; or covering them with the shame of holding a language which their actions belie. By what pretence, we ask them, can you attempt to resist our conclusions? Will not the ballot render voting independent and honest; which you allow it is not at present, so perfectly at least as were to be wished. Will it not effectually annihilate expense of elections, as well as bribery and corruption? Will it not, in this manner, effect all which you conceive to be necessary to render the representative system of England perfect? It is, if your conception be right, a perfectly radical reform of parliament; and that by means to which no artifice can attach the idea either of difficulty or danger. The change of open into secret voting excites no disturbance; weakens the security of no man's rights; takes away no influence of property, except its immoral influence: while it is attended with two effects of unspeakable importance; it brings into action the only security for good government; and it puts an end to the most demoralizing traffic between the leading men of the community and the body of the people, that ever had existence upon the face of the earth.

The language which some of them sometimes employ to meet, and resist all this body of evidence is truly astonishing. If it was not seen, it would not be credible, that men could be found who without any necessity would stand up and shew such weakness.

"The ballot is not English;" that is one of their phrases, in speaking against it. Why not English? Upon what ground do you take upon you to refuse the use of the term "English" in conjunction with the word "ballot?" If the ballot be a necessary means to the most important of all ends, and the word "English" is not applicable to it, the word "English" is then not applicable to one of the best of things – that is all. But the word "English," we suppose, is truly applicable to the system of suborning, and prostituting, votes, by which the character of Englishmen is depraved, and the interests of the English nation are trafficked away; and if so , it is applicable to one of the worst of things. Assuredly, the men who treat the word "English" in this fashion, are not the men who use it with the greatest honour.

The state of mind, however, of the man who, in the great council of the nation, when a solemn question is opened, whether a certain expedient is or is not necessary to secure the best interests of the community, gets up and pretends to terminate the whole deliberation, by refusing the application of the word "English," must be regarded through all time as a curiosity.

This is a new test of good and evil. In point of handiness, it certainly would be, if fit to be trusted, a very desirable one. Is any man in doubt, at any time, about the goodness or badness of anything. Only touch it with the word "English": immediately, as when the Devil was touched by the spear of Ithuriel, it starts up in its real shape and dimensions; and all uncertainty about it is dispelled. There is, however, one objection to it, and that a serious one. It would supersede the use of wisdom, in the great council of the nation; and would entirely put an end to the veneration which is now, on account of its wisdom, so justly bestowed upon that august assembly, by all who enjoy the spectacle of its proceedings, or have the happiness of tasting their effects.

We fear also it is a test, the use of which ought to be confined to the privileged hands; for if the people were allowed to apply it, as well as their rulers, there might be strange diversity. That might appear very English to the one, which would be very un-English to the other. For example, the people might think every thing which was really good toward saving them from the curse of misrule, was most perfectly English; and of course the ballot itself, if it was a thing of that admirable tendency. They might be led the more easily into that mistake, in respect to the ballot, by observing what is the English practice; that the ballot universally obtains where those, who have the power of determining the mode of voting, have a real interest, however slight, in the freedom and independence of the votes.

The men who themselves are in the habit of using the ballot, on small and on great occasions, during the whole course of their lives, stand up and say to an assembly of men who are all doing the same thing, that they ought to reject the ballot in parliamentary elections, because it is not English! Did we not speak true, when, towards the beginning of this discourse, we said, that the pleas of the enemies of the ballot had not even the look of honest arguments? that it was impossible to consider them as any thing but the pretexts; which must be found, when a position, which cannot be supported by reason, is to be maintained in spite of it?

Among the opponents of the ballot in parliament are some who cannot so much be said to argue, as to groan, and use inarticulate cries against it. Of this kind are those who say, They hope that they shall not live to witness the time, when Englishmen shall not have the spirit to deliver their vote in the face of day. It would be as honest, and about as wise, to say, they hope not to live to witness the time, when every Englishman shall not have his carriage and pair. If they were to say, which would be the only thing to the purpose, that they hoped not to live to see the day when an Englishman would not go to the hustings, and fearlessly vote for the man of his choice, without regard to the dictation of any person upon earth; the falsehood of the pretext would be too glaring to be successful, even in a country where as much is done by hypocrisy as in England. It is matter of fact, notorious and undisputed, that a great majority of those who vote for members of parliament in England, proceed to the hustings under the influence of what they either hope to receive, or dread to suffer, and prostitute themselves in the most infamous manner, by voting, not according to the dictates of their own minds, but like crouching slaves, at the will of another. Are these the circumstances in which votes are commonly given in England, and are men found who say they hope not to live to see the day when Englishmen will be afraid to vote openly? Patience would be found to hear them, in no assembly, we think, upon earth, but one composed of the very men who suborn such votes. Courage to vote as Englishmen vote, at the command of those by whom they are bought, or driven, is the courage of the slave, when he lends his body to the lash. Are there men, who pretend a horror at the prospect of parting with this, and receiving in exchange for it the protection of secrecy, because secrecy would degrade the people?

A wish for elevating the minds of the people is an admirable wish, and the profession of it is truly a pretty profession; but the true character of the profession is known by the character of the things which follow. Is the wish not to see Englishmen vote secretly, a wish that Englishmen should have sufficient independence of mind to vote as they please, though all the world should know in what manner they vote? We also entertain that wish most fervently. We have another strong wish; that all Englishmen were above being paupers. We appreciate, however, it would little answer any good purpose for us to use the *formula* of those who level their wishes against the ballot, and say, they hope not to live to see the day when Englishmen will live upon charity. Poverty makes the people of England willing to live on charity. Dependent circumstances make them willing to prostitute their votes. Your choice lies between prostitute voting and secret voting. There is the deepest degradation in prostitute voting. Not only is there no degradation in secret voting, but it saves from all the degradation inseparable from prostitute voting; all men, therefore, who deprecate the degradation of the people, not with hypocrisy, but in earnest, are of course the advocates of the ballot.

But, on what authority, we shall be asked, do we make the assertion, that there is no degradation in secret voting? On the authority, we reply of those very men who say that there is. What! do the same men, who say that secret voting is degrading, say also that it is not degrading? They do; as you, and as they, and as all men, are perfectly aware. You see them constantly practising the ballot, and introducing the use of ballot, without a thought of self-degradation, wherever it is really their wish that the vote should be protected from external influence. In order to protect themselves from the trifling inconvenience of displeasing somebody, by black-balling an improper candidate for admission into a club, they themselves take the benefit of secret voting. Can there be a more perfect proof that they do not regard it as degrading? Can there be a more perfect proof that when they refuse to the honest voter for a member of parliament the same protection against far more serious consequences, on the pretence that it is degrading, they are not sincere? Observe, too, the difference of the ends. That improper members may not be admitted into a club, the secret voting is needful in the one case. That improper members may not be admitted into the legislature, it is needful in the other. Do you dare to say, that the use of it is not degrading in the former of these two cases, that it is degrading in the latter? That the end sanctifies the means in the former case, not in the latter?

"I cannot abide muffling up," says one honourable gentleman; and by such an appeal to sentimentality, manfully proposes to decide one of the most important questions of legislation. If a great end is to be gained by muffling up, why should there not be muffling up? The nature of the pretext is so manifest, that it would seem not to be worth exposing; and yet there are persons for whose sake it may be proper to attract a little attention to it. If there were any argument in these words, it would rest upon this, that all secrecy is bad. If some secrecy is good, the man who says he does not like it, renders us one good service; he gives us full warning against taking him for a guide. Every body knows, this honourable gentleman knows, that, in itself, secrecy is neither good, nor bad. It is good, when it is the means to a good end; bad, when it is the means to a bad end. It is not base in the General, it is meritorious, to "muffle up" his designs from the enemy. The more perfectly he can, by concealment, stratagem, dissimulation, guile, delude their expectation, the more is he admired. It is not base in negotiation for the statesman to conceal with the utmost care the extent of the concessions he would make, rather than fail in the attainment of his object. Every government makes a point of concealing such part of its proceedings, and, as far as possible, such particulars in the national affairs, as it would be detrimental to the nation to let other nations know. If it be detrimental to the nation, that the mode should be known in which a man gives his vote for a member of parliament, that also, for the same reason, ought most assuredly to be kept from being known. One is ashamed to feel oneself obliged to contend against such puerilities.

There are some persons, who make a bold use of certain assertions with regard to the American United States, in opposition to the ballot. Some people have been there, and on the strength of a drive through the country, performed in a few months, give us their assurance, that, in the United States, the ballot does not answer expectation. Others have derived the same insight from conversations had with people of the United States. – What is the value of such assertions? Just nothing at all. Vague, hazarded declarations, respecting the interior and hidden working of the institutions of a foreign country, put forth in a debate to silence an adversary, declarations no man would repose even the smallest confidence in, if the question regarded a matter, about the truth of which he was really in earnest; the prudence, or imprudence, for example, of investing his fortune in the United States. He would go to other evidence, than the second-hand testimony of the one, or the reports, delivered by the other, of what was seen by the eyes, respecting a thing not to be understood by the eyes.

This, in itself, is a point of importance. It cannot be passed without notice. It is not generally understood of how very small a number of men the statements, respecting countries they have seen, can be received with moderate reliance. The number of accurate observers in the world is exceedingly small. It is well known to all those persons who have occasion for accurate information, to judges, for example, and others, who take evidence in courts of justice, how inconsiderable the proportion of persons is who see and hear accurately, or can, by the utmost exertion of their wills, give a true account of some ordinary and not very complicated scene, in which they have been present. The merit of the judge consists, not in relying upon the statement of one witness, or the statement of another, but in confronting the statements, and from the knowledge he has of the laws of human nature, and the order of human transactions, divining the truth.

If such is the inferiority of individual testimony in the ordinary transactions of ordinary life, what must it be in the accounts we receive of countries and nations? Here the men who have occasion for accurate knowledge; the historian, for example, of a country, the state of which he is obliged to expound to readers who have but little previous acquaintance with it have most remarkable experience of the necessity of the deductive process, in order to arrive at the truth. It is not this or that man's testimony, but the result of all the testimonies, which affords any sure ground of reliance. Individual testimony here is beyond measure less perfect than that which is delivered before the judge; both because it relates to matters, of which it is infinitely more difficult to give correct testimony, and because it is delivered in circumstances far less favourable to accuracy. By combining the whole, and interpreting one thing by another, certain leading points are made out, and a philosophical acquaintance with human nature is the guide to the rest. In all history, the great, the public, notorious facts, alone, are known with certainty. The minute particulars almost always rest upon very indifferent evidence. The great, the leading facts, therefore, interpreted by a philosophical knowledge of human nature, comprehend the whole amount of the information which history bestows.

We have the very fortunate advantage of high authority upon this subject. M. Talleyrand, whose character will not be challenged as a practical man, even by those who misunderstand the value of what they distinguish by that application, passed, as is well known, a part of the time of his emigration in the United States. His testimony will be regarded by every body as possessing peculiar value. What is it that he tells us? That there are certain grand leading facts, known to all the world; and that he who is capable of interpreting these facts, knows more about the United States, in whatsoever part of the world he may be, than the ordinary man who is upon the spot, examining every thing with his five senses.

There is a letter which Madame de Genlis received from this extraordinary man, during his residence in the United States, from which we extract the following passage:

> Ce pays-ci est une terre où les honnêtes gens peuvent prosperer, pas cependant aussi bien que les fripons, qui comme de raison, ont beaucoup d'avantages. J'avois envie d'ecrire quelque chose sur l'Amerique et de vous l'envoyer; mais je me suis aperçu que c'etait un projet insensé. Je renvoie le peu d'observations que j'ai faites aux conversations que j'espere avoir quelque jour dans les longues soirées avec vous. L'Amerique est comme tous les autres pays: il y a quelques grands faits que tout le monde connaît, et avec les quels on peut d'un cabinet de Copenhague deviner l'Amerique toute entiere. Vous savez quelle est la forme du gouvernement; vous savez qu'il y a de grands et immenses terrains inhabités où chacun peut acquérir une propriété à un prix qui n'a aucun rapport avec les terres d'Europe: vous connoissez la nouveauté du pays, point de capitaux, et beaucoup d'ardeur pour faire fortune; point de manufactures, parceque la main-d'œuvre y est et y sera encore long-temps trop chère. Combinez tout cela, et

vous savez l'Amerique mieux que la majorité des voyageurs, y compris M. de L. – – qui est ici faisant des notes, demandant des pièces, ecrivant des observations, et plus questionneur milles fois que le voyageur inquisitif dont parle Sterne.*

When certain persons, therefore, affirm to us, that the experiment of the ballot has been unsuccessful in the United States, our reply is, that we do not believe them. Why do we not believe them? Because, when we weigh the evidence which is contained in their assertions, and the evidence in opposition to them, we find the latter to preponderate. In the first place, with regard to the assertions, we know not how far those who make them do themselves rely upon them. House of Commons' morality does not imply the existence of many men who will keep back an assertion, useful for their purpose, because they know little or nothing about the evidence on which it rests. In the next place, if we knew that they were sincere, we know not what sort of observers they are; but we do know that few observers are to be trusted. We know not from what circumstances they have deduced their inference; or, if they rest their assertions upon the declarations of other people, from what sort of people they received them. Any man, who pleases, may resort to a pretty certain test of the value which ought to be attached to what ordinary people deliver about the condition of a country. Let him but ask himself this question. To how many, of all the men he knows, would he confide the task of giving an account, on which he would rely, of the country in which they were born and bred? Of the uncertainty of men's observations, even when confined to a single point, the controversies of every day afford the most glaring evidence. Can we find a better example than that which we have all had recently before us? The people of England have been divided into two parties, about the distresses of the country. One would imagine that this was not one of those circumstances which it required eyes of an extraordinary keenness to discern. Yet if you asked a man of one of those parties, whether the country was in distress, he would affirm it; if you asked a man of the other, he would deny it; and both with equal confidence. Upon the experience of which are you to rely? Of neither; because the bulk of the persons who form opinions upon such subjects are led to them by partial observations. Men judge of an object by the things in it to

*Memoires de Madame de Genlis, t. 5, p. 55.

which they direct their attention. A strong bias of the mind directs the attention to that part of the circumstances to which the bias inclines; and upon that part exclusively the opinions of ordinary men are formed.

What trifling, then, is it, to go to uncertain testimony, of which we know only that it is of no value, when the great circumstances of the case, decisive of the question, are perfectly known to us? We know well what secret voting is; and we know that it may be rendered a complete security against external influence, in voting for members of parliament. If the Americans did use it badly, that would be no argument against the thing itself. The Americans have little motive to the accurate use of it, because, by two circumstances in their situation, the general wealth of the people, and the great rarity of large fortunes, the means are wanting of placing more than an insignificant portion of them in dependence. There would be no wonder, then, if the Americans were not very nice about the machinery of the ballot, and cared but little whether it was so used as to work with much, or with little accuracy. Their case and ours are in this respect diametrically opposite; they do not depend upon the ballot for independent voting, we cannot possibly obtain it by any other means.

But beside all this, we know upon better evidence than the assertions made in parliament, that the Americans do esteem the ballot. It is evidence enough that they continue to use it. Why should they, unless they liked it? The Americans are not in our miserable condition. They cannot have institutions, under which they suffer, fastened upon them for ages in spite of their inclinations. What, then, is the fact? So far from being diminished, the use of the ballot has been continually extended in America. Some of the States, in which, originally, it was not employed, have, upon the revision of their constitutions, introduced it; and in not one, in which it has ever been used, has the thought been entertained of discontinuing it. Nothing can be more worthless, therefore, than the pretence that America affords experience against the benefit of secret voting.

Of all the assertions, however, adventured in parliament, to oppose the argument for the ballot, there is certainly not one, the audacity of which is more worthy of our admiration, than what we are next to mention; – that secret voting has no tendency to ensure independent voting. This is an infallible test of character. We strongly recommend the use of it, in the case of public men, to all who desire to understand them. We may be perfectly certain, that the man who makes this assertion will make any other assertion whatsoever, if he believes it useful to his purpose; that twice two, for example, make not four, but four hundred. Take either supposition, that he does not see the truth, or that he sees it and belies it. You, probably, will not affirm, that the man who sees the truth and belies it, in one instance, because it suits his purpose, will not, when it suits his purpose, do so again. And, if any man's intellect be in such a state that he cannot perceive the connection between secret voting and independent voting, either from its native weakness, or its readiness to be blinded by the feeling of interest, we really see no security against a similar effect from similar causes, in the case of a simple arithmetical proposition.

What we have already said upon this subject contains all the evidence necessary to determine the question. An independent vote is a vote, given in such circumstances, that good or evil, at the will of another, does not depend upon the manner of giving it. A man votes as he pleases, when nothing good is to come to him from his voting in one way, nothing evil from his voting in another. Such, necessarily, is the effect of voting in secrecy. If a man promises, or gives, a bribe to another who votes in secret, he clearly sees what he purchases; he gives his money for a certain chance that the man will vote for him; to the man who votes, the case is the same, whether he votes the one way or the other. The man who would inflict evil for a vote given against him, cannot inflict evil for its being given against him, when he cannot know but it was given for him. In these circumstances, the independence of the vote is complete, and we have already seen, that upon independent voting all the blessings of good government, and deliverance from all the unspeakable evils of bad government, inseparably depend.

It is of no consequence to tell us of certain combinations of circumstances, in which the happy and natural effect of secret voting would be eluded. We know them. We know also that under the present distribution of the suffrage in England, there are cases in which the secrecy would have no effect. Take Old Sarum for an example. Wherever the electors are so few, that good can be extended to the whole body, if the result is in one way, evil if it is in another, independence may be prevented in spite of secrecy. But these cases are a very insignificant proportion. In all counties, and in most boroughs, no such power can be pretended. Wherever the voters consist of thousands, or even of a good many hundreds, a sum to each sufficiently large to secure their votes, would exceed the share of the national plunder which any individual could hope to attain; and the power of evil over larger numbers is more limited still. No man can afford to turn out the numerous tenants, either of his lands or his houses, without a serious calamity to himself.

This being the nature of the case, as all men cannot but see, those of our representatives who tell us, that bribery and intimidation would just as much prevail under secret as open voting, must be prepared to affirm, that Englishmen will choose to be slaves, when they may be free; that they will choose to send men to parliament, who will perpetuate the evils of misrule, rather than men who would remove them; even when they can derive no advantage individually from sending the first sort, nor evil individually from sending the latter. They who can believe this, if any such there be, and they who pretend to believe it, are clearly beyond the reach of argument.

A certain set of cases, however, are held forth to countenance this monstrous pretension; which are so far from being cases in point, that they are mere examples of a gross abuse, – the employment of secrecy in circumstances in which it is a protection, not to pure, but to impure voting. This is a point, upon the elucidation of which a few words will be not ill-bestowed; as it is one of the principal sources of obscurity, and hence of sophistry, on the subject of the ballot. There are two sets of circumstances in which votes are given. These two sets of circumstances are so very different in their nature, that in the one of them open voting always tends to good, secret voting tends to evil; in the other secret voting alone tends to good, open voting tends to evil. These two sets of circumstances were not very difficult to discover, and yet we do not know that they were ever distinctly pointed out, till Mr. Mill found the explanation necessary in his History of British India.*

There is one set of circumstances in which, if men voted free from external influence, they would vote well; another set of circumstances in which, if they voted free from external influence, they would vote ill. We see that in one of the most recent discussions on the subject of

---

*The distinction has been subsequently presented to view in an admirable pamphlet, entitled "Statement of the Question of Parliamentary Reform," and published by Baldwin, Cradock, and Co. in 1821. [This pamphlet was written, at Mill's urging, by his young friend George Grote. – Ed.]

the ballot in parliament, Sir Robert Peel tried the effect of a sophism which rested on the confounding these two sets of circumstances together. He brought forward a case of the ill-effect of the ballot in that set of circumstances in which its tendency is to produce evil, whence to infer that it could produce none but ill effects in that set of cases in which its tendency is to produce good. He adduced an instance of the corrupt use of secret voting, by members of parliament in the business of parliament, in order to prove that electors would make a bad use of it in choosing the representatives of the nation.

He was ignorant, so we are willing to believe, that the circumstances of the two cases were not only not the same, but diametrically opposite. In the case of members of parliament in the business of parliament there is no security for good voting without the publicity of the voting. In the case of electors voting for representatives the only security for good voting is the secrecy of the voting.

The difference in the two cases is constituted by the difference of the interests. In the one case, the voter has an interest in bad voting, and will vote ill, if he is not prevented. In the other case, the voter has an interest in voting well, and will vote well, if he is not prevented. The member of parliament, who has an interest in abusing, for his own advantage, the powers of government intrusted to him, needs to be restrained. Restraint is found in the power of publicity. The electors, who have an interest in good representatives, need to be saved from the influence of men, who, if returned under that influence, would not be good. They can be saved by secrecy.

To express the circumstances generally; we say, that in that set of circumstances, in which the voter's own interest would lead him to vote well, but other men are likely to create an interest for him which would lead him to vote ill, the vote should be given in secret: in that set of cases, in which the voter's own interest would lead him to vote ill, but public opinion would act upon him as an inducement to vote well, the vote should be given in public. The effect of secrecy in the two cases is perfectly contrary. In the one case it is protection for the operation of the sinister interest; in the other it is protection against it. In the one case it is the safeguard of the public interest; in the other it is the removal of that safeguard.

To maintain the pretence, that perfect secrecy in voting for members of parliament would not annul the power of influencing the vote by annexing the prospect either of the matter of good to the giving it in one way, or the matter of evil to the giving it in another; it must be affirmed, in the one case, that the man who has received a bribe, or the promise of one, will vote contrary to his inclination, though the receipt of the bribe cannot in the least degree be affected by his voting according to his inclination; that is to say, he will vote against his inclination totally without a motive, which is a moral impossibility: And in all other, it must be affirmed, that the man who is threatened with evil, if he votes in a particular way, will vote against his inclination, though he knows that he is not in the smallest degree more likely to suffer the evil if he votes according to his inclination; that is to say, he will vote contrary to his inclination totally without a motive, which is the same moral impossibility as before. No *reductio ad absurdum* is more perfect than this.

The last resource, therefore, of these controvertists is, to deny the possibility of secrecy. How do they make that out? They do not make it out at all. They make out nothing; nor try to do so. That is not their way. They assert; sometimes more nakedly, sometimes more covertly, but still only assert. Please, then, to inform us in what way the secrecy is to be violated; for if it be to be violated, there must be some mode of doing it.

Voters will shew in what way they vote.

Your word *shew* has a double meaning; and is here employed in your usual, that is, equivocating way. It means either seeing or hearing. If you say, that the voter will let it be seen how he votes, we can take perfect security against that. If you say that the man would tell how he votes; we answer, that the man may do so, as much as he pleases; but the secrecy of the vote will be just as perfect as ever; since it must for ever be a secret whether or not he speaks the truth. At any rate the man who proclaims the knavery of giving a prostitute vote, cannot be depended upon for speaking the truth.

We affirm, then, and upon ground which seems impregnable; 1st. that voting may be rendered perfectly secret; 2nd. that secret voting is a perfect security for independent voting; 3rd. that without independent voting all hope of good government is vain; and 4th, that in England there cannot be independent voting without secret voting. If so, we have a pretty complete argument for the ballot.

The language which is held by the enemies of the ballot is wonderful in almost every part of it; but we do not think there is any thing in it, which excites an odder mixture of feelings, in the intelligent mind, than what they say about the high moral consequences of the tumult and uproar of an election. The excitement, they tell us, produced in the people, by such proceedings, is of an admirable tendency. Their minds are thereby filled with the principles of virtue. Tumultuous elections are a kind of school, a *gymnasium*, for the training of patriots.

In the various pretexts which are made use of to decry secret voting, that indispensable foundation of a good representative system, in all countries in which the mass of the people are not in circumstances which place them above dependence; there is nothing which more deserves our attention than the *animus* displayed by them; the peculiar combination of intellectual and moral qualities, which alone seems competent to usher them into the world.

If what is thus affirmed were true, or if the men who affirm it believe it to be true, we should see them endeavouring to turn this admirable instrument of virtue to the greatest account. Every quiet election would, upon this principle, be an evil; it would defraud the country of so much virtue. Every close borough would not only be a blot in the constitution, but a principle of immorality; a cause why the standard of virtue, in the breasts of Englishmen, is so low as it is. Every compromise in a county, by which, for avoiding of contests, a whig member and a tory member step quietly in, would, in truth, be a flagitious conspiracy against the virtue of the country. If the men who are parties to such compromise should defend it, as they commonly do, by saying that it preserves the peace of the county; that it avoids the excitement of hostile affections, which render men bad neighbours, bad relations, bad landlords, bad tenants, bad magistrates, bad masters, and bad servants; that it saves from those scenes of profligacy, that intemperance, that ferocity, that falsehood, that perjury, that prostitution, that open contempt of all moral ties, which are the grand features of a contested election; if, we say, the men who find all these advantages in what they call the peace of the county, are the very men who tell us the ballot ought to be rejected, because it tends to prevent the golden virtues which are generated by a contested election, – they will not, at any rate, we hope, pretend to be consistent. If contested and exciting elections were thus efficacious in elevating the standard of public morality, the opulent men of the nation ought to have no object nearer their hearts, than to take effectual measures for preventing any election from ever being peaceable. This would be one of the highest services they could render to their country. Nor is this all. If contested, and exciting elections, made to be universal in the country, by the virtue of our opulent men, would produce so much virtue in the people, occurring, as they do, but once in seven years; how much higher would our virtue be raised, if we had the benefit of them every year? There are other elections, too, in the country, beside the elections for members of parliament. They ought undoubtedly all of them to be made to contain as much as possible of that which, in elections for members of parliament, is found to be the cause of such admirable effects; namely, their tumultuousness. All parish vestries ought to be open vestries. Yet here again we have occasion to deplore the little care of their consistency which is taken by our public men. There is nothing which they are more attached to than select vestries; which attachment has misled them so far, notwithstanding their love of tumultuous elections, that they have made the House of Commons the perfect model of a select vestry. The same thing nearly may be said, of all elections of magistrates in corporate towns. These elections please our public men, in proportion as they are on the plan of a select vestry. Yet of how much virtue is the nation thus deprived, which would be surely generated in it, according to the same theory of our public men, if all these elections were tumultuous? We cannot avoid carrying our views even farther. There are various states and conditions, to which men are raised by various incidents, most improperly, if the process of tumultuous elections are so salutary upon the public mind. The appointment of clergymen, for example, not only for parochial duties, but to all the dignities, and all the riches, which some of them enjoy, ought to be made in the way which is most conducive to virtue. The peerage, so great a prize, ought assuredly not to be thrown away, by depending either upon individual choice, or the accident of birth, if so much benefit might be derived from it, in making it depend upon a tumultuous election. Nay the sovereignty itself ought to be elective, since, if the virtue generated by the small contest for a member of parliament be an object of any value, that generated by a choice of such ineffable importance to the nation, would be of infinitely greater value.

So much for the *argumentum ad hominem*; which, in this particular case, all discerning men will see to be of much more importance, than that sort of argument generally is. The intrinsic merits of the question are immediately seen, by a recurrence to the actual business done. There are two parties at an election; one, that of those who give prostitute votes; the other, that of those who suborn them. It is of no use to tell us that there are honest votes at elections; there might be more than any body will pretend there are, without affecting the truth of our description. The honest votes, taking the country as a whole, are a miserable exception. Now, then, draw the consequence. A scene got up for the most deeply immoral and degrading of all human purposes, for the perpetration of a great act of treachery to the nation, for delivering it into the hands of a small number of men, interested in all the abuses of misrule, contrary to the most solemn of all engagements, in the midst of fraud, perjury, and every other abomination, there are men who tell us is a scene, in which Englishmen have to learn their public virtue, and of which, from consideration of their virtues, it would be most dangerous to deprive them. – Those virtues in them, which fit them for the purposes of their suborners, they do learn there in great perfection. That is a truth beyond all dispute. No wonder the school should have patrons, in a class of men so deeply interested in its success.

One objection still remains, which, though we shall be able to shew that it rests entirely on misapprehension, we regard with far more respect than any of those which we have previously noticed; because the point of morality to which it refers is of the utmost importance, and because we know that it affects the minds of some men, who, on account both of their intellectual and moral qualities, are entitled to our highest esteem. These men say, that secret voting, to make it answer its end, supposes mendacity. The man who is bribed, promises to vote one way, and actually votes another. The man who may be turned out of his house, or his farm, or suffer any other evil, votes one way, while he says that he votes another. This violation of truth, they say, is so odious, that it renders odious and ineligible whatever is necessarily combined with it.

This objection requires the more words to shew the nature of it truly, because the evil which it points at is all upon the surface, and is easily seen; the evil which is prevented lies deep, and can only be seen by an attentive observer. – Of two evils choose the least, – is, nevertheless, the proper rule, in this, as in every other case of human deliberation.

Of so much importance is it to mankind, that they should be able to confide in what is said to them by one another, that no violation of the truth which would affect that end, can be justified.

There are circumstances, however, in which another man is not entitled to the truth; and these circumstances create a radical distinction. The cases in which men are not entitled to the truth constitute a class by themselves; subject to rules altogether different from the class of cases in which they are entitled to the truth.

Men are not entitled to the truth, when they would make a bad use of it. This is a maxim sanctioned by the moral judgment and the practice of all ages and nations. When men withhold the truth from such parties, they in fact do not violate the rule of veracity; they neither feel conscious of any guilt in themselves, nor is any ever imputed to them by others. The rule of veracity does not consist in giving information to a villain which he will employ in forwarding his villainous ends. Wrong information, for the prevention of evil, and, in certain circumstances, for the promotion of good, has rarely been classed among forbidden means by any set of men, civilized or barbarian. Who that saw a fellow-creature hiding himself from his intruding murderer, but would say to the ruffian whatever was most likely to mislead him in his pursuit? Instances might be multiplied without end. Take one of an ordinary sort. The Physician is not blamed, he does not consider himself as violating the sacred rule of veracity, when he assures his patient that he is in no danger, though he knows him to be in the greatest.

In no instance is wrong information conducive to the prevention of evil of such magnitude, as when it is conducive to the prevention of misrule. In no instance is any man less entitled to right information, than when he would employ it for the perpetration of misrule. If in every conceivable instance wrong information is not to be considered a violation of the rule of veracity, not a breach of morality, but on the contrary a meritorious act, it is when it is necessary to defeat such a purpose as this.

Among the gross inconsistencies which crowd the minds of Englishmen, one of the most remarkable is that which exists between the abhorrence of the ballot, on account of the supposed mendacity connected with it, and the habitual conduct of the men who express that abhorrence. The same mendacity, exactly, if they persist in calling it mendacity, which a voter may use to baffle his corrupter, they themselves practise every day from the slightest motives. Every time they write "obedient, humble servant," at the bottom of a letter, they tell a lie, if lie it must be called, of the very same description. Every time they direct a servant to say at their door to the people who want them, that they are not at home, when they are at home, they not only lie themselves, but in this instance have no scruple at all in making another person lie, notwithstanding the intolerable pollution they ascribe to it in the case of the ballot. It surely is not necessary for us to go on shewing how much of the whole business of life, in this purest of countries, is carried on by lying, if words and actions conveying false information deserve this opprobrious name. Let us look to more solemn occasions. The law hardly does any thing but by means of a lie; witness the writs which give commencement to a suit; and witness, to go no farther, pleadings of almost all descriptions. Not only breaches of veracity, but breaches of oath, are committed with the utmost indifference. How common is it, for jurors on their oaths, to declare an article worth but a few shillings, which they know to be worth, perhaps, ten times as many pounds, only that they may not subject a criminal to a greater punishment than he deserves; how necessarily does the law requiring unanimity in juries, compel a part of the jury in almost all doubtful cases to perjure themselves? We need but allude to the daily use of fiscal oaths, and theological oaths, to be reminded of the perfect callousness with which false swearing is practised and regarded. Nay, remarkable as it must be esteemed, we on no occasion lie more grossly, and habitually, than in our devotions; in our addresses to God himself, at the very time that we are professing with our lips that we believe him omniscient, and acquainted with our innermost thoughts. Do we not hear people daily telling God in their prayers that they renounce the pomps and vanities of the world, when we know their hearts are filled with nothing else? Does not every man who repeats the prayer, called the Lord's, tell the Deity, that he wishes "not to be led into temptation?" And do we not know many such men devoting all their thoughts to the accumulating of riches, or the acquisition of worldly grandeur, which the scripture tells them are the greatest of temptations; since it is easier for a camel to go through the eye of a needle than for a rich man to enter into the Kingdom of heaven? – Need we go on? – Surely not.

And yet have we men, who, after seeing to how great a degree the whole tissue of our lives is formed of lying, and after being themselves inured to it, profess so violent a hatred of the falsehood accidental to a vote rendered independent by secrecy, as to account the independence, and all the inestimable benefits which flow from it, less than an equivalent? We should have accounted this one of the most perfect of all possible specimens of Tartuffizing, if we did not know that there are valuable men, who have formed with the false information, which may occasionally be necessary to obtain the independence of which secrecy is the means such an association of ideas, as they do unhappily mistake for moral disapprobation.

But beside the proof we have given, that the wrong information incidental to the ballot belongs not to the class of cases in which the moral rule of veracity is concerned; beside the certainty of the rule, that the least of two evils is to be chosen; and the perfect proof by the practice of Englishmen, that in innumerable instances they regard the use of falsehood as little or no evil, while bad government is acknowledged to be the worst of all evils; beside all this, we have still to observe that the objection assumes what is not true. It assumes that every vote which would be suborned, if openly given, would be attended with mendacity if given secretly.

First observe, that if this were so, the cases, in respect of mendacity, would only be equal. Every suborned vote is by the supposition a mendacious vote. What ground then is there for any preference on the score of veracity; and what ground is there not for preference on the score of national good? This objection, drawn from the love of veracity, is thus clearly seen to be utterly worthless.

Such, however, is the admirable working of the ballot, that it would preclude the occasion for mendacity in many, in probably a great majority of instances, from the beginning; and in the end would utterly abolish it. If men never continue to do any thing in vain, men will not seek promises from others, in circumstances in which the promise is of no use to them. Where there is no promising at all, there can be no false promising. The ballot, therefore, is really the means of delivering votes from mendacity. One of the arguments in favour of secret voting springs from the very source, from which this mistaken objection is drawn.

Suppose a man to go about, asking promises from electors who vote in secret. He obtains them, of course, from all the men, from whom he would have obtained a prostitute vote in the case of publicity. An act of mendacity is necessary in either case, whether the promise is kept or broken. But of two lies, equal to a man in other respects, he may pretty surely be expected to prefer that which favours his own inclinations. The promise, therefore, is to the man who exacts it no security for the attainment of his object. It is obviously the reverse, if the attempt to impose an odious chain be felt as an injury by the man who is sought to be degraded. Every man from whom a promise is exacted to vote in one way, has received a new motive to vote in the opposite way, by this badge of slavery nefariously fastened upon him. It is abundantly certain, that the exaction of promises, – in these circumstances more than useless, – would soon be abandoned, and voting would be as pure of falsehood as it would be of dependence.

Nor would this be the only moral effect of secret voting; it would have others of the greatest extent, and importance. This, undoubtedly, is one of the most interesting points of view in which the subject can be considered. Take away from the men of property the power of obtaining the suffrages of the people by improper means, and you may deem it certain that they will immediately apply themselves to the obtaining of them by proper means.

It is impossible not to be delighted with the idea of the consequences which would result from such a change. Whereas, at present, the traffic which takes place between the parties who give and the parties who obtain votes, corrupts them both; the intercourse between them, in the other case which we have supposed, would operate most powerfully to their mutual improvement.

The evidence of this we think is incontestible. The moment it was seen that the people gave their suffrages only to those whom they regarded as best endowed with the qualities which fit men for the duties of legislation, the men of property would exert themselves to attain and to display those qualities. They would then have a motive for their attainment, of which at present they are nearly destitute. Stores of knowledge, habits of mental application, of self-denial, of preferring the public interest to the private interest, whenever there is incompatibility between them, are not easily acquired; and never will be acquired (barring remarkable exceptions) by those who have not a strong motive to acquire them.

We think, that putting the elective suffrage on a proper footing would afford that motive to the men of property in England. Men of property love distinction; but the distinction of property, where it is not connected with political power, or strongly associated with the idea of it, is insignificant. The great desire of men of property, therefore, always will be for the distinction connected with public services.

But, if they had an adequate motive for the acquisition, in a superior degree, of the high mental qualities, which fit men for the discharge of public duties, it cannot be doubted that they have great, and peculiar advantages, for the accomplishment of their purpose. Other men, even those who are not confined to mechanical drudgery, are under the necessity of employing the greater part of their lives, in earning the means either of subsistence or independence. The men who are born to a property which places them above such necessity, can employ the whole of their lives in acquiring the knowledge, the talents, and the virtues, which would entitle them to the confidence of their fellow citizens. With equal motive, and superior advantages, they would, of course, in general, have superior success. They would be the foremost men in the country, and so they would be esteemed.

And says Plato: "A man has peculiar advantages for attaining the highest excellence of his nature, when he is above the necessity of labouring for the means of subsistence."

The man who is placed in these circumstances, has not only the whole of his time to bestow, in early life, upon the acquisitions which fit him for the business of legislation and government; he alone, and not the man without fortune, who is still engaged in other pursuits, can bestow his time and attention, undivided, upon the public services with which he is intrusted. Our opinion, therefore, is, that the business of government is properly the business of the rich; and that they will always obtain it, either by bad means, or good. Upon this every thing depends. If they obtain it by bad means, the government is bad. If they obtain it by good means, the government is sure to be good. The only good means of obtaining it are, the free suffrage of the people.

Radical Reformers are commonly stigmatized in the lump; and, as names of peculiar opprobrium among the suborners of votes, they are called Democrats, and Republicans. We see not why either of these names, unless misconstrued, should be dishonourable. For our parts, however, we are Aristocrats. We think it best, that government should be placed in the hands of the Ἀριστοι; not only in the sense of the Greeks, who understood by that term the Βελτιστοι; but in that of the moderns, who understand by it only the Rich. We only desire that it be placed in the hands of the rich upon such terms as will make them the Ἀριστοι and Βελτιστοι. Whoever are the Ἀριστοι and Βελτιστοι, we desire to be governed by them; and, with the suffrage upon a proper footing, we have no doubt that they would be the Rich.

If the effect of placing the suffrage upon a proper footing would be thus salutary, with regard to the intellectual and moral qualities of the rich; let us inquire next what it would be in regard to the rest of the community.

We have seen that, while votes are liable to be suborned, and while the rich obtain their purpose with the people by corrupting them, they do corrupt them. The consequence is inevitable; and neither the insensibility to moral evil which habit produces, nor all the refinements of modern disguise, can hinder any fair observer from understanding the Tragi-comedy of which we are the spectators.

But, if the business of the rich is to corrupt the people, when they can obtain their purpose by corrupting them, it will no less certainly be their endeavour to improve them, if you render it impossible for them to obtain their purpose with the people by any other means than improving them.

Who will deny that this would be the consequence of placing the suffrage upon a proper foundation? When the people are under no inducement to choose representatives from any other consideration than that of their fitness, it becomes immediately the interest of the rich, that none but the fittest should be chosen. Whenever the benefits of misrule are taken out of the hands of the rich, the rich have then the strongest interest in good government. Good government, however, nothing but the good choice of the people can procure.

But the more wise and the more virtuous the people can be rendered, the goodness of their choice is rendered the more certain. It becomes, immediately, therefore, the interest of the rich, to employ their endeavours to raise the intellects and morals of the people to the highest pitch; that no artifice may be able to deceive, or interest to seduce them, either in regard to what is best to be done for their country, or the men who are fittest to promote it.

But, if the men of power and influence in the country, along with sufficient motives to take the utmost pains with their own intellects and morals, had the like motives to take pains with the intellects and morals of the people; to do whatever could be done for rendering their early education perfect; to take the utmost care of their morals through life, by a correct use of their approbation and disapprobation, as well as their power of giving and withholding good; to watch over the instruction given to them; to take them out of the hands of those who have an interest in giving them wrong opinions, to use the press with skill and activity, for the producing all sorts of salutary impressions, and obviating every impression of a different kind; what delightful consequences would ensue? We should then have a community, through which wisdom and virtue would be universally diffused; and of which the different classes would be knit together by the ties of mutual benefaction. In those circumstances, the order and harmony of society would be perfect. The business of government would be carried on with the utmost simplicity, because purely for the good of all. Every individual would exert himself in his sphere to provide for his own wants, and have wherewithal to benefit others; and few men would be destitute of that prudence and energy which would place, and keep him, in that situation.

Nor in all this is there one Utopian idea. There is not a consequence here anticipated, which does not flow from the principles of human nature, as necessarily as the actual effects, so woefully different, which we now experience. All that is necessary is, so to alter the position of the leading classes with respect to the rest of the community, that they may have an interest in the wisdom and virtue both of themselves and others. It is not more extraordinary, than true, that this is to be accomplished, and all its admirable consequences may be insured, by placing the Suffrage for Representatives on a proper foundation.

The evidence of all this is so clear and irrefragable, that it ought to obtain attention. The time is coming when it will obtain all the attention which it deserves. At present we believe it has little chance.

APPENDIX:
Macaulay *vs.* Mill

Mill on Government (March 1829)

T. B. Macaulay

Of those philosophers who call themselves Utilitarians and whom others generally call Benthamites, Mr. Mill is, with the exception of the illustrious founder of the sect, by far the most distinguished. The little work now before us contains a summary of the opinions held by this gentleman and his brethren on several subjects most important to society. All the seven essays of which it consists abound in curious matter. But at present we intend to confine our remarks to the Treatise on Government, which stands first in the volume. On some future occasion, we may perhaps attempt to do justice to the rest.

It must be owned that to do justice to any composition of Mr. Mill is not, in the opinion of his admirers, a very easy task. They do not, indeed, place him in the same rank with Mr. Bentham; but the terms in which they extol the disciple, though feeble when compared with the hyperboles of adoration employed by them in speaking of the master, are as strong as any sober man would allow himself to use concerning Locke or Bacon. The essay before us is perhaps the most remarkable of the works to which Mr. Mill owes his fame. By the members of his sect, it is considered as perfect and unanswerable. Every part of it is an article of their faith; and the damnatory clauses, in which their creed abounds far beyond any theological symbol with which we are acquainted, are strong and full against all who reject any portion of what is so irrefragably established. No man, they maintain, who has understanding sufficient to carry him through the first proposition of Euclid, can read this master-piece of demonstration and honestly declare that he remains unconvinced.

We have formed a very different opinion of this work. We think that the theory of Mr. Mill rests altogether on false principles, and that even on those false principles he does not reason logically. Nevertheless, we do not think it strange that his speculations should have filled the Utilitarians with admiration. We have been for some time past inclined to suspect that these people, whom some regard as the lights of the world and others as incarnate demons, are in general ordinary men, with narrow understandings and little information. The contempt which they express for elegant literature is evidently the contempt of ignorance. We apprehend that many of them are persons who, having read little or nothing, are delighted to be rescued from the sense of their own inferiority by some teacher who assures them that the studies which they have neglected are of no value, puts five or six phrases into their mouths, lends them an odd number of the Westminster Review, and in a month transforms them into philosophers. Mingled with these smatterers, whose attainments just suffice to elevate them from the insignificance of dunces to the dignity of bores, and to spread dismay among their pious aunts and grandmothers, there are, we well know, many well-meaning men who have really read and thought much; but whose reading and meditation have been almost exclusively confined to one class of subjects; and who, consequently, though they possess much valuable knowledge respecting those subjects, are by no means so well qualified to judge of a great system as if they had taken a more enlarged view of literature and society.

Nothing is more amusing or instructive than to observe the manner in which people who think themselves wiser than all the rest of the world fall into snares which the simple good sense of their neighbours detects and avoids. It is one of the principal tenets of the Utilitarians that sentiment and eloquence serve only to impede the pursuit of truth. They therefore affect a quakerly plainness, or rather a cynical negligence and impurity, of style. The strongest arguments, when clothed in brilliant language, seem to them so much wordy nonsense. In the meantime they surrender their understandings, with a facility found in no other party, to the meanest and most abject sophisms, provided those sophisms come before them disguised with the externals of demonstration. They do not seem to know that logic has its illusions as well as rhetoric, – that a fallacy may lurk in a syllogism as well as in a metaphor.

Mr. Mill is exactly the writer to please people of this description. His arguments are stated with the utmost affectation of precision; his divisions are awfully formal; and his style is generally as dry as that of Euclid's Elements. Whether this be a merit, we must be permitted to doubt. Thus much is certain: that the ages in which the true principles of philosophy were least understood were those in which the ceremonial of logic was most strictly observed, and that the time from which we date the rapid progress of the experimental sciences was also the time at which a less exact and formal way of writing came into use.

The style which the Utilitarians admire suits only those subjects on which it is possible to reason *à priori*. It grew up with the verbal sophistry which flourished during the dark ages. With that sophistry it fell before the Baconian philosophy in the day of the great deliverance of the human mind. The inductive method not only endured but required greater freedom of diction. It was impossible to reason from phœnomena up to principles, to mark slight shades of difference in quality, or to estimate the comparative effect of two opposite considerations, between which there was no common measure, by means of the naked and meagre jargon of the schoolmen. Of those schoolmen Mr. Mill has inherited both the spirit and the style. He is an Aristotelian of the fifteenth century, born out of due season. We have here an elaborate treatise on Government, from which, but for two or three passing allusions, it would not appear that the author was aware that any governments actually existed among men. Certain propensities of human nature are assumed; and from these premises the whole science of politics is synthetically deduced! We can scarcely persuade ourselves that we are not reading a book written before the time of Bacon and Galileo, – a book written in those days in which physicians reasoned from the nature of heat to the treatment of fever, and astronomers proved syllogistically that the planets could have no independent motion, – because the heavens were incorruptible, and nature abhorred a vacuum!

The reason, too, which Mr. Mill has assigned for taking this course strikes us as most extraordinary.

"Experience," says he, "if we look only at the outside of the facts, appears to be *divided* on this subject. Absolute monarchy, under

273

Neros and Caligulas, under such men as the Emperors of Morocco and Sultans of Turkey, is the scourge of human nature. On the other side, the people of Denmark, tired out with the oppression of an aristocracy, resolved that their king should be absolute; and, under their absolute monarch, are as well governed as any people in Europe."

This Mr. Mill actually gives as a reason for pursuing the *à priori* method. But, in our judgment, the very circumstances which he mentions irresistibly prove that the *à priori* method is altogether unfit for investigations of this kind, and that the only way to arrive at the truth is by induction. *Experience* can never be divided, or even appear to be divided, except with reference to some hypothesis. When we say that one fact is inconsistent with another fact, we mean only that it is inconsistent with *the theory* which we have founded on that other fact. But, if the fact be certain, the unavoidable conclusion is that our theory is false; and, in order to correct it, we must reason back from an enlarged collection of facts to principles.

Now here we have two governments which, by Mr. Mill's own account, come under the same head in his *theoretical* classification. It is evident, therefore, that, by reasoning on that theoretical classification, we shall be brought to the conclusion that these two forms of government must produce the same effects. But Mr. Mill himself tells us that they do not produce the same effects. Hence he infers that the only way to get at truth is to place implicit confidence in that chain of proof *à priori* from which it appears that they must produce the same effects! To believe at once in a theory and in a fact which contradicts it is an exercise of faith sufficiently hard: but to believe in a theory *because* a fact contradicts it is what neither philosopher nor pope ever before required. This, however, is what Mr. Mill demands of us. He seems to think that, if all despots, without exception, governed ill, it would be unnecessary to prove, by a synthetical argument, what would then be sufficiently clear from experience. But, as some despots will be so perverse as to govern well, he finds himself compelled to prove the impossibility of their governing well by that synthetical argument which would have been superfluous had not the facts contradicted it. He reasons *à priori*, because the phœnomena are not what, by reasoning *à priori*, he will prove them to be. In other words, he reasons *à priori*, because, by so reasoning, he is certain to arrive at a false conclusion!

In the course of the examination to which we propose to subject the speculations of Mr. Mill we shall have to notice many other curious instances of that turn of mind which the passage above quoted indicates.

The first chapter of his Essay relates to the ends of government. The conception on this subject, he tells us, which exists in the minds of most men is vague and undistinguishing. He first assumes, justly enough, that the end of government is "to increase to the utmost the pleasures, and diminish to the utmost the pains, which men derive from each other." He then proceeds to show, with great form, that "the greatest possible happiness of society is attained by insuring to every man the greatest possible quantity of the produce of his labour." To effect this is, in his opinion, the end of government. It is remarkable that Mr. Mill, with all his affected display of precision, has here given a description of the ends of government far less precise than that which is in the mouths of the vulgar. The first man with whom Mr. Mill may travel in a stage coach will tell him that government exists for the protection of the *persons* and property of men. But Mr. Mill seems to think that the preservation of property is the first and only object. It is true, doubtless, that many of the injuries which are offered to the persons of men proceed from a desire to possess their property. But the practice of vindictive assassination as it has existed in some parts of Europe – the practice of fighting wanton and sanguinary duels, like those of the sixteenth and seventeenth centuries, in which bands of seconds risked their lives as well as the principals; – these practices, and many others which might be named, are evidently injurious to society; and we do not see how a government which tolerated them could be said "to diminish to the utmost the pains which men derive from each other." Therefore, according to Mr. Mill's very correct assumption, such a government would not perfectly accomplish the end of its institution. Yet such a government might, as far as we can perceive, "insure to every man the greatest possible quantity of the produce of his labour." Therefore, such a government might, according to Mr. Mill's subsequent doctrine, perfectly accomplish the end of its institution. The matter is not of much consequence, except as an instance of that slovenliness of thinking which is often concealed beneath a peculiar ostentation of logical neatness.

Having determined the ends, Mr. Mill proceeds to consider the means. For the preservation of property some portion of the community must be intrusted with power. This is Government; and the question is, how are those to whom the necessary power is intrusted to be prevented from abusing it?

Mr. Mill first passes in review the simple forms of government. He allows that it would be inconvenient, if not physically impossible, that the whole community should meet in a mass; it follows, therefore, that the powers of government cannot be directly exercised by the people. But he sees no objection to pure and direct Democracy, except the difficulty which we have mentioned.

"The community," says he, "cannot have an interest opposite to its interests. To affirm this would be a contradiction in terms. The community within itself, and with respect to itself, can have no sinister interest. One community may intend the evil of another; never its own. This is an indubitable proposition, and one of great importance."

Mr. Mill then proceeds to demonstrate that a purely aristocratical form of government is necessarily bad.

> The reason for which government exists is, that one man, if stronger than another, will take from him whatever that other possesses and he desires. But if one man will do this, so will several. And if powers are put into the hands of a comparatively small number, called an aristocracy, – powers which make them stronger than the rest of the community, they will take from the rest of the community as much as they please of the objects of desire. They will thus defeat the very end for which government was instituted. The unfitness, therefore, of an aristocracy to be intrusted with the powers of government, rests on demonstration.

In exactly the same manner Mr. Mill proves absolute monarchy to be a bad form of government.

> If government is founded upon this as a law of human nature, that a man, if able, will take from others any thing which they have and he desires, it is sufficiently evident that when a man is called a king he does not change his nature, so that when he has got power to enable him to take from every man what he pleases, he will take whatever he pleases. To suppose that he will not, is to affirm that government is unnecessary, and that human beings will abstain from injuring one another of their own accord.
>
> It is very evident that this reasoning extends to every modification of the smaller number. Whenever the powers of government

are placed in any hands other than those of the community, whether those of one man, of a few, or of several, those principles of human nature which imply that government is at all necessary, imply that those persons will make use of them to defeat the very end for which government exists.

But is it not possible that a king or an aristocracy may soon be saturated with the objects of their desires, and may then protect the community in the enjoyment of the rest? Mr. Mill answers in the negative. He proves, with great pomp, that every man desires to have the actions of every other correspondent to his will. Others can be induced to conform to our will only by motives derived from pleasure or from pain. The infliction of pain is of course direct injury; and even if it take the milder course, in order to produce obedience by motives derived from pleasure, the government must confer favours. But as there is no limit to its desire of obedience, there will be no limit to its disposition to confer favours; and as it can confer favours only by plundering the people, there will be no limit to its disposition to plunder the people. "It is therefore not true that there is in the mind of a king, or in the minds of an aristocracy, any point of saturation with the objects of desire."

Mr. Mill then proceeds to show that, as monarchical and oligarchical governments can influence men by motives drawn from pain, as well as by motives drawn from pleasure, they will carry their cruelty, as well as their rapacity, to a frightful extent. As he seems greatly to admire his own reasonings on this subject, we think it but fair to let him speak for himself.

> The chain of inference in this case is close and strong to a most unusual degree. A man desires that the actions of other men shall be instantly and accurately correspondent to his will. He desires that the actions of the greatest possible number shall be so. Terror is the grand instrument. Terror can work only through assurance that evil will follow any failure of conformity between the will and the actions willed. Every failure must therefore be punished. As there are no bounds to the mind's desire of its pleasure, there are, of course, no bounds to its desire of perfection in the instruments of that pleasure. There are, therefore, no bounds to its desire of exactness in the conformity between its will and the actions willed; and by consequence to the strength of that terror which is its procuring cause. Even the most minute

failure must be visited with the heaviest infliction; and as failure in extreme exactness must frequently happen, the occasions of cruelty must be incessant.

We have thus arrived at several conclusions of the highest possible importance. We have seen that the principle of human nature, upon which the necessity of government is founded, the propensity of one man to possess himself of the objects of desire at the cost of another, leads on, by infallible sequence, where power over a community is attained, and nothing checks, not only to that degree of plunder which leaves the members (excepting always the recipients and instruments of the plunder) the bare means of subsistence, but to that degree of cruelty which is necessary to keep in existence the most intense terrors.

Now no man who has the least knowledge of the real state of the world, either in former ages or at the present moment, can possibly be convinced, though he may perhaps be bewildered, by arguments like these. During the last two centuries, some hundreds of absolute princes have reigned in Europe. Is it true, that their cruelty has kept in existence the most intense degree of terror; that their rapacity has left no more than the bare means of subsistence to any of their subjects, their ministers and soldiers excepted? Is this true of all of them? Of one half of them? Of one tenth part of them? Of a single one? Is it true, in the full extent, even of Philip the Second, of Louis the Fifteenth, or of the Emperor Paul? But it is scarcely necessary to quote history. No man of common sense, however ignorant he may be of books, can be imposed on by Mr. Mill's argument; because no man of common sense can live among his fellow-creatures for a day without seeing innumerable facts which contradict it. It is our business, however, to point out its fallacy; and happily the fallacy is not very recondite.

We grant that rulers will take as much as they can of the objects of their desires; and that, when the agency of other men is necessary to that end, they will attempt by all means in their power to enforce the prompt obedience of such men. But what are the objects of human desire? Physical pleasure, no doubt, in part. But the mere appetites which we have in common with the animals would be gratified, almost as cheaply and easily as those of the animals are gratified, if nothing were given to taste, to ostentation, or to the affections. How small a portion of the income of a gentleman in easy circumstances is laid out merely in giving pleasurable sensations to the body of the possessor! The greater part even of what is spent on his kitchen and his cellar goes, not to titillate his palate, but to keep up his character for hospitality, to save him from the reproach of meanness in housekeeping, and to cement the ties of good neighbourhood. It is clear that a king or an aristocracy may be supplied to satiety with mere corporal pleasures, at an expense which the rudest and poorest community would scarcely feel.

Those tastes and propensities which belong to us as reasoning and imaginative beings are not indeed so easily gratified. There is, we admit, no point of saturation with objects of desire which come under this head. And therefore the argument of Mr. Mill will be just, unless there be something in the nature of the objects of desire themselves which is inconsistent with it. Now, of these objects there is none which men in general seem to desire more than the good opinion of others. The hatred and contempt of the public are generally felt to be intolerable. It is probable that our regard for the sentiments of our fellow-creatures springs, by association, from a sense of their ability to hurt or to serve us. But, be this as it may, it is notorious that, when the habit of mind of which we speak has once been formed, men feel extremely solicitous about the opinions of those by whom it is most improbable, nay absolutely impossible, that they should ever be in the slightest degree injured or benefited. The desire of posthumous fame and the dread of posthumous reproach and execration are feelings from the influence of which scarcely any man is perfectly free, and which in many men are powerful and constant motives of action. As we are afraid that, if we handle this part of the argument after our own manner, we shall incur the reproach of sentimentality, a word which, in the sacred language of the Benthamites, is synonymous with idiocy, we will quote what Mr. Mill himself says on the subject, in his Treatise on Jurisprudence.

> Pains from the moral source are the pains derived from the unfavourable sentiments of mankind . . . These pains are capable of rising to a height with which hardly any other pains incident to our nature can be compared. There is a certain degree of unfavourableness in the sentiments of his fellow-creatures, under which hardly any man, not below the standard of humanity, can endure to live.

The importance of this powerful agency, for the prevention of

injurious acts, is too obvious to need to be illustrated. If sufficiently at command, it would almost supersede the use of other
means . . .

To know how to direct the unfavourable sentiments of
mankind, it is necessary to know in as complete, that is, in as
comprehensive, a way as possible, what it is which gives them
birth. Without entering into the metaphysics of the question, it is
a sufficient practical answer, for the present purpose, to say that
the unfavourable sentiments of man are excited by every thing
which hurts them.

It is strange that a writer who considers the pain derived from the
unfavourable sentiments of others as so acute that, if sufficiently at
command, it would supersede the use of the gallows and the tread-
mill, should take no notice of this most important restraint when
discussing the question of government. We will attempt to deduce a
theory of politics in the mathematical form, in which Mr. Mill
delights, from the premises with which he has himself furnished us.

PROPOSITION I. THEOREM.

No rulers will do any thing which may hurt the people.

This is the thesis to be maintained; and the following we humbly
offer to Mr. Mill, as its syllogistic demonstration.

No rulers will do that which produces pain to themselves.

But the unfavourable sentiments of the people will give pain to
them.

Therefore no rulers will do any thing which may excite the
unfavourable sentiments of the people.

But the unfavourable sentiments of the people are excited by every
thing which hurts them.

Therefore no rulers will do any thing which may hurt the people.
Which was the thing to be proved.

Having thus, as we think, not unsuccessfully imitated Mr. Mill's
logic, we do not see why we should not imitate, what is at least equally
perfect in its kind, his self-complacency, and proclaim our Εὐρηκα
in his own words: "The chain of inference, in this case, is close and
strong to a most unusual degree."

The fact is, that, when men, in treating of things which cannot be
circumscribed by precise definitions, adopt this mode of reasoning,

when once they begin to talk of power, happiness, misery, pain, pleasure, motives, objects of desire, as they talk of lines and numbers, there is no end to the contradictions and absurdities into which they fall. There is no proposition so monstrously untrue in morals or politics that we will not undertake to prove it, by something which shall sound like a logical demonstration, from admitted principles.

Mr. Mill argues that, if men are not inclined to plunder each other, government is unnecessary; and that, if they are so inclined, the powers of government, when intrusted to a small number of them, will necessarily be abused. Surely it is not by propounding dilemmas of this sort that we are likely to arrive at sound conclusions in any moral science. The whole question is a question of degree. If all men preferred the moderate approbation of their neighbours to any degree of wealth or grandeur, or sensual pleasure, government would be unnecessary. If all men desired wealth so intensely as to be willing to brave the hatred of their fellow-creatures for six-pence, Mr. Mill's argument against monarchies and aristocracies would be true to the full extent. But the fact is, that all men have some desires which impel them to injure their neighbours, and some desires which impel them to benefit their neighbours. Now, if there were a community consisting of two classes of men, one of which should be principally influenced by the one set of motives and the other by the other, government would clearly be necessary to restrain the class which was eager for plunder and careless of reputation: and yet the powers of government might be safely intrusted to the class which was chiefly actuated by the love of approbation. Now, it might with no small plausibility be maintained that, in many countries, *there are* two classes which, in some degree, answer to this description; that the poor compose the class which government is established to restrain, and the people of some property the class to which the powers of government may without danger be confided. It might be said that a man who can barely earn a livelihood by severe labour is under stronger temptations to pillage others than a man who enjoys many luxuries. It might be said that a man who is lost in the crowd is less likely to have the fear of public opinion before his eyes than a man whose station and mode of living render him conspicuous. We do not assert all this. We only say that it was Mr. Mill's business to prove the contrary; and that, not having proved the contrary, he is not entitled to say, "that those principles which imply that government is at all necessary, imply that an aristocracy will make use of its power to defeat the end for which governments exist." This is not true, unless it be true that a rich man is as likely to covet the goods of his neighbours as a poor man, and that a poor man is as likely to be solicitous about the opinions of his neighbours as a rich man.

But we do not see that by reasoning *à priori* on such subjects as these, it is possible to advance one single step. We know that every man has some desires which he can gratify only by hurting his neighbours, and some which he can gratify only by pleasing them. Mr. Mill has chosen to look only at one-half of human nature, and to reason on the motives which impel men to oppress and despoil others, as if they were the only motives by which men could possibly be influenced. We have already shown that, by taking the other half of the human character, and reasoning on it as if it were the whole, we can bring out a result diametrically opposite to that at which Mr. Mill has arrived. We can, by such a process, easily prove that any form of government is good, or that all government is superfluous.

We must now accompany Mr. Mill on the next stage of his argument. Does any combination of the three simple forms of government afford the requisite securities against the abuse of power? Mr. Mill complains that those who maintain the affirmative generally beg the question; and proceeds to settle the point by proving, after his fashion, that no combination of the three simple forms, or of any two of them, can possibly exist.

> From the principles which we have already laid down it follows that, of the objects of human desire, and, speaking more definitely, of the means to the ends of human desire, namely, wealth and power, each party will endeavour to obtain as much as possible.
>
> If any expedient presents itself to any of the supposed parties effectual to this end, and not opposed to any preferred object of pursuit, we may infer with certainty that it will be adopted. One effectual expedient is not more effectual than obvious. Any two of the parties, by combining, may swallow up the third. That such combination will take place appears to be as certain as any thing which depends upon human will; because there are strong motives in favour of it, and none that can be conceived in opposition to it . . . The mixture of three of the kinds of government, it is thus evident, cannot possibly exist . . . It may be proper to inquire whether an union may not be possible of two of them . . .

Let us first suppose, that monarchy is united with aristocracy. Their power is equal or not equal. If it is not equal, it follows, as a necessary consequence, from the principles which we have already established, that the stronger will take from the weaker till it engrosses the whole. The only question therefore is, What will happen when the power is equal?

In the first place, it seems impossible that such equality should ever exist. How is it to be established? or, by what criterion is it to be ascertained? If there is no such criterion, it must, in all cases, be the result of chance. If so, the chances against it are as infinity to one. The idea, therefore, is wholly chimerical and absurd . . .

In this doctrine of the mixture of the simple forms of government is included the celebrated theory of the balance among the component parts of a government. By this it is supposed that, when a government is composed of monarchy, aristocracy, and democracy, they balance one another, and by mutual checks produce good government. A few words will suffice to show that, if any theory deserves the epithets of "wild, visionary and chimerical," it is that of the balance. If there are three powers, how is it possible to prevent two of them from combining to swallow up the third?

The analysis which we have already performed will enable us to trace rapidly the concatenation of causes and effects in this imagined case.

We have already seen that the interest of the community, considered in the aggregate, or in the democratical point of view, is, that each individual should receive protection; and that the powers which are constituted for that purpose should be employed exclusively for that purpose . . . We have also seen that the interest of the king and of the governing aristocracy is directly the reverse. It is to have unlimited power over the rest of the community, and to use it for their own advantage. In the supposed case of the balance of the monarchical, aristocratical, and democratical powers, it cannot be for the interest of either the monarchy or the aristocracy to combine with the democracy; because it is the interest of the democracy, or community at large, that neither the king nor the aristocracy should have one particle of power, or one particle of the wealth of the community, for their own advantage.

The democracy or community have all possible motives to endeavour to prevent the monarchy and aristocracy from exercising power, or obtaining the wealth of the community for their own advantage. The monarchy and aristocracy have all possible motives for endeavouring to obtain unlimited power over the persons and property of the community. The consequence is inevitable: they have all possible motives for combining to obtain that power.

If any part of this passage be more eminently absurd than another, it is, we think, the argument by which Mr. Mill proves that there cannot be an union of monarchy and aristocracy. Their power, he says, must be equal or not equal. But of equality there is no criterion. Therefore the chances against its existence are as infinity to one. If the power be not equal, then it follows, from the principles of human nature, that the stronger will take from the weaker, till it has engrossed the whole.

Now, if there be no criterion of equality between two portions of power there can be no common measure of portions of power. Therefore it is utterly impossible to compare them together. But where two portions of power are of the same kind, there is no difficulty in ascertaining, sufficiently for all practical purposes, whether they are equal or unequal. It is easy to judge whether two men run equally fast, or can lift equal weights. Two arbitrators, whose joint decision is to be final, and neither of whom can do any thing without the assent of the other, possess equal power. Two electors, each of whom has a vote for a borough, possess, in that respect, equal power. If not, all Mr. Mill's political theories fall to the ground at once. For, if it be impossible to ascertain whether two portions of power are equal, he never can show that, even under a system of universal suffrage, a minority might not carry every thing their own way, against the wishes and interests of the majority.

Where there are two portions of power differing in kind, there is, we admit, no criterion of equality. But then, in such a case, it is absurd to talk, as Mr. Mill does, about the stronger and the weaker. Popularly, indeed, and with reference to some particular objects, these words may very fairly be used. But to use them mathematically is altogether improper. If we are speaking of a boxing-match, we may say that some famous bruiser has greater bodily power than any man in England. If we are speaking of a pantomime, we may say the same of some very agile harlequin. But it would be talking nonsense to say, in general, that the power of Harlequin either exceeded that of the pugilist, or fell short of it.

If Mr. Mill's argument be good as between different branches of a legislature, it is equally good as between sovereign powers. Every government, it may be said, will, if it can, take the objects of its desires from every other. If the French government can subdue England it will do so. If the English government can subdue France it will do so. But the power of England and France is either equal or not equal. The chance that it is not exactly equal is as infinity to one, and may safely be left out of the account; and then the stronger will infallibly take from the weaker till the weaker is altogether enslaved.

Surely the answer to all this hubbub of unmeaning words is the plainest possible. For some purposes France is stronger than England. For some purposes England is stronger than France. For some, neither has any power at all. France has the greater population, England the greater capital; France has the greater army, England the greater fleet. For an expedition to Rio Janeiro or the Philippines, England has the greater power. For a war on the Po or the Danube, France has the greater power. But neither has power sufficient to keep the other in quiet subjection for a month. Invasion would be very perilous; the idea of complete conquest on either side utterly ridiculous. This is the manly and sensible way of discussing such questions. The *ergo*, or rather the *argal*, of Mr. Mill cannot impose on a child. Yet we ought scarcely to say this; for we remember to have heard a *child* ask whether Bonaparte was stronger than an elephant!

Mr. Mill reminds us of those philosophers of the sixteenth century who, having satisfied themselves *à priori* that the rapidity with which bodies descended to the earth varied exactly as their weights, refused to believe the contrary on the evidence of their own eyes and ears. The British Constitution, according to Mr. Mill's classification, is a mixture of monarchy and aristocracy; one House of Parliament being composed of hereditary nobles, and the other almost entirely chosen by a privileged class who possess the elective franchise on account of their property, or their connection with certain corporations. Mr. Mill's argument proves that, from the time that these two powers were mingled in our government, that is, from the very first dawn of our history, one or the other must have been constantly encroaching. According to him, moreover, all the encroachments must have been on one side. For the first encroachment could only have been made by the stronger; and that first encroachment would have made the stronger stronger still. It is, therefore, matter of absolute demonstration, that either the Parliament was stronger than the Crown in the reign of Henry the Eighth, or that the Crown was stronger than the Parliament in 1641. "Hippocrate dira ce que lui plaira," says the girl in Molière; "mais le cocher est mort." Mr. Mill may say what he pleases; but the English Constitution is still alive. That since the Revolution the Parliament has possessed great power in the state, is what nobody will dispute. The King, on the other hand, can create new peers, and can dissolve Parliaments. William sustained severe mortifications from the House of Commons, and was, indeed, unjustifiably oppressed. Anne was desirous to change a ministry which had a majority in both Houses. She watched her moment for a dissolution, created twelve Tory peers, and succeeded. Thirty years later, the House of Commons drove Walpole from his seat. In 1784, George the Third was able to keep Mr. Pitt in office in the face of a majority of the House of Commons. In 1804, the apprehension of a defeat in Parliament compelled the same King to part from his most favoured minister. But, in 1807, he was able to do exactly what Anne had done nearly a hundred years before. Now, had the power of the King increased during the intervening century, or had it remained stationary? Is it possible that the one lot among the infinite number should have fallen to us? If not, Mr. Mill has proved that one of the two parties must have been constantly taking from the other. Many of the ablest men in England think that the influence of the Crown has, on the whole, increased since the reign of Anne. Others think that the Parliament has been growing in strength. But of this there is no doubt, that both sides possessed great power then, and possess great power now. Surely, if there were the least truth in the argument of Mr. Mill, it could not possibly be a matter of doubt, at the end of a hundred and twenty years, whether the one side or the other had been the gainer.

But we ask pardon. We forget that a fact, irreconcilable with Mr. Mill's theory, furnishes, in his opinion, the strongest reason for adhering to the theory. To take up the question in another manner, is it not plain that there may be two bodies, each possessing a perfect and entire power, which cannot be taken from it without its own concurrence? What is the meaning of the words stronger and weaker, when applied to such bodies as these? The one may, indeed, by physical force, altogether destroy the other. But this is not the question. A third party, a general of their own, for example, may, by physical force, subjugate them both. Nor is there any form of government, Mr. Mill's utopian democracy not excepted, secure from such an occurrence. We are speaking of the powers with which the constitution invests the two branches of the legislature; and we ask Mr. Mill how, on his own principles, he can maintain that one of them will be able to encroach on the other, if the consent of the other be necessary to such encroachment?

Mr. Mill tells us that, if a government be composed of the three simple forms, which he will not admit the British Constitution to be, two of the component parts will inevitably join against the third. Now, if two of them combine and act as one, this case evidently resolves itself into the last; and all the observations which we have just made will fully apply to it. Mr. Mill says, that "any two of the parties, by combining, may swallow up the third;" and afterwards asks, "How it is possible to prevent two of them from combining to swallow up the third?" Surely Mr. Mill must be aware that in politics two is not always the double of one. If the concurrence of all the three branches of the legislature be necessary to every law, each branch will possess constitutional power sufficient to protect it against any thing but that physical force from which no form of government is secure. Mr. Mill reminds us of the Irishman, who could not be brought to understand how one juryman could possibly starve out eleven others.

But is it certain that two of the branches of the legislature will combine against the third? "It appears to be as certain," says Mr. Mill, "as any thing which depends upon human will; because there are strong motives in favour of it, and none that can be conceived in opposition to it." He subsequently sets forth what these motives are. The interest of the democracy is that each individual should receive protection. The interest of the King and the aristocracy is to have all the power that they can obtain, and to use it for their own ends. Therefore the King and the aristocacy have all possible motives for combining against the people. If our readers will look back to the passage quoted above, they will see that we represent Mr. Mill's argument quite fairly.

Now we should have thought that, without the help of either history or experience, Mr. Mill would have discovered, by the light of his own logic, the fallacy which lurks, and indeed scarcely lurks, under this pretended demonstration. The interest of the King may be opposed to that of the people. But is it identical with that of the aristocracy? In the very page which contains this argument, intended to prove that the King and the aristocracy will coalesce against the people, Mr. Mill attempts to show that there is so strong an opposition of interest between the King and the aristocracy that if the powers of government are divided between them the one will inevitably usurp the power of the other. If so, he is not entitled to conclude that they will combine to destroy the power of the people merely because their interests may be at variance with those of the people. He is bound to show, not merely that in all communities the interest of a king must be opposed to that of the people, but also that, in all communities, it must be more directly opposed to the interest of the people than to the interest of the aristocracy. But he has not shown this. Therefore he has not proved his proposition on his own principles. To quote history would be a mere waste of time. Every schoolboy, whose studies have gone so far as the Abridgments of Goldsmith, can mention instances in which sovereigns have allied themselves with the people against the aristocracy, and in which the nobles have allied themselves with the people against the sovereign. In general, when there are three parties, every one of which has much to fear from the others, it is not found that two of them combine to plunder the third. If such a combination be formed, it scarcely ever effects its purpose. It soon becomes evident which member of the coalition is likely to be the greater gainer by the transaction. He becomes an object of jealousy to his ally, who, in all probability, changes sides, and compels him to restore what he has taken. Everybody knows how Henry the Eighth trimmed tween Francis and the Emperor Charles. But it is idle to cite examples of the operation of a principle which is illustrated in almost every page of history, ancient or modern, and to which almost every state in Europe has, at one time or another, been indebted for its independence.

Mr. Mill has now, as he conceives, demonstrated that the simple forms of government are bad, and that the mixed forms cannot possibly exist. There is still, however, it seems, a hope for mankind.

> In the grand discovery of modern times, the system of representation, the solution of all the difficulties, both speculative and practical, will perhaps be found. If it cannot, we seem to be forced upon the extraordinary conclusion, that good government is impossible. For, as there is no individual or combination of individuals, except the community itself, who would not have an interest in bad government if intrusted with its powers, and as the

community itself is incapable of exercising those powers, and must intrust them to certain individuals, the conclusion is obvious: the community itself must check those individuals; else they will follow their interest and produce bad government. But how is it the community can check? The community can act only when assembled; and when assembled, it is incapable of acting. The community, however, can choose representatives.

The next question is – How must the representative body be constituted? Mr. Mill lays down two principles, about which, he says, "it is unlikely that there will be any dispute."

"First, The checking body must have a degree of power sufficient for the business of checking."

"Secondly, it must have an identity of interest with the community. Otherwise, it will make a mischievous use of its power."

The first of these propositions certainly admits of no dispute. As to the second, we shall hereafter take occasion to make some remarks on the sense in which Mr. Mill understands the words "interest of the community."

It does not appear very easy, on Mr. Mill's principles, to find out any mode of making the interest of the representative body identical with that of the constituent body. The plan proposed by Mr. Mill is simply that of very frequent election. "As it appears," says he, "that limiting the duration of their power is a security against the sinister interest of the people's representatives, so it appears that it is the only security of which the nature of the case admits." But all the arguments by which Mr. Mill has proved monarchy and aristocracy to be pernicious will, as it appears to us, equally prove this security to be no security at all. Is it not clear that the representatives, as soon as they are elected, are an aristocracy, with an interest opposed to the interest of the community? Why should they not pass a law for extending the term of their power from one year to ten years, or declare themselves senators for life? If the whole legislative power is given to them, they will be constitutionally competent to do this. If part of the legislative power is withheld from them, to whom is that part given? Is the people to retain it, and to express its assent or dissent in primary assemblies? Mr. Mill himself tells us that the community can only act when assembled, and that, when assembled, it is incapable of acting. Or is it to be provided, as in some of the American republics, that no change in the fundamental laws shall be made without the consent of a convention, specially elected for the purpose? Still the difficulty recurs: Why may not the members of the convention betray their trust, as well as the members of the ordinary legislature? When private men, they may have been zealous for the interests of the community. When candidates, they may have pledged themselves to the cause of the constitution. But, as soon as they are a convention, as soon as they are separated from the people, as soon as the supreme power is put into their hands, commences that interest opposite to the interest of the community which must, according to Mr. Mill, produce measures opposite to the interests of the community. We must find some other means, therefore, of checking this check upon a check; some other prop to carry the tortoise, that carries the elephant, that carries the world.

We know well that there is no real danger in such a case. But there is no danger only because there is no truth in Mr. Mill's principles. If men were what he represents them to be, the letter of the very constitution which he recommends would afford no safeguard against bad government. The real security is this, that legislators will be deterred by the fear of resistance and of infamy from acting in the manner which we have described. But restraints, exactly the same in kind, and differing only in degree, exist in all forms of government. That broad line of distinction which Mr. Mill tries to point out between monarchies and aristocracies on the one side, and democracies on the other, has in fact no existence. In no form of government is there an absolute identity of interest between the people and their rulers. In every form of government, the rulers stand in some awe of the people. The fear of resistance and the sense of shame operate, in a certain degree, on the most absolute kings and the most illiberal oligarchies. And nothing but the fear of resistance and the sense of shame preserves the freedom of the most democratic communities from the encroachments of their annual and biennial delegates.

We have seen how Mr. Mill proposes to render the interest of the representative body identical with that of the constituent body. The next question is, in what manner the interest of the constituent body is to be rendered identical with that of the community. Mr. Mill shows that a minority of the community, consisting even of many thousands, would be a bad constituent body, and, indeed, merely a numerous aristocracy.

"The benefits of the representative system," says he, "are lost, in all cases in which the interests of the choosing body are not the same with those of the community. It is very evident, that if the community itself were the choosing body, the interest of the community and that of the choosing body would be the same."

On these grounds Mr. Mill recommends that all males of mature age, rich and poor, educated and ignorant, shall have votes. But why not the women too? This question has often been asked in parliamentary debate, and has never, to our knowledge, received a plausible answer. Mr. Mill escapes from it as fast as he can. But we shall take the liberty to dwell a little on the words of the oracle. "One thing," says he, "is pretty clear, that all those individuals whose interests are involved in those of other individuals, may be struck off without inconvenience . . . In this light women may be regarded, the interest of almost all of whom is involved either in that of their fathers, or in that of their husbands."

If we were to content ourselves with saying, in answer to all the arguments in Mr. Mill's essay, that the interest of a king is involved in that of the community, we should be accused, and justly, of talking nonsense. Yet such an assertion would not, as far as we can perceive, be more unreasonable than that which Mr. Mill has here ventured to make. Without adducing one fact, without taking the trouble to perplex the question by one sophism, he placidly dogmatizes away the interest of one half of the human race. If there be a word of truth in history, women have always been, and still are, over the greater part of the globe, humble companions, playthings, captives, menials, beasts of burden. Except in a few happy and highly civilized communities, they are strictly in a state of personal slavery. Even in those countries where they are best treated, the laws are generally unfavourable to them, with respect to almost all the points in which they are most deeply interested.

Mr. Mill is not legislating for England or the United States; but for mankind. Is then the interest of a Turk the same with that of the girls who compose his harem? Is the interest of a Chinese the same with that of the woman whom he harnesses to his plough? Is the interest of an Italian the same with that of the daughter whom he devotes to God? The interest of a respectable Englishman may be said, without any impropriety, to be identical with that of his wife. But why is it so? Because human nature is *not* what Mr. Mill conceives it to be; because civilized men, pursuing their own happiness in a social state, are not Yahoos fighting for carrion; because there is a pleasure in being loved and esteemed, as well as in being feared and servilely obeyed. Why does not a gentleman restrict his wife to the bare maintenance which the law would compel him to allow her, that he may have more to spend on his personal pleasures? Because, if he loves her, he has pleasure in seeing her pleased; and because, even if he dislikes her, he is unwilling that the whole neighbourhood should cry shame on his meanness and ill-nature. Why does not the legislature, altogether composed of males, pass a law to deprive women of all civil privileges whatever, and reduce them to the state of slaves? By passing such a law they would gratify what Mr. Mill tells us is an inseparable part of human nature, the desire to possess unlimited power of inflicting pain upon others. That they do not pass such a law, though they have the power to pass it, and that no man in England wishes to see such a law passed, proves that the desire to possess unlimited power of inflicting pain is not inseparable from human nature.

If there be in this country an identity of interest between the two sexes, it cannot possibly arise from any thing but the pleasure of being loved, and of communicating happiness. For, that it does not spring from the mere instinct of sex, the treatment which women experience over the greater part of the world abundantly proves. And, if it be said that our laws of marriage have produced it, this only removes the argument a step further; for those laws have been made by males. Now, if the kind feelings of one half of the species be a sufficient security for the happiness of the other, why may not the kind feelings of a monarch or an aristocracy be sufficient at least to prevent them from grinding the people to the very utmost of their power?

If Mr. Mill will examine why it is that women are better treated in England than in Persia, he may perhaps find out, in the course of his inquiries, why it is that the Danes are better governed than the subjects of Caligula.

We now come to the most important practical question in the whole essay. Is it desirable that all males arrived at years of discretion should vote for representatives, or should a pecuniary qualification be required? Mr. Mill's opinion is, that the lower the qualification the better; and that the best system is that in which there is none at all.

> "The qualification," says he, "must either be such as to embrace the majority of the population, or something less than

the majority. Suppose, in the first place, that it embraces the majority, the question is, whether the majority would have an interest in oppressing those who, upon this supposition, would be deprived of political power? If we reduce the calculation to its elements, we shall see that the interest which they would have of this deplorable kind, though it would be something, would not be very great. Each man of the majority, if the majority were constituted the governing body, would have something less than the benefit of oppressing a single man. If the majority were twice as great as the minority, each man of the majority would only have one half the benefit of oppressing a single man . . . Suppose, in the second place, that the qualification did not admit a body of electors so large as the majority, in that case taking again the calculation in its elements, we shall see that each man would have a benefit equal to that derived from the oppression of more than one man; and that, in proportion as the elective body constituted a smaller and smaller minority, the benefit of misrule to the elective body would be increased, and bad government would be insured.

The first remark which we have to make on this argument is, that, by Mr. Mill's own account, even a government in which every human being should vote would still be defective. For, under a system of universal suffrage, the majority of the electors return the representative, and the majority of the representatives make the law. The whole people may vote, therefore; but only the majority govern. So that, by Mr. Mill's own confession, the most perfect system of government conceivable is one in which the interest of the ruling body to oppress, though not great, is something.

But is Mr. Mill in the right when he says that such an interest could not be very great? We think not. If, indeed, every man in the community possessed an equal share of what Mr. Mill calls the objects of desire, the majority would probably abstain from plundering the minority. A large minority would offer a vigorous resistance; and the property of a small minority would not repay the other members of the community for the trouble of dividing it. But it happens that in all civilized communities there is a small minority of rich men, and a great majority of poor men. If there were a thousand men with ten pounds apiece, it would not be worth while for nine hundred and ninety of them to rob ten, and it would be a bold attempt for six hundred of them to rob four hundred. But, if ten of them had a hundred thousand pounds apiece, the case would be very different. There would then be much to be got, and nothing to be feared.

"That one human being will desire to render the person and property of another subservient to his pleasures, notwithstanding the pain or loss of pleasure which it may occasion to that other individual, is," according to Mr. Mill, "the foundation of government." That the property of the rich minority can be made subservient to the pleasures of the poor majority will scarcely be denied. But Mr. Mill proposes to give the poor majority power over the rich minority. Is it possible to doubt to what, on his own principles, such an arrangement must lead?

It may perhaps be said that, in the long run, it is for the interest of the people that property should be secure, and that therefore they will respect it. We answer thus: – It cannot be pretended that it is not for the immediate interest of the people to plunder the rich. Therefore, even if it were quite certain that, in the long run, the people would, as a body, lose by doing so, it would not necessarily follow that the fear of remote ill consequences would overcome the desire of immediate acquisitions. Every individual might flatter himself that the punishment would not fall on him. Mr. Mill himself tells us, in his Essay on Jurisprudence, that no quantity of evil which is remote and uncertain will suffice to prevent crime.

But we are rather inclined to think that it would, on the whole, be for the interest of the majority to plunder the rich. If so, the Utilitarians will say, that the rich *ought* to be plundered. We deny the inference. For, in the first place, if the object of government be the greatest happiness of the greatest number, the intensity of the suffering which a measure inflicts must be taken into consideration, as well as the number of the sufferers. In the next place, we have to notice one most important distinction which Mr. Mill has altogether overlooked. Throughout his essay, he confounds the community with the species. He talks of the greatest happiness of the greatest number: but, when we examine his reasonings, we find that he thinks only of the greatest number of a single generation.

Therefore, even if we were to concede that all those arguments of which we have exposed the fallacy are unanswerable, we might still deny the conclusion at which the essayist arrives. Even if we were to grant that he had found out the form of government which is best for the majority of the people now living on the face of the earth, we might still without inconsistency maintain that form of government to be pernicious to mankind. It would still be incumbent on Mr. Mill to prove that the interest of every generation is identical with the interest of all succeeding generations. And how on his own principles he could do this we are at a loss to conceive.

The case, indeed, is strictly analogous to that of an aristocratic government. In an aristocracy, says Mr. Mill, the few, being invested with the powers of government, can take the objects of their desires from the people. In the same manner, every generation in turn can gratify itself at the expense of posterity, – priority of time, in the latter case, giving an advantage exactly corresponding to that which superiority of station gives in the former. That an aristocracy will abuse its advantage, is, according to Mr. Mill, matter of demonstration. Is it not equally certain that the whole people will do the same; that, if they have the power, they will commit waste of every sort on the estate of mankind, and transmit it to posterity impoverished and desolated?

How is it possible for any person who holds the doctrines of Mr. Mill to doubt that the rich, in a democracy such as that which he recommends, would be pillaged as unmercifully as under a Turkish Pacha? It is no doubt for the interest of the next generation, and it may be for the remote interest of the present generation, that property should be held sacred. And so no doubt it will be for the interest of the next Pacha, and even for that of the present Pacha, if he should hold office long, that the inhabitants of his Pachalic should be encouraged to accumulate wealth. Scarcely any despotic sovereign has plundered his subjects to a large extent without having reason before the end of his reign to regret it. Every body knows how bitterly Louis the Fourteenth, towards the close of his life, lamented his former extravagance. If that magnificent prince had not expended millions on Marli and Versailles, and tens of millions on the aggrandisement of his grandson, he would not have been compelled at last to pay servile court to low-born moneylenders, to humble himself before men on whom, in the days of his pride, he would not have vouchsafed to look, for the means of supporting even his own household. Examples to the same effect might easily be multiplied. But despots, we see, do plunder their subjects, though history and experience tell them that, by prematurely exacting the means of profusion, they are in fact devouring the seed-corn from which the future harvest of revenue is to spring. Why then should we suppose that the people will be deterred from procuring immediate relief and enjoyment by the fear of distant calamities, of calamities which perhaps may not be fully felt till the times of their grandchildren?

These conclusions are strictly drawn from Mr. Mill's own principles: and, unlike most of the conclusions which he has himself drawn from those principles, they are not, as far as we know, contradicted by facts. The case of the United States is not in point. In a country where the necessaries of life are cheap and the wages of labour high, where a man who has no capital but his legs and arms may expect to become rich by industry and frugality, it is not very decidedly even for the immediate advantage of the poor to plunder the rich; and the punishment of doing so would very speedily follow the offence. But in countries in which the great majority live from hand to mouth, and in which vast masses of wealth have been accumulated by a comparatively small number, the case is widely different. The immediate want is, at particular seasons, craving, imperious, irresistible. In our own time it has steeled men to the fear of the gallows, and urged them on the point of the bayonet. And, if these men had at their command that gallows and those bayonets which now scarcely restrain them, what is to be expected? Nor is this state of things one which can exist only under a bad government. If there be the least truth in the doctrines of the school to which Mr. Mill belongs, the increase of population will necessarily produce it everywhere. The increase of population is accelerated by good and cheap government. Therefore, the better the government, the greater is the inequality of conditions: and the greater the inequality of conditions, the stronger are the motives which impel the populace to spoliation. As for America, we appeal to the twentieth century.

It is scarcely necessary to discuss the effects which a general spoliation of the rich would produce. It may indeed happen that, where a legal and political system full of abuses is inseparably bound up with the institution of property, a nation may gain by a single convulsion, in which both perish together. The price is fearful. But, if, when the shock is over, a new order of things should arise under which property may enjoy security, the industry of individuals will soon repair the devastation. Thus we entertain no doubt that the Revolution was, on the whole, a most salutary event for France. But would France have gained if, ever since the year 1793, she had been governed by a democratic convention? If Mr. Mill's principles be sound, we say that almost her whole capital would by this time have been annihilated. As soon as the first explosion was beginning to be forgotten, as soon as wealth again began to germinate, as soon as the poor again began to compare their cottages and salads with the hotels and banquets of the rich, there would have been another scramble for property, another maximum, another general confiscation, another reign of terror. Four or five such convulsions following each other, at intervals of ten or twelve years, would reduce the most flourishing countries of Europe to the state of Barbary or the Morea.

The civilized part of the world has now nothing to fear from the hostility of savage nations. Once the deluge of barbarism has passed over it, to destroy and to fertilize; and in the present state of mankind we enjoy a full security against that calamity. That flood will no more return to cover the earth. But is it possible that in the bosom of civilization itself may be engendered the malady which shall destroy it? Is it possible that institutions may be established which, without the help of earthquake, of famine, of pestilence, or of the foreign sword, may undo the work of so many ages of wisdom and glory, and gradually sweep away taste, literature, science, commerce, manufactures, every thing but the rude arts necessary to the support of animal life? Is it possible that, in two or three hundred years, a few lean and half-naked fishermen may divide with owls and foxes the ruins of the greatest European cities – may wash their nets amidst the relics of her gigantic docks, and build their huts out of the capitals of her stately cathedrals? If the principles of Mr. Mill be sound, we say, without hesitation, that the form of government which he recommends will assuredly produce all this. But, if these principles be unsound, if the reasonings by which we have opposed them be just, the higher and middling orders are the natural representatives of the human race. Their interest may be opposed in some things to that of their poorer contemporaries; but it is identical with that of the innumerable generations which are to follow.

Mr. Mill concludes his essay, by answering an objection often made to the project of universal suffrage – that the people do not understand their own interests. We shall not go through his arguments on this subject, because, till he has proved that it is for the interest of the people to respect property, he only makes matters worse by proving that they understand their interests. But we cannot refrain from treating our readers with a delicious *bonne bouche* of wisdom, which he has kept for the last moment.

The opinions of that class of the people who are below the middle rank are formed, and their minds are directed, by that intelligent, that virtuous rank, who come the most immediately in contact with them, who are in the constant habit of intimate communication with them, to whom they fly for advice and assistance in all their numerous difficulties, upon whom they feel an immediate and daily dependence in health and in sickness, in infancy and in old age, to whom their children look up as models for their imitation, whose opinions they hear daily repeated, and account it their honour to adopt. There can be no doubt that the middle rank, which gives to science, to art, and to legislation, itself their most distinguished ornaments, and is the chief source of all that has exalted and refined human nature, is that portion of the community, of which, if the basis of representation were ever so far extended, the opinion would ultimately decide. Of the people beneath them, a vast majority would be sure to be guided by their advice and example.

This single paragraph is sufficient to upset Mr. Mill's theory. Will the people act against their own interest? Or will the middle rank act against its own interest? Or is the interest of the middle rank identical with the interest of the people? If the people act according to the directions of the middle rank, as Mr. Mill says that they assuredly will, one of these three questions must be answered in the affirmative. But, if any one of the three be answered in the affirmative, his whole system falls to the ground. If the interest of the middle rank be identical with that of the people, why should not the powers of government be entrusted to that rank? If the powers of government were entrusted to that rank, there would evidently be an aristocracy of wealth; and "to constitute an aristocracy of wealth, though it were a very numerous one, would," according to Mr. Mill, "leave the community without protection, and exposed to all the evils of unbridled power." Will not the same motives which induce the middle classes to abuse one kind of power induce them to abuse another? If their interest be the same with that of the people they will govern the people well. If it be opposite to that of the people they will advise the people ill. The system of universal suffrage, therefore, according to Mr. Mill's own account, is only a device for doing circuitously what a representative system, with a pretty high qualification, would do directly.

So ends this celebrated Essay. And such is this philosophy for which the experience of three thousand years is to be discarded; this philosophy, the professors of which speak as if it had guided the world to the knowledge of navigation and alphabetical writing; as if, before its dawn, the inhabitants of Europe had lived in caverns and eaten each other! We are sick, it seems, like the children of Israel, of the objects of our old and legitimate worship. We pine for a new idolatry. All that is costly and all that is ornamental in our intellectual treasures must be delivered up, and cast into the furnace – and there comes out this Calf!

Our readers can scarcely mistake our object in writing this article. They will not suspect us of any disposition to advocate the cause of absolute monarchy, or of any narrow form of oligarchy, or to exaggerate the evils of popular government. Our object at present is, not so much to attack or defend any particular system of polity, as to expose the vices of a kind of reasoning utterly unfit for moral and political discussions; of a kind of reasoning which may so readily be turned to purposes of falsehood that it ought to receive no quarter, even when by accident it may be employed on the side of truth.

Our objection to the essay of Mr. Mill is fundamental. We believe that it is utterly impossible to deduce the science of government from the principles of human nature.

What proposition is there respecting human nature which is absolutely and universally true? We know of only one: and that is not only true, but identical; that men always act from self-interest. This truism the Utilitarians proclaim with as much pride as if it were new, and as much zeal as if it were important. But in fact, when explained, it means only that men, if they can, will do as they choose. When we see the actions of a man we know with certainty what he thinks his interest to be. But it is impossible to reason with certainty from what *we* take to be his interest to his actions. One man goes without a dinner that he may add a shilling to a hundred thousand pounds: another runs in debt to give balls and masquerades. One man cuts his father's throat to get possession of his old clothes: another hazards his own life to save that of an enemy. One man volunteers on a forlorn hope: another is drummed out of a regiment for cowardice. Each of these men has, no doubt, acted from self-interest. But we gain nothing by knowing this, except the pleasure, if it be one, of multiplying useless words. In fact, this principle is just as recondite and just as important as the great truth that whatever is, is. If a philosopher were always to state facts in the following form – "There is a shower: but whatever is, is; therefore, there is a shower," – his reasoning would be perfectly sound, but we do not apprehend that it would materially enlarge the circle of human knowledge. And it is equally idle to attribute any importance to a proposition which, when interpreted, means only that a man had rather do what he had rather do.

If the doctrine, that men always act from self-interest, be laid down in any other sense than this – if the meaning of the word self-interest be narrowed so as to exclude any one of the motives which may by possibility act on any human being, – the proposition ceases to be identical; but at the same time it ceases to be true.

What we have said of the word "self-interest" applies to all the synonymes and circumlocutions which are employed to convey the same meaning; pain and pleasure, happiness and misery, objects of desire, and so forth.

The whole art of Mr. Mill's essay consists in one simple trick of legerdemain. It consists in using words of the sort which we have been describing first in one sense and then in another. Men will take the objects of their desire if they can. Unquestionably: – but this is an identical proposition: for an object of desire means merely a thing which a man will procure if he can. Nothing can possibly be inferred from a maxim of this kind. When we see a man take something we shall know that it was an object of his desire. But till then we have no means of judging with certainty what he desires or what he will take. The general proposition, however, having been admitted, Mr. Mill proceeds to reason as if men had no desires but those which can be gratified only by spoliation and oppression. It then becomes easy to deduce doctrines of vast importance from the original axiom. The only misfortune is, that by thus narrowing the meaning of the word desire the axiom becomes false, and all the doctrines consequent upon it are false likewise.

When we pass beyond those maxims which it is impossible to deny without a contradiction in terms, and which, therefore, do not enable us to advance a single step in practical knowledge, we do not believe that it is possible to lay down a single general rule respecting the motives which influence human actions. There is nothing which may not, by association or by comparison, become an object either of desire or of aversion. The fear of death is generally considered as one of the strongest of our feelings. It is the most formidable sanction which legislators have been able to devise. Yet it is notorious that, as Lord Bacon has observed, there is no passion by which that fear has not been often overcome. Physical pain is indisputably an evil; yet it has been often endured, and even welcomed. Innumerable martyrs have exulted in torments which made the spectators shudder; and, to use a more homely illustration, there are few wives who do not long to be mothers.

Is the love of approbation a stronger motive than the love of wealth? It is impossible to answer this question generally even in the case of an individual with whom we are very intimate. We often say, indeed, that a man loves fame more than money or money more than fame. But this is said in a loose and popular sense: for there is scarcely a man who would not endure a few sneers for a great sum of money, if he were in pecuniary distress; and scarcely a man, on the other hand, who, if he were in flourishing circumstances, would expose himself to the hatred and contempt of the public for a trifle. In order, therefore, to return a precise answer even about a single human being, we must know what is the amount of the sacrifice of reputation demanded and of the pecuniary advantage offered, and in what situation the person to whom the temptation is proposed stands at the time. But, when the question is propounded generally about the whole species, the impossibility of answering is still more evident. Man differs from man; generation from generation; nation from nation. Education, station, sex, age, accidental associations, produce infinite shades of variety.

Now, the only mode in which we can conceive it possible to deduce a theory of government from the principles of human nature is this. We must find out what are the motives which, in a particular form of government, impel rulers to bad measures, and what are those which impel them to good measures. We must then compare the effect of the two classes of motives; and, according as we find the one or the other to prevail, we must pronounce the form of government in question good or bad.

Now let it be supposed that, in aristocratical and monarchical states, the desire of wealth and other desires of the same class always tend to produce misgovernment, and that the love of approbation and other kindred feelings always tend to produce good government. Then, if it be impossible, as we have shown that it is, to pronounce generally which of the two classes of motives is the more influential, it is impossible to find out, *à priori*, whether a monarchical or aristocratical form of government be good or bad.

Mr. Mill has avoided the difficulty of making the comparison, by very coolly putting all the weights into one of the scales, – by reasoning as if no human being had ever sympathized with the feelings, been gratified by the thanks, or been galled by the execrations, of another.

The case, as we have put it, is decisive against Mr. Mill; and yet we have put it in a manner far too favourable to him. For, in fact, it is impossible to lay it down as a general rule that the love of wealth in a sovereign always produces misgovernment, or the love of approbation good government. A patient and far-sighted ruler, for example, who is less desirous of raising a great sum immediately than of securing an unencumbered and progressive revenue, will, by taking off restraints from trade and giving perfect security to property, encourage accumulation and entice capital from foreign countries. The commercial policy of Prussia, which is perhaps superior to that of any country in the world, and which puts to shame the absurdities of our republican brethren on the other side of the Atlantic, has probably sprung from the desire of an absolute ruler to enrich himself. On the other hand, when the popular estimate of virtues and vices is erroneous, which is too often the case, the love of approbation leads sovereigns to spend the wealth of the nation on useless shows, or to engage in wanton and destructive wars. If then we can neither compare the strength of two motives, nor determine with certainty to what description of actions either motive will lead, how can we possibly deduce a theory of government from the nature of man?

How, then, are we to arrive at just conclusions on a subject so important to the happiness of mankind? Surely by that method which, in every experimental science to which it has been applied, has signally increased the power and knowledge of our species, – by that method for which our new philosophers would substitute quibbles scarcely worthy of the barbarous respondents and opponents of the middle ages, – by the method of Induction; – by observing the present state of the world, – by assiduously studying the history of past ages, – by sifting the evidence of facts, – by carefully combining and contrasting those which are authentic, – by generalizing with judgment and diffidence, – by perpetually bringing the theory which we have constructed to the test of new facts, – by correcting, or altogether abandoning it, according as those new facts prove it to be partially or fundamentally unsound. Proceeding thus, – patiently, – diligently, – candidly, – we may hope to form a system as far inferior in pretension to that which we have been examining and as far superior to it in real utility as the prescriptions of a great physician, varying with every stage of every malady and with the constitution of every patient, to the pill of the advertising quack which is to cure all human beings, in all climates, of all diseases.

This is that noble Science of Politics, which is equally removed from the barren theories of the Utilitarian sophists, and from the petty craft, so often mistaken for statesmanship by minds grown narrow in habits of intrigue, jobbing, and official etiquette; – which of all sciences is the most important to the welfare of nations, – which of all sciences most tends to expand and invigorate the mind, – which draws nutriment and ornament from every part of philosophy and literature, and dispenses in return nutriment and ornament to all. We are sorry and surprised when we see men of good intentions and good natural abilities abandon this healthful and generous study to pore over speculations like those which we have been examining. And we should heartily rejoice to find that our remarks had induced any person of this description to employ, in researches of real utility, the talents and industry which are now wasted on verbal sophisms, wretched of their wretched kind.

As to the greater part of the sect, it is, we apprehend, of little consequence what they study or under whom. It would be more amusing, to be sure, and more reputable, if they would take up the old republican cant and declaim about Brutus and Timoleon, the duty of killing tyrants and the blessedness of dying for liberty. But, on the whole, they might have chosen worse. They may as well be Utilitarians as jockeys or dandies. And, though quibbling about self-interest and motives, and objects of desire, and the greatest happiness of the greatest number, is but a poor employment for a grown man, it certainly hurts the health less than hard drinking and the fortune less than high play; it is not much more laughable than phrenology, and is immeasurably more humane than cock-fighting.

Reply to Macaulay
From *A Fragment on Mackintosh*
(1835)

James Mill

On [my] treatise on government, Sir James [Mackintosh] delivers his wisdom thus:

> Mr. Mill, for example, derives the whole theory of government from the single fact, that every man pursues his interest, when he knows it; which he assumes to be a sort of self evident practical principle, if such a phrase be not contradictory. That a man's pursuing the interest of another, or indeed any other object in nature, is just as *conceivable* as that he should pursue his own interest, is a proposition which seems never to have occurred to this acute and ingenious writer. Nothing, however, can be more certain than its truth, if the term interest be employed in its proper sense of general well-being, which is the only acceptation in which it can serve the purpose of his arguments. If indeed the term be employed to denote the gratification of a predominant desire, his proposition is self-evident, but wholly unserviceable in his argument; for it is clear that individuals and multitudes often desire what they know to be most inconsistent with their general welfare. A nation, as much as an individual, and sometimes more, may not only mistake its interest, but, perceiving it clearly, may prefer the gratification of a strong passion to it. The whole fabric of his political reasoning seems to be overthrown by this single observation; and instead of attempting to explain the immense

variety of political facts, by the simple principle of a contest of interests, we are reduced to the necessity of once more referring them to that variety of passions, habits, opinions, and prejudices, which we discover only by experience.

And in a note Sir James says, "The same mode of reasoning has been adopted by the writer of a late criticism on Mr. Mill's Essay. – See Edinburgh Review, No. 97, March 1829." – This is convenient; because the answer, which does for Sir James, will answer the same purpose with the Edinburgh Review.*

All that is here alledged against Mr. Mill, in the way of matter, is – that men do not always act in conformity with their true interest, sometimes mistaking it, and sometimes impelled by passion to disregard it. Sir James says, and according to him, "the writer of a late criticism in the Edinburgh Review" says, that this "overthrows the whole fabric of Mr. Mill's political reasoning." So far is this from being true, that Mr. Mill's "political reasoning" is in perfect conformity with it. We have had experience enough of Sir James, not to be surprised that he should commit this trifling mistake. But with respect to Mr. Mill, his vindication is complete; unless the assertion I have now made be successfully contradicted.

Sir James's wording, however, is here a matter of curiosity. He says, that the fact of men's acting sometimes without an immediate view to their own interest, never occurred to Mr. Mill, as a thing conceivable. Did Sir James expect any body to believe him, when he made this assertion?

To come a little nearer to the point; is there a single proposition of Mr. Mill's which implies an ignorance of this fact? Or is there one of his conclusions which is vitiated by inattention to it?

To Mr. Mill, considering as he did that the principles of government mean the principles by which men are governed, and the principles by which men are governed mean the principles by which their acts are determined, it was not only necessary, it was indispensable, that he should ask himself, what is that within a man which has the principal influence in determining his actions. – The answer of Mr. Mill was, – "the man's view of his own interest." Would Sir James have had him return any other answer? Sir James abstains from

---

*[Mill refers here to T. B. Macaulay's "Mill on Government," *Edinburgh Review*, March 1829; reprinted in the present volume. – Ed.]

saying this. But he loudly condemns Mr. Mill for what he did answer.

I am not at all disposed to quibble with Sir James, about the meaning of the word "interest." It is very obvious, to any one who has read Mr. Mill's Treatise, in what sense he uses it. He uses it, neither in the refined sense of a man's best interest, or what is most conducive to his happiness upon the whole; nor to signify every object which he desires, though that is a very intelligible meaning too. Mr. Mill uses it, in its rough and common acceptation, to denote the leading objects of human desire; Wealth, Power, Dignity, Ease; including escape from the contrary, Poverty, Impotence, Degradation, Toil.

I suppose nobody, at least nobody now alive, will dispute, that, taking men generally, the bulk of their actions is determined by consideration of these objects. As little, I suppose, will it be disputed, that in deliberating on the best means for the government of men in society, it is the business of philosophers and legislators (what title had Sir James to meddle with the business of either?) – to look to the more general laws of their nature, rather than the exceptions. The bearing of Sir James's talk (you can seldom gather more from it than its bearing) is to recommend attention principally to the exceptions. At least, his whole complaint of Mr. Mill is that he did not confine his attention to the exceptions.

Sir James, though he had no ideas of his own to set him right, might have derived from his memory, which was reported as good (*i.e.* for words and dates – possibly enough it did not extend to ideas), that Mr. Mill, if in error, in this matter, is in good company.

Bishop Berkeley says, "Self-love being a principle of all others the most universal, and the most deeply engraven on our hearts, it is natural for us to regard things as they are fitted to augment or impair our own happiness; and accordingly we denominate them *good* or *evil*."* This is a very comprehensive decision; the very terms *good* and *evil* derive their meaning from self-interest.

The following quotation from David Hume is of the more importance; because it teaches the very same application of the same general law, for which, carried out into detail, Mr. Mill is accused, as shewing his ignorance, at once, of the most notorious facts in human nature, and of the proper mode of philosophising.

*Berkeley's Works, ii. p. 7. Ed. 4to.

Political writers have established it as a maxim, that, in contriving any system of government, and fixing the several checks and controls of the constitution, every man ought to be supposed a knave, and to have no other end, in all his actions, than private interest. By this interest we must govern him, and by means of it make him, notwithstanding his insatiable avarice and ambition, co-operate to public good. Without this, say they, we shall in vain boast of the advantages of any constitution, and shall find in the end, that we have no security for our liberties and possessions, except the good will of our rulers; that is, we shall have no security at all.

It is, therefore, a just political maxim, that every man must be supposed a knave; though at the same time, it appears somewhat strange, that a maxim should be true in politics which is false in fact. But to satisfy us on this head, we may consider, that men are generally more honest in their private than in their public capacity, and will go greater lengths to serve a party, than when their own private interest is alone concerned. Honour is a great check upon mankind; but when a considerable body of men act together, this check is in a great measure removed; since a man is sure to be approved of by his own party for what promotes the common interest; and he soon learns to despise the clamours of adversaries. To which we may add, that every court or senate is determined by the greater number of voices; so that, if self-interest influences only the majority (as it will always do), the whole senate follows the allurements of this separate interest, and acts as if it contained not one member who had any regard to public interest and liberty.

When there offers, therefore, to our censure and examination, any plan of government, real or imaginary, where the power is distributed among several courts and several orders of men, we should always consider the separate interest of each court and each order; and if we find that, by the skilful division of power, this interest must necessarily, in its operation, concur with the public, we may pronounce that government to be wise and happy. If, on the contrary, separate interests be not checked, and be not directed to the public, we ought to look for nothing but faction, disorder, and tyranny, from such a government. In this opinion I am justified by experience, as well as by the authority of all philosophers and politicians, both ancient and modern.*

*[David Hume], Essay on the Independency of Parliament.

Did Sir James consider this an example of the error of the Cartesians? Did he condemn Mr. Hume, because he "derived the whole theory of government from the single fact, that every man pursues his own interest when he knows it; which he assumes to be a sort of self-evident practical principle, if such a phrase be not contradictory."

The common experience of mankind is well expressed by the old dramatic writer:–

> Verum illud verbum est, vulgo quod dici solet,
> Omnes sibi malle melius esse, quam alteri.
> *Teren. Andr. Act* ii. *Sc.* 5.

The next quotation I deem of importance; both on account of the reputation the author enjoys, as being what they call a practical man; and from the striking manner in which he puts and applies the very fact, which we have to guard against Sir James's perversion.

> As the Creator is a being, not only of infinite power and wisdom, but also of infinite goodness, he has been pleased so to contrive the constitution and frame of humanity, that we should want no other prompter to inquire after and pursue the rule of right, but only our own self-love, that universal principle of action. For he has so intimately connected, so inseparably interwoven, the laws of eternal justice with the happiness of each individual, that the latter cannot be obtained but by observing the former; and, if the former be punctually obeyed, it cannot but induce the latter. In consequence of which mutual connexion of justice and human felicity, he has not perplexed the law of nature with a multitude of abstracted rules and precepts, referring merely to the fitness or unfitness of things, as some have gravely surmised; but has graciously reduced the rule of obedience to this one paternal precept, "*that man should pursue his own happiness.*" This is the foundation of what we call ethics, or natural law. For the several articles into which it is branched in our system, amount to no more than demonstrating, that this or that action tends to man's real happiness, and therefore, very justly concluding that the performance of it is a part of the law of nature; or, on the other hand, that this or that action is destructive of man's real happiness, and therefore, that the law of nature forbids it. This law of nature, being coeval with mankind, and dictated by God himself, is of course superior in obligation to any other. It is binding over all the globe, in all countries, and at all times. No human laws are of any validity, if contrary to this: and such of

them as are valid derive all their force, and all their authority, mediately or immediately from this original.*

In the opinion of Blackstone; self-love is not only *the universal principle of action*, but, what is necessarily consequent upon this, *the sole principle of moral obligation*. If the theory of government is not built upon the universal principle of action, I should like to know on what foundation Sir James would place it.

Sir James would have done well to observe what is said by Blackstone about the law of nature, and the authority of human laws: that the law of nature commands what is favourable, forbids what is unfavourable to man's happiness: and that no human law, which is contrary to this law of nature, is of any validity. Did Sir James not think that this is giving a pretty extensive operation to the principle of utility?

Mr. Mill, going upon what thus appears, notwithstanding the contradiction of Sir James, to be pretty sure ground, inferred, that if the interest of those who rule could, by any contrivance, be made to coincide with the interest of those who obey, we should have the best security, which the nature of man affords, that the interest of the community would be steadily pursued by rulers; because we should have the security of their own interest. And though it may perhaps be true of certain individuals out of a multitude, that they are not habitually governed by their own interest; yet, as is truly remarked by Mr. Hume, it may be affirmed of all bodies of men, that they are guided by the principle of interest invariably.

The necessity, which those who examine what is the best form of government are under, of building on this foundation, is the leading position in Mr. Mill's discourse. The truth of it is self-evident. But, for the due exposure of the ignorance and presumption of Sir James, who derides it, a reference may be useful to some of those who have had occasion expressly to teach it.

The whole of Plato's Republic may be regarded as a development, and, in many of its parts, a masterly development, of the principle applied by Mr. Mill; that identity of interests between the governors and the governed affords the only security for good government. In the third book, after a long and beautiful deduction of the qualities required in the rulers (guardians, he calls them) of the state, the result

*Blackstone's Commentaries on the Laws of England, Introd. §2.

is exhibited in [several] striking expressions, [the] meaning [of which] is, that those chosen guardians should have three grand qualities; wisdom adapted to their trust; power adapted to their trust; and above all, care for the interests of the community: That a man's care, however, of other interests than his own, is then best secured, when both are promoted by the same events; because when any one expects that every addition to the happiness of others will be attended with a similar addition to his own, he pursues their happiness with the same constancy as his own.

Such is "the fabric of political reasoning," which Sir James tells us, for our edification, is overthrown by his sapient remark, that "a nation, as much as an individual, and sometimes more, may not only mistake its interest, but, perceiving it clearly, may prefer the gratification of a strong passion to it."

Does it, according to his logical head, follow, that because a nation may sometimes mistake its true interest, therefore its best security for good government is not to be found in effecting an identity of interests between those who govern, and itself?

"Nothing," says Mr. Burke, "is security to any individual, but the common interest of all."*

Without identity of interest with those they rule, the rulers, Plato says, instead of being the guardians of the flock, become wolves and its devourers . . .

[Two long excerpts, in Greek, from Books III and v of Plato's *Republic*, follow. Since Mill goes on to paraphrase their meaning, these passages have been omitted. – Ed.]

Not daring to attempt a translation of this passage, I shall endeavour shortly to express its meaning. "There is no evil in a community so great, as that which disunites, and makes it several, instead of one; nor any good so great, as that which makes it one, instead of several. The means of effecting this unity, is so to regulate the component parts, that what is a cause of pleasure or pain to one or a few, shall be so to all, or as many as possible. On the contrary, when interests are disunited, so that from the same political events, one portion of the community derives pleasure, another pain, this state of things, by inevitable consequence, leads to the dissolution of states."

*Letter to the Sheriffs of Bristol. Burke's Works. Ed. in 4to. vol. ii. p. 112.

It is mortifying to find one's self under the necessity of vindicating the wisdom of ages, from the pitiful objections of a man who, finding it stated in some quarter which he disliked, that identity of interests with the community is the best security the community can have for the good conduct of its rulers; gives out a proposition which has no bearing on the matter, and cries out, "*There!* I have demolished your best security: men sometimes mistake their true interest: therefore, the identity of the interests of the rulers with the interests of the community is not the best security for care of the interests of the community."

Well reasoned! Would it not be a still better connected conclusion to say, that individuals sometimes mistake their true interest; therefore, no individual should manage his own affairs, but every man those of some other?

Plato, seeing thus clearly the necessity of identifying the interests of the guardians with the interests of the guarded, bent the whole force of his penetrating mind, to discover the means of effecting such identification; but being ignorant, as all the ancients were, of the divine principle of representation, found himself obliged to have recourse to extraordinary methods. He first of all prescribes a very artificial system of education for the class of guardians: a system of such vigilance, begun so early, and continued so long, as to make of them a very different sort of beings from the ordinary race of mortals, to make of them, in short, philosophers, Plato laying it down as a universal truth, that there can be no happiness for states, until either philosophers are the rulers, or the rulers philosophers. In the next place, in order to prevent the existence of any private interest militating against that of the community, in the breasts of the guardians, he thought it necessary that they (he did not say the rest of the people, that is a vulgar error), should have nothing belonging to them individually, not even wives and children. This system of means, for the attainment of that identity of interests between the guardians and the guarded, on which good guardianship depends, has been the subject of much ignorant ridicule; but if the principle of representation, unknown to Plato, be excluded, it will not be easy to find another combination of means better adapted to the end; and surely that end is of sufficient importance to render it expedient to employ the most extraordinary means for its attainment, if other and simpler means are not to be found. Besides, Plato had an example of something nearly as extraordinary as the means he proposed, actually before his eyes, at Sparta. And the inhabitants of modern Europe have had examples of something still more extraordinary in the whole set of monastic institutions; above all that of the Jesuits.

Aristotle lays down the same doctrine; but, as his manner is, in a more abstract way; where he treats of ends, τελη, in the most comprehensive sense.

It is illustrated also, at great length, and with great beauty, in many parts of the writings of Xenophon. It is the great theme of two of his most exquisite and instructive productions, his Institution of Cyrus, and his Economics; and is touched upon with great effect in some of the dialogues in the Memoirs of Socrates.

Mr. Mill, it is necessary to observe, confines his inquiry to one department of government. The only thing he takes in hand, is, to shew, by what means good legislation can be effected. He certainly took it for granted, not having duly fathomed the intellects of such men as Sir James, that it was necessary for this end to establish an identity of interests between the community and those to whom they intrust the power of legislating for them.

And next he found, that the same means precisely which produce a true representation; that is, a body of representatives, the real, and not the pretended, choice of the people; produce most happily, indeed wonderfully, the identity of interest, on which good legislation depends; and that exactly in proportion as the system of representation falls short of this perfection, it fails in producing that effect. No wonder, that the class who were permitted to rule, without that identity of interests, in other words, to misrule, were very angry at hearing this doctrine; and that they who sought their favour were eager to signalize themselves by reviling both the doctrine and its author.

Let the vehicles of aristocratical opinions, and of the advocation of aristocratical interests in England, for the last fifty years, be consulted; it will be found with what perseverance the necessity of that identification has been reprobated. It will also be found, what wrath has been poured upon those who maintained its importance. They would not repose confidence in public men. That was the complaint. The not reposing confidence in public men, is another name for requiring that their interests should be identified with the interests of those whom they govern. And the confidence itself is another name for scope to misrule. The author of Hudibras said well; all that the knave stands in need of is to be trusted; after that, his business does itself. Sir James stood in the first rank of those who called out for confidence in public men, and poured contumely on those who sought the identity of interests.

The words in which Sir James has unfolded his sapience would afford the reader some sport. But the work is getting bulky; and I shall only notice an expression or two, which contain something like new matter of accusation.

Sir James gives us his opinion about two things; one of which he says is right, the other wrong; and the wrong he lays to the charge of Mr. Mill. But Mr. Mill has no concern with either. Sir James's wrong thing may be either wrong or right, his right thing may be either right or wrong; and Mr. Mill's reasoning stands unaffected in either case.

It is a wrong thing, he says, to attempt to explain the immense variety of political facts, by the simple element of a contest of interests.

Be it so, to please Sir James; but Mr. Mill has not sought to explain the immense variety of political facts at all. All that Mr. Mill attempted was, to shew how a community could obtain the best security for good legislation; and that he said, was, by establishing, as far as possible, an identity of interests between the law-makers and themselves.

Does Sir James dispute that position?

Sir James's bad thing we have thus seen. His good thing is, to refer the immense variety of political facts (these are surely all the facts of history) to that variety of passions, habits, opinions and prejudices, which we discover only by experience. Sir James's enumeration, far as he thinks it goes beyond Mr. Mill, is by no means complete. Sir James, for example, does not include reason among the principles in human nature, which account for historical facts. I, on the contrary, am of opinion, and I have no doubt that Mr. Mill is with me, that the whole nature of man must be taken into account, for explaining the "immense variety" of historical facts.

But, between this proposition, that the whole of human nature is to be taken into account, in explaining the immense variety of historical facts: and this other proposition, that the best security for good government is found in the identity of interest between the governors and the governed, did Sir James perceive any contrariety?

The European public has been a good deal occupied of late, in discussing the fact, and considering the reasons, of the decline of the Physical Sciences in England. The degraded state of the moral sciences is a thing still more lamentable. Of our sad condition in this respect, the work of Sir James is a monument. Any thing so discreditable to the literature of England, as such a book, allowed to pretend to the highest honors, in its highest department, is new in its history.

This first of the instances adduced by Sir James to prove that the advocates of utility philosophize in the wrong way, turns out, therefore, to be an instance of philosophizing in the right way . . .

Index

This is, in the main, an analytical index keyed to central concepts or ideas and proper names. It includes the Mill and Macaulay texts and the editor's introduction, but not other editorial matter.

CAMBRIDGE TEXTS IN THE
HISTORY OF POLITICAL THOUGHT

Titles published in the series thus far

Aristotle *The Politics* (edited by Stephen Everson)
Bakunin *Statism and Anarchy* (edited by Marshall Shatz)
Bentham *A Fragment on Government* (introduction by Ross Harrison)
Bossuet *Politics Drawn from the Very Words of Holy Scripture* (edited by
Patrick Riley
Cicero *On Duties* (edited by M. T. Griffin and E. M. Atkins)
Constant *Political Writings* (edited by Biancamaria Fontana)
Filmer *Patriarcha and Other Writings* (edited by Johann P. Sommerville)
Hegel *Elements of the Philosophy of Right* (edited by Allen W. Wood and
H. B. Nisbet)
Hobbes *Leviathan* (edited by Richard Tuck)
Hooker *Of the Laws of Ecclesiastical Polity* (edited by A. S. McGrade)
John of Salisbury *Policraticus* (edited by Cary Nederman)
Kant *Political writings* (edited by H. S. Reiss and H. B. Nisbet)
Leibniz *Political Writings* (edited by Patrick Riley)
Locke *Two Treatises of Government* (edited by Peter Laslett)
Luther and Calvin on Secular Authority (edited by Harro Höpfl)
Machiavelli *The Prince* (edited by Quentin Skinner and Russell Price)
James Mill *Political Writings* (edited by Terence Ball)
J. S. Mill *On Liberty*, with *The Subjection of Women* and *Chapters on Socialism*
(edited by Stefan Collini)
Milton *Political Writings* (edited by Martin Dzelzainis)
Montesquieu *The Spirit of the Laws* (edited by Anne M. Cohler,
Basia Carolyn Miller and Harold Samuel Stone)
More *Utopia* (edited by George M. Logan and Robert M. Adams)
Nicholas of Cusa *The Catholic Concordance* (edited by Paul E. Sigmund)
Paine *Political Writings* (edited by Bruce Kuklick)
Pufendorf *On the Duty of Man and Citizen according to Natural Law*
(edited by James Tully)
The Radical Reformation (edited by Michael G. Baylor)
Vitoria *Political Writings* (edited by Anthony Pagden)